No. 511
$12.95

How To Sell Radio Advertising

By Si Willing

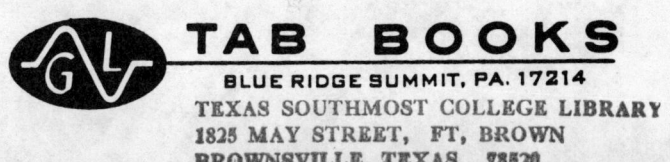
BLUE RIDGE SUMMIT, PA. 17214

TEXAS SOUTHMOST COLLEGE LIBRARY
1825 MAY STREET, FT. BROWN
BROWNSVILLE, TEXAS. 78520

FIRST EDITION

FIRST PRINTING — NOVEMBER 1970

Copyright © 1970 by TAB BOOKS

Printed in the United States
of America

Reproduction or publication of the content in any manner, without express permission of the publisher, is prohibited. No liability is assumed with respect to the use of the information herein.

Library of Congress Card Number: 70-105972

Preface

Find a need and fill it! sums up the salesman's efforts. Find a cavity and drill it is every dentist's dream. But, from the need to the fill and from the cavity to the drill are countless years of study and research. In the following pages we chart the course of progressive steps that a salesman of broadcast advertising must take in order to develop his expertise. The attempts, the failures, the successes. We will explore the methods, the techniques and homework that go into the development of a salesman.

It is absolutely necessary to accept the fact that you must be prepared to cope with the countless objections that are raised by prospective advertisers. You must condition yourself to not only listen to these objections but also dissolve them so that you can make the sale.

If selling were easy, radio stations could simply hire high school boys, give them order blanks and assign them the job of taking orders for schedules. There are many radio stations that work on this "cafeteria style." Order takers cave in when they are confronted with resistance from sponsors. Their life is limited because they have not been trained to overcome resistance in an intelligent manner. There should be no trickery or sorcery involved in a sales effort. Sponsors should buy your product based on its quality and the job it can perform. It is hoped that this book will chart the course of the beginner; open new vistas for the dedicated, and correct the abuses of the salesmen who do their best work in the "gray areas" of broadcast advertising.

SALES IS FACT, NOT FICTION:

It is based on my carefully documented chronicle of experience on the firing line from Main Street right up on to Madison Avenue. This is not a scientific journal. It contains no magic formula nor do we wave magic wands to create sales. It is an account of personal confrontations with merchants and time buyers.

A Radio Advertising Account Executive must be part engineer and part chemist so that he can plan his sales based on the chemical reaction that takes place when people meet. **He must have a sense of humor but not be a comedian!**

I acknowledge with thanks the suggestions, contributions, and Golden Nuggets of Wisdom supplied by the following authors and publications:

George N. Kahn (Ten Biggest Mistakes Salesman Make)
Neil Terrell (Effective Closing Techniques)
Frank Kingdon & Millard Bennett (Attitudes, The Key To More Sales)
Tasset du Pont (Selling With Psycochek)
Auren Uris (Discover Your Inner Self)
Wallace K. Lewis (How To Make Yourself A Born Salesman)
Edward Berman (Successful Low Pressure Salesmanship)
Harry Simmons (How To Talk Your Way To Success)
Willard A Pleuthner (460 Secrets Of Advertising Experts)
Broadcasting Magazine
BM-E (Broadcast Management-Engineering)
Broadcaster South Magazine
Broadcast Engineering Magazine
Fame & Fortune Selling
LAB (Louisiana Association of Broadcasters)
NAB (National Association of Broadcasters)
RAB (Radio Advertising Bureau, Inc.)
Research & Review Service of America, Inc.
S.R.D.S. (Standards Rate and Data Service)
The Wall Street Journal
The Christophers

Most of the information from the above sources was assimilated by me through the years and for this reason I express my thanks publicly. Contributions from salesmen in radio broadcasting are published in full with my grateful acknowledgement.

S A L E S is dedicated to my wife Fran and daughter, Michele who are:
Sweet
And
Lovely
Encouraging
Sincere

Si Willing
KMAR
Winnsboro, La.

Contents

1 Start — 11

First Things First—Know Thyself—The Job Ahead—Lukewarm Salesmen—How To Begin—The Launching Pad—Important Orientation—Sell That Sponsor—The "Time" Salesman—What Is A Sales Message—Radio Persuades Listeners—Handle With Care—The Salesman's Market Place—Tough Competition—Market Study—Advantage & Disadvantage—The Heart Of Your Market—Living Methods—No Alternative—Popular Methods Of Compensation—The Tools Of The Trade—Coverage Map—Rate Cards—The Brochure—How To Get Brochure Information—Letters Of Testimonial—Typical Forms—Rates—Detailed Rate Cards—Spot Announcements—Frequency Discounts—Time Buyers & Representatives—Advertising Agencies—"Double Clipping" Agencies—Short Rate & Rebate Policy—Barting, Trading, Swapping—Collection Debit

2 Advance — 51

Big Bad Bully—If You Can't Budge It, Budget—How To Sequestor—Jellybeans—The Objection—Rate Cutters—You Have One Product To Sell—Operating Cost Plus Profit—One Way To Deal With A Rate Cutter—Work With The Tools At Hand—More Market Study—Sources Of Information—Manufacturing What You Sell—Y-O-U Equals You—Types Of People—Classify Your Prospects—Fear, How To Overcome It—Your Personal Chart—Keep Eyes And Ears Open—Goal To Go!—Top Priority, Get The Big Accounts First—Be Creative—The Action Begins—How To Make It Stick—Go After Smaller Accounts Also—How To Right Mr. Wrong—Short Shots—Character—Skirmish—Counter Attack—Innocent Victim—Team Work—Victory

3 Lead 83

Mannerisms — Handshakes — Variegated Varieties — More Do's & Don'ts—Closing The Sale—Timidity—Study The Prospects Weakness—Comedy Relief—Use Strategy, Not Deception—How To Beat Lack Of Interest—The Emotional Bully—The False Objection—Fact, A Negative & A Positive Must Produce A Charge—Keep Your Temper—Easy Does It—Time To Firm Up—Keep Calm—Sudden Shocks—Needs & Wants—Combatting Indecision—Enthusiasm—Be A Realist—Of Time & Timing & Squelching People—Personal Standards—Real Life Drama—Join The Five Percent—Surveys—Effective Use Of Audience Surveys—Promoting Your Station—Public Relations—Letters Of Testimonial—The Difference Between Publicity & Advertising—Making The Best Of Every Opportunity—Borderline Sales Promos—P.I. Deals—Never Take Things For Granted—Triple Play—Getting Better—If At First You Don't Succeed—The Importance Of Keeping Seconds—Reminder Memo

4 Excel 149

Why Radio Advertising Is Necessary—Sponsors Buy Ideas—Change With The Times—Action, Reaction—Off Beat Media—Be Wise, Merchandise—As Advertised On Radio—Lead Don't Follow—Intra-Competition—Understanding & Being Understood—The Advantages Of Being A Salesman—The Man Who Couldn't Give Away A Million Dollars—Head On Collision—Products & Services—Of Piques & Boos—Friends, Friendly People & Acquaintances—Salesmen Appreciate—Brain Power—Know Your W's—Organize Or Agonize—The Promissory Note—The Buddy-Buddy System—Exchanging Accounts—Making Sales Reports—House Accounts—Sales Techniques—The Big Difference—Short & Long Range Goals—Flesh On The Skeleton—Memorable Messages—The Customer Is Always Right—One Kind Of Salesman Who Died—Don't Flatter, Compliment—Keep A Morgue—Don't Be A Hit & Run Salesman—Big Shot Salesman—Hollow Shells—Patience Hath It's Own Reward—Weigh It, Before You Say It—I.O.U.—Attacking Problems—Solutions—Use Your Problem Solving Scapel—Don't Borrow, Worry Or Trouble—Here's An Ice Cream Scoop—Don't Be A Vulture—Illustrate, Don't Demonstrate—Notice To Rate Cutters—Does Your Rate Raise Rate a Raise?—Challenge Inherited Knowledge—A Challenge To Reject—Switch List Advertising & Lotteries—Things To Remember—Build A Prison; Become Your Own Jailer—Boredom, The Poison Of Mankind—Build On Your Experience—Take No

For An Answer—Salesmanship Ingredients—Nothing New Under The Sun—Turning Points—Consideration—Listen And Hear—Opinion Making—Know It, Or Blow It—Chain Reaction—Reasoning To The Rescue—Follow Up And Follow Through—Search For New Business—Don't Neglect Your Sponsor—Build A Firm Foundation—Joiner, But Don't Be A Joiner—Effective Communications By Mail—Letters Are Forever—Effective Phone Communications—The Importance Of Our Trade Organizations—The importance Of Trade Papers—Attending Conventions—A Job Worth Doing Is Worth Doing Well—Make It Count—Distractions—Recognize People—Health Don't Neglect It—The Missing Link—The Vegetable People—Parasites The Theives Of Time—Extra Effort Makes The Difference—Things Get Old Fast—Be A Do It Yourself Thinker—Reasons Why Sponsors Quit Advertising—How To Sell A Newscast—Diagonal Placement—Prime Time—Copy Writing Techniques—Vital Statistics—We Learn From Each Other

5 Surpass 227

How It's Done—A Success Story—I'll Call You—Wrong Time Of Year—I Don't Need To Advertise—One Station Is All We Can Afford—I'll Give It A Try—I Don't Like Your Music—With Newspapers I Always Get Results—How To Side Step Objections—Demolish Objections—Sell Your Station As Well As Advertising—The Numbers Racket—Determine The True Objections—The Opportune Moment—Helpful Suggestions—Remote Broadcasts—Change Of Pace—It Is Better To Give Than Receive—Salvage—Converting A No Into A Yes—One Line Disposals—Speed Reading—Leave Your Name—Goodwill Builder—Be Considerate—Miss Or Mrs.—Service Without Servitudes—Servitude Without Service—See The Top Man—Variations On Thieves—Give The Complete Sales Story—Sell The Use Of Your Product—Nick A Nickname—Don't Forget To Remember—One Detail Can Make The Sale—See More Sponsors—Confirm Every Order—Take Personal Inventory—Automotivate Or You'll Be Automated—Be A Pseudo Detective—Don't Be A Whirlwind—Don't Waste Your Time—Responsibility Of A Single Station Market—Be A Showman—Gain Your Sponsors Confidence—Don't Cave In To Price Cutting—Dare To Be Different—Simplicity Pays Off—Eager Beaver Selling—Don't Buy Your Sponsors—Clip The Gossip—How To Analyze Objections—Wear A Different Hat—Two Man Selling—Dare To Deviate—Analyze—How The Entire Team Functions—McAlister Broadcasting Operations

Section 1

Start
SALES

FIRST THINGS FIRST

A broadcast salesman must know his product and his market. Just like in algebra, you must solve two equations before you can find the third unknown. What we're after is making the sale and that's the third equation in the game of selling. A salesman's product is the sound of his station. The music. The news. The personality. The sales messages. The people in it. And these things are so variable. Someone aptly described his radio station to me; he said "My station is as good or as bad as the last announcement, the last record played, or the last newscast given." This keen analysis was an extension of Shakespeare's famous line, "The good that men do is oft interred in their bones, the evil they do lives after them."

Know Thyself

There is another factor involved: The salesman must know himself and how he relates to his station and market. Funny, but we live a lifetime and scarcely know anything about ourselves. Most of us have never taken the time to do personal research. There's more to being a salesman than you think. Homework is the key to unlocking the doors that hold mysteries we seek to solve. "Knowledge makes you free!" Explore and explore some more. And be prepared for some rude awakenings. Once you accept some basic realities, you'll be more able to envelope yourself in an aura of enthusiasm and optimism; these are necessary ingredients in the formula.

The Job Ahead

The effort to get my message across compares with the eulogy preached by the pastor. He must persuade the survivors of the deceased that their loved one has gone to a far better place and will be free from the cares and worries of this cruel world. Yet, at the same time, he must convince the survivors that they must carry on because life is worth living. I compare my thesis on being expert in preparing yourself to become a salesman with the preacher's sermon because I am trying to reach those who are just beginning and those who are set in sloppy habits.

Lukewarm Salesmen

Bad habits produce "lukewarm" salesmen. These are the men (and women) who are considered to be professional salesmen. They've had years of experience in sales and have managed to earn livable wages from their commissions and-or salaries. They are satisfied with their earnings and rally to the mistaken idea that "The more that you earn, the more the station earns." This serves as the panacea for sales incentive. But such lukewarm salesmen have never really made an effort to find their real potential as salesmen. They have never been given a real training course in salesmanship.

Well, maybe they have but they listened without actually hearing. Their attitude was one of indifference. "Heck, if Jones won't buy from me, I'll sell Smith" is the way tepid salesmen reason. Quotas? Goals? "Sure I've got 'em. My quota is to bring in enough sales to satisfy my goal." But, when you ask some of these men to explain what their goal is, they talk in vagaries. For example: "My goal is to some day own a radio station." Another answer goes like this: "My goal is to earn enough money to retire young and live it up." Then we pose the big question: "How do you plan to reach your goal and what is the target date?" The answers come back: "By earning enough money to buy a station." "By working hard, making more sales, consequently more commission and saving enough so I can retire young and live the way I want to live."

You Must Plan Your Goal

Having a goal without a plan is like having no destination at all. A goal under these conditions is more like wishful thinking. It's DAY-dreaming; not DO-dreaming. The neophyte salesman is easier to teach because he has not yet become contaminated with "the easy way to do things." We want him to understand that constant homework is necessary in the field of selling. Now we come to grips with the problem of trying to persuade alleged experienced salesmen to "unlearn" their bad habits and at the same time attempt to get the newcomers into orbit; a two-pronged message, the same as our preacher friends give.

HOW TO BEGIN

The very fact that you have this book in your hands indicates your interest in being a salesman. That's the very first ingredient, **your interest in selling!** If you are presently an announcer, you are a salesman whether you know it or not. If no one has ever told you this, or, if you have never realized it, you have no place in the announcing field. The misnomer "disc jockey" or "deejay" has muddied up the waters of professional radio broadcasting. If you still don't believe it, I ask you this question: "What are you doing when you announce a sales message for a sponsor if not selling?" Also, aren't you selling yourself when you make any announcement. Aren't you competing for higher ratings when you do a good tight program? When you give a good newscast? Every time you talk on the air you're selling. Obvious as this is, few announcers will accept the fact that they are salesmen, or at least, they should be.

The Launching Pad

The best launching pad into selling advertising for a radio station is from the announcer's booth. The announcer is exposed to the daily program log. He sees the results of the advertising sales that have already been made. He knows that some announcements are guaranteed to be adjacent to programs that will have audiences that are interested in those products. An example of this is Jones' Sports Center announcement given immediately before or after the 10-minute sports roundup. Smith's Supermarket is scheduled next to the Woman's Program and so on. He's also getting an idea of how the traffic manager works with the sales department in placing these announcements in strategic positions on the log. He can discern how the program director works with the sales department and the traffic manager to create the best possible material to sell to sponsors. Yes, the wise announcer who wants to make more money has an advantage because he has a bird's-eye view of the entire organization, except, of course, the bookkeeping or business that the manager must indulge himself in with the FCC, civic clubs, etc.

Important Orientation

Announcers who graduate into sales do not necessarily make good salesmen when it comes down to eyeball-to-eyeball selling on Main Street or in agencies. Even though he did have the advantage to learn about his station, he probably didn't learn about the technique of face-to-face selling. I merely pointed up the fact that as an announcer he had an advantage that most salesmen don't ever get, unless they learn the make-up of the station they will represent on their own. Most stations in small, medium, and large markets (I didn't say all stations) scarcely ever take enough time or trouble to orient their salesmen. The battle cry is "Men, this station has to produce revenue in order to exist. Here is a list of accounts for you, for you, and for you." Each salesman takes his list and they go in all directions to start making sales. Very seldom is care or attention given to the make-up of the market place, nor the composition of the station's programming format. Practically never is a salesman briefed about what his prospects are like.

Sell That Sponsor!

The order of the day is to "sell schedules of spot announcements to merchants and agencies and sell 'em as much as you can." That's just like telling them to venture out into a field of quicksand and try to stay afloat. If some of the salesmen sink out of sight, there are always others to replace them. Whether or not this thought is openly expressed, it nevertheless does prevail. How else do you account for the transient salesmen who float from station to station and eventually out of the business altogether. Why are the leading trade papers cluttered with ads screaming for good salesmen? The beginning of a good salesman is first becoming interested in being a good salesman and then his determination to make that desire become a reality.

THE "TIME" SALESMAN

The expression "selling radio time" came into being when it was presumed that a salesman was selling the time consumed in giving a sales message. Somebody labeled the product "time" and that description took root and still prevails. This definition is so deeply ingrained in the broadcasting world that it seems almost impossible to change it. But, if you analyze what is actually being sold, you must agree that "time" is not really the product; rather, it is **sales messages** that are being sold. It's the same thing as when Columbus sailed forth to bring back spices and other good things from India. He landed on this continent and labeled the Aborigines "Indians." Columbus had no way of knowing that he was wrong because he had never set foot in India and he couldn't tell the difference anyway. But in broadcasting, advertising became a necessary part of the industry because revenue was (and is still) very much needed. So it is important that we understand what we're selling.

On The Spot

As the broadcasting profession mushroomed and became one of the most dominant advertising media, the theory that "time" was the product became a fact. But when you consider that time is merely the capsule that contains the sales message, you can see why there are really no "time" salesmen but only people who persuade sponsors to put their sales messages on the air. Then, as if the "time" hangup wasn't enough, the job of the salesman became even more complicated when a sales message was labeled "spot announcement." The reason for this misnomer was to distinguish between programs and sales messages. We shall soon see how these hastily named commodities have handicapped the broadcasting profession.

WHAT IS A SALES MESSAGE?

Words make up a sales message, but the job of translating those words into meaningful, compelling announcements that move people to action is most important. It compares with the script of a play. The author of the play can only express himself in print; it depends upon the director and the cast to bring that script to life. It is frightening when you consider that you must persuade thousands of radio listeners to take action as the result of a 60-second or less sales message. Seldom, if ever, is a retail sale made in that brief space of time. So the job of getting a message across over the radio seems to be almost an impossibility. Yet, millions upon millions of commercials in varying lengths anywhere from 10 seconds up to 60 seconds have been broadcast and will continue to be broadcast as long as the medium of radio exists.

Radio Persuades Listeners

A mistaken idea about radio advertising is that it sells merchandise or services. This is not so. An announcement on the air can only move people to the product that was advertised. The product must measure up to the claims that were made on its behalf; otherwise, no sale. That is why integrity is the hidden ingredient in the announcement formula. That is why it behooves all of us to accept only clean, honest advertising from reputable sponsors. Customers identify the quality of the merchandise with the advertising medium. If a radio station indulges itself with advertising questionable goods or services, listeners quickly blame the source of advertising for misrepresentation.

Now you can see why there must be rapport among the various departments in the radio station. Dwell on this for a moment: A salesman goes through the process of developing the sales campaign with his sponsor. He gives that information to the copywriter who in turn entrusts the finished commercial copy to the announcers. If there isn't complete understanding among all parties concerned, the finished announcements could be well off course and out of orbit.

Consequently, you have a dissatisfied sponsor and another strike against the station.

FRAGILE! HANDLE WITH CARE!

The most fragile thing about radio is the sound. It can perish for lack of care. The **sound** of your station can be tuned out. Ponder this now: A fraction of an inch on the radio dial is the margin of lifeline that spells success or doom for your station. I tremble when I think how simple it is for bored listeners to flip dials to other stations. That is why we nourish our stations with programs that include up-to-the-minute news, accurate information, entertaining music, exciting contests, etc. Conversely, a radio receiver is an inexpensive, durable, hardy instrument. No moving parts, scarcely any maintenance. Tubes last indefinitely; transistors are practically imperishable. You can buy a combination AM-FM radio for very little and enjoy a wide selection of stations. So, with the listener having the overwhelming advantage of station selectivity, it becomes everybody's job at the radio station to go the extra mile in service to hold every listener's attention. Loyal listeners create faithful advertisers.

THE SALESMAN'S MARKETPLACE

People make up the marketplace of any broadcasting facility. This is such an obvious truism that it is often ignored by sales managers and salesmen. Who can deny that without listeners, you not only cannot survive but you cannot even get an FCC license to operate. In order to get FCC permission to build a radio station, you must first prove that you can render a service to your community. The Federal Communications Commission is custodian of the airlanes through which your radio waves travel. Therefore, you must satisfy the commission that you will provide wholesome and meaningful radio fare to the market. The Commission cares not a whit whether you make a profit; they are concerned with your promise of performance. They check up on every station every three years when licenses come up for renewal. Every station must prove that it kept its original promise. If programming changes become necessary, the Commission must be notified. There must be valid reasons for program changes. It is to the point (at this writing) where certain members of the FCC are advocating that people or groups other than the present licensees be encouraged to file for the same existing frequencies if they feel (and can prove) that they can serve the community better than the people who now hold the FCC license.

SALES DEVELOPMENT PROJECT

From your sales manager or prospect list, get the name of an advertiser who spends heavily in competitive media but very little, or nothing at all, in radio.

1. Describe the "Image" the advertiser is striving to create in the public's mind.

2. Discuss the prospect's strengths.

3. Discuss the prospect's weaknesses.

4. What is your prospect's most serious marketing or merchandising problem? Explain fully.

5. Describe the benefits a buyer might reasonably expect to enjoy by doing business with your prospect.

6. Why should the prospect advertise on radio? Discuss fully.

7. Why should the prospect advertise on your station? Discuss fully.

8. Describe the advantages of your station over local competitive media — in terms of your prospect's goals.

9. Specify commercial position and frequency that would be best for your prospect. Explain.

10. Write, or describe the essential content of, one 60-second and one 30-second commercial for your prospect. Be sure the commercials contain selling propositions that are clearly attributable to your prospect.

The above excerpt from the radio time sales course (RAB) is designed to achieve the following objectives: 1. Outline essential elements of basic marketing technique. 2. Illustrate that selling blunders are rooted in poor planning, inadequate preparation, or ignorance of basic selling techniques. 3. Acquaint the salesman with a selling procedure that may be utilized with his more important prospects. (See Appendix.)

Tough Competition

Competition is becoming very keen; that's because practically every frequency in the spectrum is taken. With the ever increasing crunch of competition, not only from other radio stations but also from every other kind of medium such as newspapers, magazines, record players, television, tape machines, etc., the struggle to keep your share of the market becomes more difficult almost every day. A salesman, therefore, must know the market in which he is expected to sell.

MARKET STUDY

Are the listeners of your station "city folks," farmers, ethnic groups, mostly elderly people, or a combination of all of these? Just who are the people your station must serve? It's easier for some stations to make this determination than others. Small stations in agricultural communities have less of a problem than stations in multiple markets of a heterogeneous population. Decisions must be made whether to cater only to the ethnic groups; the teenagers; the Geritol bunch, or what have you.

I remember when we were discussing this problem at a state convention, one manager rose to his feet to recount his dilemma. He said that his was the ninth station to be licensed in his city. The competition had sliced the market up pretty well. Each station was already catering to a segment of the audience; there weren't any segments left. The manager said he solved his problem by making it an all-music station. The music was neither fast nor slow. "Right down the middle" was the way he put it. Whereupon I asked whether they were playing just "half-fast" music. That drew a chuckle from the assembly, including our manager friend.

Advantage And Disadvantage

If you should be a charter member salesman of a station, you have a good advantage. You're on the team from the beginning and are aware of the audience the station wants to reach. Research must have been conducted in order to satisfy the FCC that a construction permit was in order. But, if you are a beginner salesman in an established station, you don't fare quite as well. If assignments are given to you without the benefit of market orientation, you should start asking questions before you even put one foot out the door. It not only is your right to know these facts but **you must know them** before you can sell a dime's worth of advertising. You must know the programming and why it was designed that way.

You should know the composition of your audience. The extent of your station's coverage, the habits of the people: When they drive to work, when they drive home. When do the factories have their lunch periods. You must know your market from east to west and from north to south. Without this arsenal of information you'll be charging a windmill like Don Quixote.

The Heart of Your Market

Your sponsors make up the heart of the market place. True, a station is licensed to perform a service but without sufficient revenue from advertisers, the station could not stay in business very long. That is the reason, very simply, why you have been hired as a salesman. That's why you decided to become a salesman. Now we wrestle with a big question: **Are profits the cause or the result of service?** In other words, are we serving our market to make a profit or is it the other way around. This may sound saccharine, but I say that if you provide the service, profits will result.

Try To Score Straight

It bears repeating that the FCC licenses stations to render a service to their communitites. A station must indicate the services it intends to perform in order to get the Commission's OK to go into business. Then, every three years, a station must prove that it operated the way it had promised. If this promise of performance satisfies the FCC, a 3-year license renewal is granted; otherwise, the Commission challenges the station to qualify its deviation from the original intent. If irregularities are very great, the Commission may issue a temporary license to operate and also conduct a hearing in Washington. If the case isn't too bad, the FCC may issue the full 3-year license with a stern warning not to repeat the transgressions. In some cases, a 7-year license renewal is granted. It all depends upon the nature of the case and the mood of the Commission.

At any rate, rendering a service to the community is a station's first order of business, officially, and whether we like it or not, this should always be number one on any station's priority list. William Shakespeare, even though he probably never knew anything about radio stations, certainly knew people. Shakespeare wrote: "There is a kind of character in thy life, that to the observer doth thy history fully unfold." Applying his observation to today's mores, he tells us to be on the ball because the eyes of the Commission are upon us.

HIRING METHODS

At this writing, there are no formal schools that teach specifically how to sell radio advertising, and precious little effort is made in the industry to create salesmen. The problem is more difficult because even the meager effort is not organized. Most stations operate independently; they recruit sales talent from their personnel corps. In most stations, from small to large, salesmen are hired in any of the following methods: 1. Announcers are given the opportunity to increase their income through the medium of sales "in their spare time." 2. A young lad who is interested in radio applies for "any kind of a job" so he is assigned to the sales department. 3. An important sponsor has a friend or relative who "wants to get into radio" so he refers him to the radio station, and right away he's put into the sales department. 4. An ad is put into leading trade magazines asking good salesmen to apply for that "once-in-lifetime-opportunity" to sell radio advertising. At the risk of offending the publishers of these trade papers, I must point out that the rank and file in radio stations do not subscribe to trade papers. In most cases, owners and managers don't let their copies of such periodicals get past their desks for fear that the help will find a better job opportunity. So, advertising for salesmen and announcers in these publications is about 80 percent waste. However, salesmen and other personnel who are looking for greener pastures should use the trade paper want ads because the people in the higher echelons do read them and they are generally the decision makers. 5. It is a tradition in the industry to look for a "hungry widow with about four kids to feed." The theory here is that whether this gal can sell or not, sheer desperation will make her sell and set the pace for the other salesmen on the force. The reasoning is that no real "he-man" will let a woman outsell him.

No Alternative

With all due respect to broadcasters everywhere, I must explain why there is hardly an alternative to this sloppy method of hiring salesmen. Radio stations are spread across the fifty United States and that's a lot of territory. Membership in the National Association of Broadcasters is optional. Also, membership in state broadcasting associations is optional. Because of this complex geography and lack of central control, organizing an industry training agency and personnel office is almost impossible. That is the reason why books of this kind are so important, they are substitutes for academic classroom training and are based on the actual experiences of the authors and voluntary contributors.

The Radio Advertising Bureau (RAB) is a fine organization that makes every effort to train salesmen for radio broadcasting. They are staffed with fine personnel who have had lots of experience in the field. Their task forces probe and analyze to find out why a category of business is not using radio to advertise. For example, they were very much concerned about a large retail chain devoting most of its budget to the print medium. It took loads of work, visitations with the top brass of this gigantic chainstore, but RAB finally convinced the top echelon to allocate some budget for radio. The results were very good and, consequently, that big chain of retail stores did include radio in its regular advertising schedule.

RAB is supported by dues-paying members; these members are owners of radio stations throughout the United States. Every radio station is eligible to join RAB. Member stations are supplied with a constant stream of good literature telling all about the successes or failures of their efforts to get big companies to use radio advertising. RAB holds regional forums and seminars and owners, managers, and salesmen can learn a lot at these sessions.

RAB is not a formal school, however. They do cover a lot of ground and disseminate a lot of information, but it's up to the individual salesman to study the material and apply it in his market. Again, complex geography and optional membership in RAB makes it difficult for them to serve as a training school for radio sales representatives who need training the most.

POPULAR METHODS OF COMPENSATION

Several methods are used to pay salesmen in the broadcasting industry. We will describe the more popular forms of payment. The amount of money you earn depends entirely upon you and the station you work for.

1. **The straight commission plan based on your sales.** Many stations pay commission based on gross sales each month. If your accounts have been approved for credit, payment to you is made based on your amount of sales. In some instances an expense account is allowed.

2. **Straight commission arrangement based on collections.** A good number of stations pay straight commissions based on your collections each month. Again, depending upon station policy, you may or may not receive an expense account.

3. **Salary draw against commissions.** This arrangement calls for a modest salary to be paid to you. If the percentage of your commissions based on gross sales or collections exceeds your salary, you get paid the difference between the salary already paid and the collections made. Expense accounts are optional, depending upon station policy.

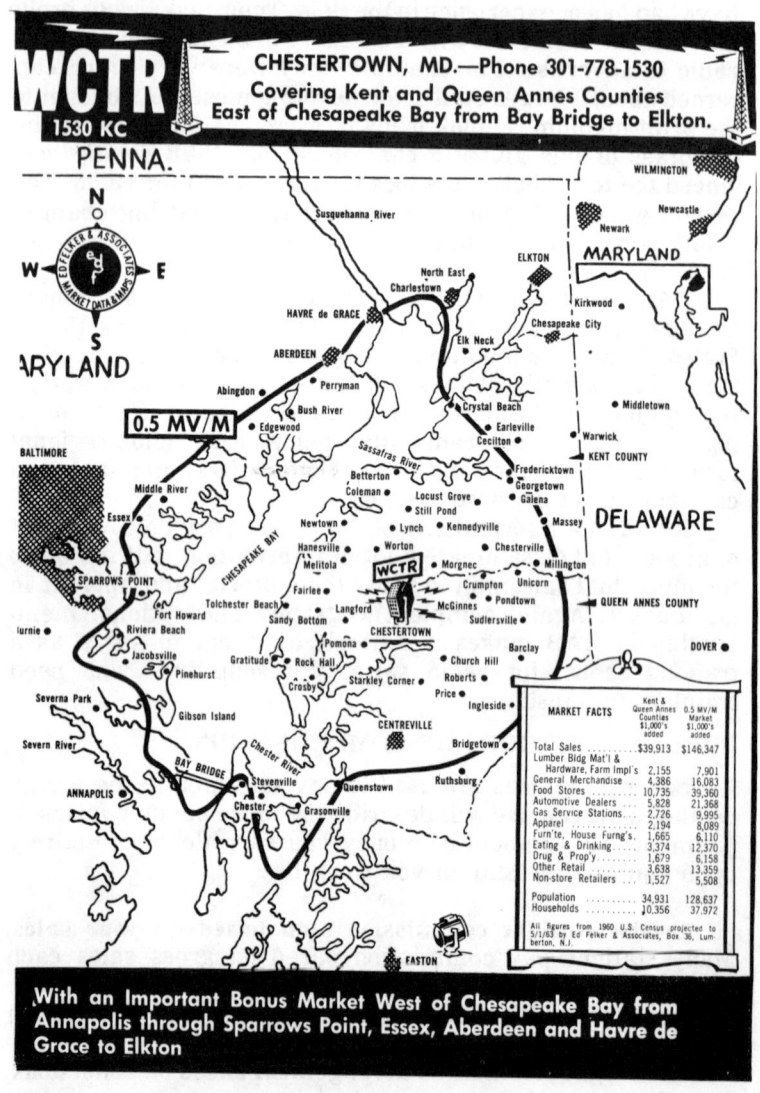

With an Important Bonus Market West of Chesapeake Bay from Annapolis through Sparrows Point, Essex, Aberdeen and Havre de Grace to Elkton

You will immediately see that W C T R more than covers the Chestertown trading area, consisting of all of Kent and most of Queen Anne's Counties; population of the trading area is 32,050; retail sales figure is $33,934,000. The main communities in this single-station market are Chestertown, Galena, Millington, Rock Hall, and Centreville. The highway system is excellent and the Bay Bridge is but a short ride from most anywhere in this area.

4. Straight salary and expense account. Some salesmen work for stations that pay a good salary plus an expense account but do not pay any commissions based on sales or collections. In some cases a year-ending bonus is also included as part of the salesman's salary.

Listed above are the more popular methods of salesman compensation. There are others, of course. The prevailing rule is this: The best salesmen can almost write their own tickets.

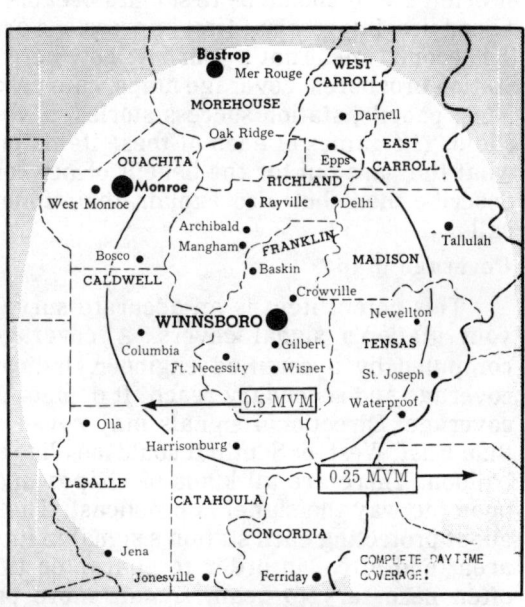

BE WISE!
K-MAR-IZE
Your Advertising
Dollar -- Prevent
it from Shrinking!

KNOWS
MARKET
ANALYSIS
RESEARCH

1570 KC
1000 Watts
Daytime
Non-Directional

MARKET DATA:	0.5 MVM Coverage	0.25 MVM Coverage
Total Population	70,700	299,500
Total Households	18,350	81,650
Radio Homes	17,580	80,050
Passenger Cars	24,560	110,350
Consumer Spendable Income	$70,137,000	367,538,000
RETAIL SALES:		
Food Stores	$11,223,000	50,621,000
Drug Stores	$ 1,968,000	9,161,000
General Merchandise	$ 3,431,000	29,702,000
Apparel Stores	$ 1,996,000	14,886,000
Home Furnishings	$ 1,132,000	9,918,000
Auto Sales	$ 8,457,000	50,664,000
Filling Stations	$ 4,815,000	24,459,000
Building Materials	$ 7,350,000	36,840,000
TOTAL RETAIL SALES	$47,159,000	258,242,000
FARM DATA:		
Farm Population	44,900	102,600
Farm Households	10,600	24,080
Farm Radio Homes	10,100	23,600
Gross Farm Income	$38,552,000	98,625,000

SOURCE: United States Census Reports on Population, Housing, Agriculture, Retail Trade; SRDS Consumer Data; REA Farm Survey Reports; RETMA. (1962-63)

KMAR

THE K-MARK OF GOOD SOUND
WINNSBORO, LOUISIANA

* Serving the Richest Cotton and Cattle Region in Louisiana!
* New Industries Moving In!
* Full-time LOCAL news coverage PLUS Associated Press National and Worldwide Coverage!
* Farm Programs given by 32 LOCAL department chiefs every month!
* Carefully selected Music!
* COMPLETE Weather News!
* Excellent Sports Reports!

Si Willing, General Manager
P. O. Box 312   Phone 435-5141
WINNSBORO, LOUISIANA

KMAR's coverage map includes pertinent market data as well as the primary and secondary areas served by the station.

You can earn a lot of money in this business but it all depends upon your talent as a salesman.

THE TOOLS OF THE TRADE

We concern ourselves here with the physical tools that are standard equipment for any broadcast salesman who takes his job seriously. First of all, you should have a good attache case or briefcase. It should be first class because it helps you make a good first impression; first impressions are difficult to make the second time. That's your kit; now here's what goes in it: Station brochures, coverage maps, rate cards, scratch paper, pens, pencils, station success stories, a vest pocket portable radio. The names of each of these items practically describe what they are but for the benefit of newcomers, I'll not only describe them but also explain their function in your sales calls.

Coverage Map

This potent item is an accurate survey of the area that your station's signal covers. A coverage map, generally computed by a certified engineer, indicates your primary coverage and secondary reach. It depicts the pattern of your coverage. Directional signals may cover more to the North than East, West, or South. It could look like a cigar or a narrow balloon. There are all kinds of shapes and sizes, depending upon the way the signal is broadcast. The FCC is very fussy about protecting each station's signal in its assigned coverage area, and often, in order to guarantee this protection, it is often necessary to beam signals more prominently in one direction than all the others. Coverage maps, informative as they are, serve only to help a salesman show his station's sphere of influence and do not, of themselves, make sales.

Rate Cards

The name is almost self-explanatory. A rate card gives all the information regarding charges made by the station for use of its facilities. There are so many kinds and shapes that they are a plague to sponsors and time buyers. There is no need to have a complicated rate card. Farther along we get into the vital part that rates play when a salesman calls on sponsors and agency time buyers. For now, we just want to define each item in the salesman's kit.

Pocket-Size Radios

Of course, you know the function of a radio receiver. That is, you did when you were just part of the huge radio audience. But, when you are a salesman, attempting to sell radio advertising, this remarkable device becomes one of the most important items in your kit. In all of my travels, lectures, and visitations, I have found very few salesmen who consider a small radio to be the sample of their product. Most salesmen consider the product of radio advertising to be "the most intangible" product in creation. They have been influenced by advertisers who generally deal in tangible merchandise that they can see, feel, or taste. But, when a sponsor takes a schedule on radio and he doesn't hear his programs or announcements, he is not aware of what he bought until the bill comes. Then, the sponsor, his wife, or somebody in the organization raises the question that usually sounds like this: "What are we paying for; I didn't hear my spots, did you?" The answer is also negative. Seems everybody was too busy to monitor the radio station, and just like ostriches, they think that because they didn't hear any of the announcements, neither did anybody else. Sponsors are reluctant in many cases to credit a boost in business to their radio advertising. Yet, that is precisely why they advertised in the first place. So, it behooves the salesman to make the sponsor fully aware of how radio produces sales messages for the advertiser.

Here is how you use your radio receiver to convert an intangible into the most tangible product going. Suppose you are calling on a new account, a man who never has been on the air. You first do some research about the prospective sponsor. You create, or have created, some hard-hitting sales messages. You arrange to have these announcements played when you call the station to give the signal. Be sure that all staff members are alerted to this plan of action. The trick is to have your timing down to perfection. You make your call when you have the full attention of the sponsor. You make it clear to your staff members that when you call and say OK the announcements are to be played on the air. Taking for granted that all gears are ready to mesh, you go through this routine: The call on the advertiser; the telephone call to the station; the playing of the announcements, preceded with a brief introduction by the announcer who says something like: "Ladies and gentlemen, we interrupt this program to bring you an announcement of great importance". He then plays the sales message or messages. This brings to life exactly what you're trying to sell, commercial messages that bring into clear focus just how potent the spoken word is. Radio excites the imagination and that's the beautiful part of it. A man who never advertised is impressed when he hears his name or the name of his company mentioned on the air. He is taken in with this method of advertising because it has saved him from a lot of trouble preparing his ad, he can better understand the impact of radio advertising. To you who have been in the trade and to those who are planning to become salesmen, use this method of presentation and you'll see that a small portable radio is indeed one of the most important sales tools you can have with you.

As an alternative, you can make several "spec" sales messages on either reel-to-reel tape or cartridge. Use your taped presentations in the same manner as you do your portable radio. Be sure to "showcase" your taped messages with a bit of programming on each side of the announcement so that the sponsor can get a truer image of how his message sounds on the air. A current supply of letters of testimonial always helps. Be certain that you don't let your letters get shopworn. Encase them in transparent holders. Discard them when they become dated. You can't sell with out-dated ammunition.

The Brochure

Brochures come in many shapes and sizes and are organized to contain all pertinent information about your station: market data, one-line testimonials, coverage map, rate card, etc. The two brochures shown should give you a good idea about the makeup of a brochure.

Your brochure should certainly have the latest market data; numbers of radio homes, consumer spendable income in your 0.5 MVM coverage and your 0.25 MVM coverage. It also should contain information regarding money spent on groceries, for cars, drugs, etc. This is important to time buyers who want to reach different kinds of audiences. If possible, you should get estimated future development of your area. If agricultural in makeup, harvest yields should be indicated. If it is an agricultural-industrial mixture, show the revenue derived from each source. For example: Cotton yield averages: 100,000 bales; soy beans: 60,000 bushels; cattle: 50,000 head, etc. Give the numbers of employees in each industry and their average wage. Yes, your brochure should show the makeup of your market.

How To Get Information For Your Brochure

Statistics are available from the U.S. Department of Commerce or from your state capitol. You can do your own research based on sales taxes paid in your area. This is a pretty good indication about how much spendable income there is. There are many ways to go about researching your market. The best source of information, however, is from local, state and federal government sources. That's why it's important to become acquainted with officials like your tax assessor, county clerk, mayor, alderman, state and federal senators and representatives. They are constantly in touch with changes in their towns, cities, counties, and states. They will be glad to help you get the information you want. I don't say that it is easy because there is a big time lapse between the gathering of the information and the publishing thereof. But, if

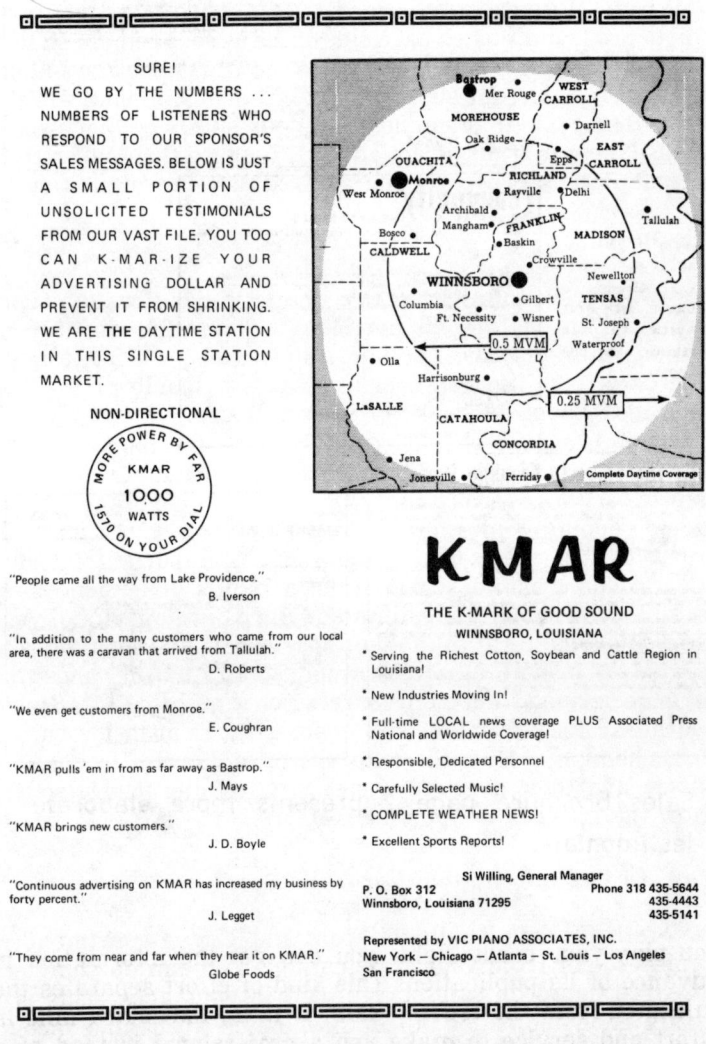

Front page of KMAR's sales brochure displays a coverage map and 1-line testimonials.

KMAR PUTS THE P⊙W! IN POWER!
HERE ARE JUST A FEW MORE TESTIMONIALS

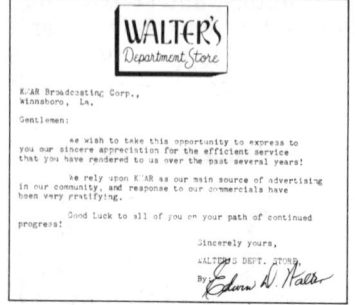

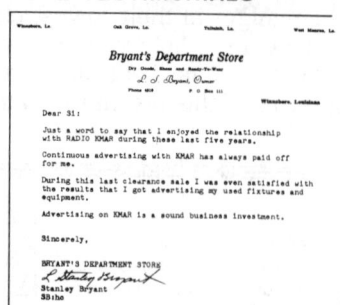

According to Mediastat, KMAR has the LARGEST share of listeners! Why? BECAUSE WE GIVE SERVICE TO OUR LISTENERS AND OUR SPONSORS!

Many of our sponsors have not missed one day of advertising since we took to the air in May of 1957.

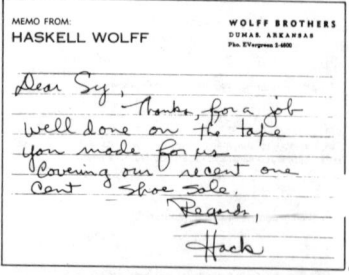

Sales brochure page 2 presents more elaborate testimonials.

you play your cards right, you can get the information in advance of its publication. This kind of effort separates the salesmen from the order takers. It takes that extra mile in effort and service to make you a professional instead of a puppet who accepts dated information and uses it until a newer report comes out.

Brochures are expensive to print, yet they should be updated periodically. If this is not done, it's the same as trying to use old gunpowder that has gotten wet. Supplementary pages can be added, others deleted; this takes a bit of planning and doing. But then again, anything worth anything at all takes time, trouble, and patience.

Industry Leadership!

The third page emphasizes management's industry leadership.

KMAR
1957

Media Code 4 219 9765 1.00
KMAR Broadcasting Corp., Box 312, Winnsboro, La., 71295. Phone 318-435-5141.

STATION'S PROGRAMMING DESCRIPTION

KMAR: Programmed for general interest.
News at :55, 5 min. Country music sign-on 9 am. Sports 6:31 am. Religious programming 7-7:30 am. Local news 7:31 am for 10 min. 9 am-noon, middle-of-the-road music. 10:45 am forestry weather news. 11:50 am, local, regional and national newscast. Noon-12:30 pm, market news such as cattle, cotton, etc. 1:15 pm, forestry weather news. 2-3 pm, music, showtunes, standard and middle-of-the-road, also, discussions, talk. 3 pm, rock and rhythm and blues. 4:30 pm, state and regional news for 10 min. Sports 5-5:10 pm. Contact Representative for further details. Rec'd 8/14/67.

1. **PERSONNEL**
   Pres. & Gen'l Mgr. — Si Willing.

2. **REPRESENTATIVES**
   Vic Piano Associates, Inc.

3. **FACILITIES**
   1,000 w. days; 1570 kc.
   Non-directional.
   Operating schedule: Sunrise to local sunset.

4. **AGENCY COMMISSION**
   15% on time only; no cash discount.

5. **GENERAL ADVERTISING —**
   See coded regulations
   NAB Radio Code Advertising Standards Apply.
   General: 1a, 2b, 3a, 4b, 4d, 5, 6a, 7b, 8.
   Rate Protection: 10a, 11c, 12a, 13a, 14a.
   Basic Rates: 20 lb;1a, 28a, 28c, 29a, 30.
   Contracts: 40a, 44a, 46, 49, 51c.
   Comb.; Cont. Discounts: 60a, 60i, 61b, 62a.
   Cancellation: 70a, 70c, 71a.
   Prod. Services: 82.

TIME RATES
Eff —— Rec'd 7/5/68.

6. **SPOT ANNOUNCEMENTS**

	1x	156x	312x
1 min. or less	$7	6	5

8. **PROGRAM TIME RATES**

	1 hr	1/2 hr	1/4 hr	5 min
1 x	$50	40	25	15
156 x	35	30	20	12
312 x	30	25	18	9

MARKET DATA: 0.5 MVM Coverage   0.25 MVM Coverage
*Estimated Consumer spendable income $100,137,000 $417,538,000

Time buyers often complain about complicated rate cards. KMAR's rates are simple, easy to remember and a pleasure to use. The more you buy, the less it costs.
*Source: U. S. Dept. Commerce: CBP-67-20-1967

On page 4 KMAR's sales brochure lists programming and other station data, plus rates.

Letters of Testimonial

If your station is doing a good job, you will receive unsolicited letters to that effect. Such letters are a valuable asset because they impress your customers, especially if these letters are from well known advertisers and organizations. This, too, is a never-ending quest; it keeps you on your toes, makes you want to do so well that your mail will be sprinkled with complimentary notes. The sad part of testimonial letters is that they have limited life in your portfolio. They are like a spent bullet once shown. You must then wait until some new ones come in.

Writing Equipment

Use a good pen. It may cost more but don't trot out a beat-up, empty pen when you get ready to write. Also, have some good, sharp pencils and a work-pad to do your figuring on. It offends a sponsor when you ask for a pen, pencil, or scrap paper. I know a salesman who didn't get the order because he started to scribble on an envelope that he picked up from the prospective sponsor's desk. The envelope had some checks in it and the would-be advertiser resented the liberty that the salesman had taken. What irked him even more was the fact that the salesman didn't have his own equipment along. These household hints may sound trivial but they are most important. It's the little things that can lose sales and alienate sponsors as well as the big-ticket faux pas. If you've had boy scout training, you know the importance of being well prepared. As we proceed with the evolution of a salesman, you'll see just how important this bit of advice can be.

Keep A Pad & Pencil Handy At All Times

It's amazing how quickly you can forget a good idea if you don't jot it down **immediately.** Many of us think of good ideas and then when it comes time to recall them, we simply cannot remember them to save our lives. Keep a pad and pencil (or pen) within reach at all times, day or night. Even if you should get an embryo of an idea in the middle of the night, write it down immediately in the pad or memo book that you keep on your night table. Don't trust your memory exclusively; **write it down before you forget it forever!**

Typical Forms

The more you learn about our industry, the better chance you'll have to get ahead. For your information, copies of some of the forms used in a radio station are illustrated.

1. **Billing & traffic log,** used by the salesman to supply all the information needed by the traffic clerk and other department heads. I dare say that there are about as many different forms as there are stations. But the main purpose of these forms is to give all the facts about each sale made.

KMAR
WINNSBORO, LA.
BILLING & TRAFFIC LOG

DATE _____

Name of Account _____
_____

Bill To _____
Start Date _____ Last Day _____
Transcription _____ Live _____
Total No. of Spots or Prgms. _____

BROADCAST SCHEDULE

SUN.	MON.	TUES.	WED.	THURS.	FRI.	SAT.

          SPOTS   **PROGRAMS**

RATES: _____ Min. @ $ _____   _____ @ $ _____
            _____ Min. @ $ _____   _____ @ $ _____
            _____ Min. @ $ _____   _____ @ $ _____

Talent _____ Line Charge _____ Other Charges _____

Remarks and Billing Instructions _____
_____
_____
_____

Salesman _____
Sponsor _____

KMAR's billing traffic log form.

2. **Simple statement,** mailed each month to sponsors who have bought schedules. Again, there are many varieties of statements.

3. **Affidavit of service,** used to testify to the fact that the schedule was given as promised. Affidavits are usually required by agencies and manufacturers who reimburse sponsors for all or portions of their advertising. This kind of advertising is called "cooperative" advertising.

STATEMENT
WE SERVE THE PUBLIC

KMAR RADIO

Phone 318 435-5141
435-5644
435-4443

KMAR BROADCASTING CORPORATION
P. O. BOX 312
WINNSBORO, LOUISIANA 71295 _____, 19____

To: _____

_____

_____

Amount Brought Forward $_____

_____Announcements for Mo. of_____ @ $____Each   Total $_____

_____Programs for Month of _____ @ $____Each   Total $_____

Additional Charges:

                      Please Pay   Total _____

Itemized Invoices
available upon request.   **THANK YOU!**

Bills rendered from first to first and payable by tenth of succeeding month.

Monthly statement form.

KMAR

KMAR BROADCASTING CORPORATION
Post Office Box 312
WINNSBORO, LOUISIANA
71295

To:_____
_____
_____

ANNOUNCEMENTS FOR MONTH OF_____

1	2	3	4	5	6	7	8	9	10	11	12	13	14	15	16

TOTAL NUMBER OF ANNOUNCEMENTS_____

PROGRAMS FOR MONTH OF_____ 19__

1	2	3	4	5	6	7	8	9	10	11	12	13	14	15	16

AFFIDAVIT OF SERVICE RENDERED

State of LOUISIANA } ss:
County of FRANKLIN

The undersigned, having been duly sworn, deposes and says that broadcasting service has been rendered by this station in accordance with the above statement:

KMAR BROADCASTING CORPORATION

By_____

Subscribed and sworn to before me,

this_____ day of_____, 19_____

_____NOTARY PUBLIC

BILLS RENDERED FROM FIRST TO FIRST AND DUE AND PAYABLE BY THE TENTH

Affidavit form.

Date_____19____

_____

_____

_____   TERMS: NET

____19____

17	18	19	20	21	22	23	24	25	26	27	28	29	30	31

_____@_____ $_____

_____

17	18	19	20	21	22	23	24	25	26	27	28	29	30	31

TOTAL NO. PROG._____@_____ $_____

TALENT CHARGES @ - - - - - - - - $_____

WIRE CHARGES - - - - - - - - - - $_____

_____ $_____

_____ $_____

AMOUNT BROUGHT FORWARD - - - $_____

TOTAL - - - - - - - - - - - - - - - $_____

OF SUCCEEDING MONTH.   THANK YOU!

OPERATOR			TRANSMITTER LOG			**KMAR**	
ON DUTY _____			_____ M				
OFF DUTY _____			_____ M	WINNSBORO, LOUISIANA _____			19 ___
ON DUTY _____			_____ M	CARRIER: — ON _____		OFF _____	
OFF DUTY _____			_____ M	ON _____		OFF _____	
ON DUTY _____			_____ M	ON _____		OFF _____	
OFF DUTY _____			_____ M	PROGRAM: — ON _____		OFF _____	
ON DUTY _____			_____ M	ON _____		OFF _____	
OFF DUTY _____			_____ M	ON _____		OFF _____	

TIME	PLATE VOLTS	PLATE CURRENT	ANTENNA CURRENT	FREC. DIV.	REMARKS

Log form used to record half hourly transmitter readings.

KMAR BROADCASTING CORPORATION
Post Office Box 312
WINNSBORO, LOUISIANA
71295

KMAR PROGRAM LOG

6. Commercial Matter or Announcement Type: Commercial Continuity (CC); Commercial Announcement (CA); Public Service Announcement (PSA); Mechanical Reproduction Announcement (MRA); Announced as Sponsored (x).
7. Program Source: Local (L); Network (Identify); Recorded (REC).
8. Program Type: Agricultural (A); Entertainment (E); News (N); Public Affairs (PA); Religious (R); Instructional (I); Sports (S); Other (O); Editorials (EDIT); Political (POL); Educational (ED).

page_____
day_____
date_____

Station Identification Time 1	PROGRAM TIME		PROGRAM TITLE — SPONSOR	Commercial Matter or Announcement		PROGRAM	
	Begin 2	End 3		Duration 5	Type 6	Source 7	Type 8

On	9. Operator or Announcer	Off	On	9. Operator or Announcer	Off
On	9. Operator or Announcer	Off	On	9. Operator or Announcer	Off
On	9. Operator or Announcer	Off	On	9. Operator or Announcer	Off

Program log form.

4. **Transmitter log**, kept by engineers and announcers to log transmitter operating information.

5. **Program log**, gives all information about programs and commercial announcements. (Transmitter and program logs are required by the FCC.)

RATES

Congress prohibits the FCC from fixing a station's advertising rates. However, at this writing, a station may not use more than 18 commercial minutes in any one hour of broadcasting. So, in effect, there is a limit imposed upon the amount of revenue a station can earn. Therefore, rates are predicated upon this limitation, taking into account the operating cost of the station to arrive at a reasonable charge in order to insure a fair profit. As you know, without making a profit, there is no incentive for a station to operate.

The rate structure in the broadcasting industry is a complex affair. Very seldom do two stations have matching rates. Some stations use a mean local rate to which they add commission should agencies and representatives be involved. Others have a local, non-commissionable rate to agencies and reps; it is, however, commissionable to their local salesmen. Such stations may also have a rate card showing their commissionable regional rates.

Regional rates and schedules apply when products advertised are germane to specific regions such as milk companies, bread products, soft drinks, etc. To qualify for the local rate, a regional advertiser must name a local retailer as the place to buy that product. If a local department store advertises its own wares and invites listeners to come into its store, it is a local advertisement. If a regional bakery, dairy, soft drink company, etc., advertises its product sans retail store mention, it is considered to be just that, a regional ad because it doesn't matter in which grocery store you buy the milk, bread, etc., so long as you buy that brand product. Regional advertisers generally have their own advertising departments and place their own ads on the several stations in their market or else they employ small agencies within the state to not only prepare the advertising but also place it with the various media. Radio stations, accordingly, have regional representatives to deal with those agencies.

There is a conflict of opinion about what rates should be charged for regional business as compared with local business. Some stations insist that one rate should prevail for all advertisers, whether they buy local, regional or national.

They say that proper adjustments should be made for commissions involved but that the station should get just one net payment. Other stations say that because regional advertisers lay claim to a larger area of coverage, those regional rates should be higher than the local rates with two commissions built into them. They also have even higher rates for national advertisers because a national advertiser doesn't care where you buy his products (Example: soaps, cigarettes, toothpaste, cosmetics, etc.) so long as you buy his brands. Because you can buy these national brands anywhere in the country, you are getting maximum mileage out of the advertising and so you should pay for total coverage.

Fortunately, the rates charged for local, regional, and national business are optional with the station owner. If they are out of line, the rates will not hold up in the market place and that's the way it should be. So, as far as this writer is concerned, if your rates are suitable for you and palatable to sponsors and agency time buyers, they are quite all right and should be used. A word of caution: Don't price yourself out of all markets; also, don't cut your margin of profit so thin that you can't make ends meet. Common sense is the best method to determine how your rates should be established. Above all, don't cut your rates. Stand firm on your charges once they become station policy. However, if you can't equate your rates with the service of your station, then you're in trouble. A high rate for a poor quality station will never do!

Detailed Rate Cards

Detailed informative cards contain all the facts about the various rates. Agency time buyers have wailed long and loud about the complex time cards created by so many stations. Trying to decipher some of these cards is like trying to read the stock market reports without being familiar with the symbols. Many stations have "package deals," combination rates such as: "if you buy 60 one-minute announcements, you may buy a package of 50 ten-second 'shorties' at a reduced rate." Or, if you buy so many programs, you may also have several 60-, 30-, and 20-second announcements for so much money.

Standard Rate and Data Service (SRDS) publishes rate cards from practically every station in the nation in book form. When you thumb through this handy manual you can appreciate why the rate maze amazes and keeps agency men in a daze. Although I am a voice crying in the wilderness, I go along with station reps and time buyers who plead for simple, uncomplicated rate cards. KMAR's national rate card is about as simple as you can find. We don't advocate a universal card, but we do say that more time buys would be made on small to medium stations if their rate cards weren't so involved and didn't require so much time to unravel.

Spot Announcements

Earlier, we said that the definition "spot announcements" is a misnomer and handicap in the industry. True, there had to be some distinction between commercial messages and programs and so a sales message was christened "spot announcement." That's how it happened but why it happened that way seems to be a mystery. I have gone to great lengths to find out who the father (or fathers) of this anathema was, but so far I haven't succeeded. Compounding the complexity of this poorly named commodity is the classification of the spot into 10-, 20-, 30- and 60-second spots. If these money-making tid-bits were entitled simply "sales messages," the business of time length would have not occured and everybody would be much better off. Our rate card puts it this way: "**KMAR's rates apply to all sales messages regardless of length but not to exceed sixty seconds.**" The premise for this is that we are creating sales messages to do the most effective job for the sponsor. Therefore, why should we encourage sponsors to make the time of the message the first consideration. If we can do the message in 21 or 32 or 47 seconds with greatest impact, why attempt to go the hard way and fit the message to a prescribed time length? You can be certain that because we elect to serve the sponsor in the best possible manner, we will always create the most compelling message regardless of length but not to exceed 60 seconds. Burden of proof is on us and that's the way it should be.

Why Stations Advocate Selling "Time"

A common argument in favor of dividing sales messages into time lengths with differing prices goes like this: "Our rate card calls for 60-second spots at $3.00 each, while the 30-second spots go for $1.75 each; quick arithmetic shows that when we sell two 30-second spots instead of one sixty, we are ahead by fifty cents. Pretty good reasoning if you don't check the other side of the coin. Look at the way we figure it: "Our rate card lists a charge of $3.00 for all sales messages, regardless of length but not to exceed 60 seconds. In most cases we can get maximum impact when we prepare these in varying lengths anywhere from 20 to 40 seconds. So, we gross $6.00 for two messages and we haven't strained the copywriter by trying to hold the message to a prescribed length of 30 seconds. The yardstick should be this: Every message should be a **total message**! If 60 seconds is needed to tell the whole story and your sponsor has bought a schedule of 30-second announcements, something is awry. The answer is quite obvious. If a station or a salesman is trying to squeeze more profits as the main objective, he **must** sacrifice quality. Translating this into more meaningful language, the price per announcement shouldn't be established **until** the copy has been completed if the station or salesman wants to proceed on the basis of selling announcements in time lengths. What if it becomes impossible to tell the full story in 30 seconds? Is it fair to penalize the sponsor because of this? And while you're at it you not only put a penalty on the sponsor but you place your station in jeopardy when you deliver partial messages. If they don't produce, you can lose sponsors. We believe in telling the full story in the shortest length of time but we never time the message until it is written, rewritten, and polished to perfection. Then we put the stopwatch to it. We make repairs **only** if it exceeds 60 seconds. Consequently, our salesmen never have to quibble about the rate card because the sponsors in our market know they are buying sales messages that most often are dynamic, compelling stories that motivate listeners.

Frequency Discounts

This following statement is trite but true, and also tried and true: The more you buy the less it costs. Bigger advertisers expect this; marginal operators oppose it. The small man wants the same price advantage as the larger sponsors; he also wants the same advantages such as guaranteed times, etc. Yes, he wants the same everything and generally yells foul when he buys a small schedule for Christmas and finds that he can't get the best time period. "He's bigger than I am," goes the complaint, "and so he gets all of the advantages!" This is not true. The consistent advertiser, who realizes that advertising is an investment and not an expense, deserves to get a discount for buying in quantity. I say that every sponsor regardless of size should be given every care and courtesy, but you cannot extend price advantages to any sponsor unless they are earned. That is why it is important to establish a firm rate card with definite frequency discounts and never deviate from that card!

Of Time Buyers and Representatives

A time buyer is a man or woman who works for an advertising agency and buys advertising on radio and televsion stations. Since that person knows very little about the majority of stations throughout the United States, he depends upon the station's national representative to sell him. It is up to the rep to have all the information about the stations he represents so that he can sell the time buyer on his clients.

Let's stop here and describe a representative. He is actually a salesman representing a number of stations throughout the country. His job is to visit time buyers at various agencies, learn what advertising is to be scheduled in those areas of the country where his clients are located, and then go about the job of showing reasons why the time buyer should place his advertising on his stations.

Actually, this is the same process that a salesman goes through on a local level. In this case, however, the salesman is attached to the radio station and he deals directly with the sponsor. The reason most stations have national reps is, again, because of the problem of geography and expense. With few exceptions, there isn't a station that can afford to have a salesman in every major city where dwell the multitude of advertising agencies. Therefore, it pays those stations to employ the services of a reputable national rep to maintain contact with agencies. Rates are adjusted upward to include the representative's 15 percent commission.

ADVERTISING AGENCIES

Many books have been written about the function of advertising agencies. If I were to go into detail, it would be like writing a play within a play. For the sake of brevity, here in a nutshell are the primary functions of advertising agencies:

1. They are hired to create, prepare, and place advertising for advertisers.
2. When the sales campaign plan is complete and approved by the sponsor, the time has come for the agency to place the advertising in the most appropriate media.
3. Sales campaigns are created for exposure in the broadcasting medium and-or the print medium.
4. Time buyers buy schedules in the broadcasting medium.
5. Space buyers buy space in the print medium.

The general method of compensation for agencies amounts to 15 percent of the total advertising budget of the sponsor. The more sponsors an agency has, the more income it gets. That's elementary arithmetic. The main point for a salesman in the broadcast field to remember is that an advertising agency is paid by the sponsor to not only prepare the sales campaign but also place that advertising campaign. The agency is very well compensated by the sponsor for performing both of these functions.

Many advertising agencies cast themselves in the role of a station representative by demanding a commission from the media in which they place the sponsor's advertising. In other words, they are "double-dipping" or collecting from both ends.

"Double-Dipping" Advertising Agencies

An advertising agency is selected by a sponsor to perform two functions: One is to create the most compelling advertising campaign that will sell the product or service of that sponsor. The other function is to place the advertising with the most appropriate media. The sponsor pays the agency the traditional 15 percent commission of the ad budget for these services. When the campaign is complete and ready to go, many agencies charge the media 15 percent for placing the schedule. This is double-dipping. To add to this unfair practice, many agencies insist that the media make their **local, net rate** available from which the 15 percent commission will be taken. I have talked to dozens of broadcasters in as many states and much to my chagrin have found that the stations have registered mild protests but did eventually capitulate because they wanted the business.

Here is an account of my own personal experience concerning three sponsors, each of whom advertised locally. They prospered and grew into regional accounts. Our station not only prepared their commercial copy but also supplied neighboring stations with that copy. We never charged the sponsor a penny for this "second-mile service." Time passed. The accounts grew so fast that they hired a regional agency to do the work of preparing the campaigns and placing the schedules. The agency then asked me to continue to advertise for those sponsors **but they wanted us to not only extend our local net rate but also pay them 15 percent commission for placing the schedules!** I protested. The agency said, "Pay us our 15 percent commission off your net, local rate or no schedule!" I brought this to the attention of the sponsors. They authorized the agency to place the schedules with us **with no commission to be paid by us** because the sponsors were paying for this service.

We commend Broadcasting Magazine for continuously challenging this double-dipping system. In an editorial the magazine said in part, "A new argument for elimination of the 15 percent commission media pay to agencies may be found in the growing use of outside commercial production specialists by agencies themselves. Increasingly they are calling in the specialists, who they say can, and apparently do, turn out commercials less expensively than the agencies' own production departments can do." This writer admonishes all media to protest directly to the sponsor when an agency insists upon a 15 percent commission for placing a schedule. After all, the process of placing schedules is part of the service that the sponsor pays for. If enough complaints are registered, double-dipping should disappear.

THE SHORT RATE & REBATE POLICY

When a sponsor contracts to use the required number of commercial announcements to guarantee him the lowest frequency discount and then doesn't honor his contract, he is subject to a "short rate." This simply means that the station can bill him for the difference between what he has already spent and the amount that he should have spent for the actual number of announcements used. For example, if the station's rates are:

1000 or less commercial announcements used in a 12 consecutive month period are $5.00 each

1001 or more commercial announcements used in a 12 consecutive month period are $3.50 each

Suppose the sponsor contracted to use 1001 or more announcements in the prescribed time. He is, therefore, billed at the lowest frequency discount of $3.50 per announcement from the inception of the contract. Let us presume that he uses only 800 announcements in this period. According to the station's rate policy, he should be charged $5.00 per announcement. Therefore:

He should have paid for 800 announcements at $5.00 each: $4000.

He actually paid for 800 announcements at $3.50 each: $2800, a difference of $1200.

The station is entitled to receive the difference of $1200.

On the other hand, if a sponsor contracts to use less than 1000 announcements with this same station but exceeds 1000, he is entitled to a rebate. For example, suppose the sponsor contracts to use 800 announcements at $5.00 each but actually uses 1200 announcements in the required 12 consecutive month period. If he was billed for:

1200 announcements at $5.00: $6000

He should have been billed for 1200 announcements at $3.50: $4200. There's a difference of $1800.

He is entitled to an $1800 rebate either in cash or advertising. If a station has a policy of "short rating," they should also have a policy of rebating. It's like bookkeeping; what you do on one side of the ledger, you must do on the other to make it balance. These facts must be made known to **all** sponsors. However, if there is a no "short rating policy," then the station is not obligated to rebate. This policy should also be made known to all sponsors. If a sponsor is undecided about what schedule he will use, many stations grant the frequency discount only when it is earned or reached with no rebate to the sponsor.

Important Terminology

Notice that I use the term "in a 12 consecutive month period," rather than a year's time. I learned from experience. Some sponsors consider a "year's time" as an accumulation of 12 months. They may use 12 months of advertising over a 2-year period and insist that it adds up to one year. Leave nothing to chance; stipulate the starting and finishing date like this:

Jones' Department Store will use 1200 commercial announcements, regardless of length **but not to exceed** 60 seconds at $3.50 each. Contract starts 12 June 1969 and ends 11 June 1970. If the sponsor does **not** use the required amount of commercial announcements to entitle him to the $3.50 rate, he is to pay the station the difference between the $3.50 rate and the $5.00 rate for the number of commercial announcements that he did use.

The same guarantee is written into a contract that calls for the $5.00 rate, like this:

Smith's Department Store will use 800 commercial announcements, regardless of length but **not to exceed** 60 seconds at $5.00 each. Contract starts 12 June 1969 and ends 11 June 1970. Should the number of announcements used exceed 1001 within this time period, the station will rebate the difference between $3.50 and $5.00 to the sponsor for **all** an-

45

nouncements that were used in that period of time. The sponsor may elect to have his refund in cash or in advertising. If the sponsor uses advertising as the method of rebate, the announcements are to be priced at the $3.50 rate.

Make Your Policy Known

The reason many stations get hooked with low rates is because they do not make their policies known, or else they simply do not have a policy. They'll start a sponsor at the lowest frequency discount. After several years, they are chagrined, perplexed, stymied, etc., because the sponsor has used just a small number of announcements and he is still paying that low, low rate. Salesmen, it's **how** you start a sponsor that determines how you'll wind up with him. **Never be afraid to state your station's policy of charging for commercial advertising.** If there is no policy in existence, respectfully suggest that a policy be instituted and **then stick to that policy!**

BARTERING, TRADING, SWAPPING

If you remember that you can't pay your bills with merchandise, then you'll quickly see the wisdom of refusing all barter, trade-outs, and swaps. There are companies that make deals calling for a no-money exchange of station jingles and promotions for commercial announcements. It goes like this: A company in the business of producing tailor-made station breaks, station jingles, promotions, etc., also makes transcribed commercial announcements for sponsors. They compute the cost of making your station's jingle, say at about $3,000. Then they offer to give you those jingles provided that you will give them $3,000 worth of commercial announcement time for their sponsors. This is commonly known as "barter." No money changes hands.

Local merchants will offer to give you an equivalent amount of their merchandise like gasoline, groceries, etc., in exchange for advertising. This is a no-money trade-out. A note of caution: The FCC looks with disfavor on this practice and if you must resort to this kind of business, be sure that you exchange checks in even amounts with your sponsor.

Avoid This Calamity

I know a station manager who loaded his commercial log but it was on a "trade-out" basis. He bought a house, car, boat and motor, all on an even-swap basis. He even conducted this kind of business with the butcher, baker, and candlestick maker. The absentee owners were delighted with his "sales" reports until they wondered why the bank deposits were so low. Before they could get to the bottom of this nefarious trade-out arrangement, they nearly were broke because they had to ante up the payroll and other station expense items out of their own pockets for so long. The manager kept writing that "he was having a terrible time collecting these accounts." Absentee owners, learn a lesson from this. Salesmen, don't indulge yourself in this awful practice or else you'll be blackballed from all jobs like the manager whom we described. A "once-in-a-blue-moon" trade-out for a nominal amount is sometimes in order but **don't make it a habit!** Even then, let **everybody** who should know about this trade-out in on the transaction. Best advice is to think twice before making any deal and then think about it some more.

One of the quickest ways to shake a sponsor's confidence in you is to forget to keep a promise that you made. First, **before** you make a promise, be **sure** that you can **keep** that promise. Second, remember to keep the promises that you make.

Jimmy Durante was once asked to give some sure signs of old age. Said The Schnozz, "there are three sure signs of old age. The first sign is a very bad memory and I can't remember the other two." Sharpen your wits and your memory. I cannot remind you often enough **to write things down and remember to refer to your notes:**

CREATE A COLLECTION DEBIT

Some sponsors are known to be good pay but they are slow. Others are well-intentioned but they have a habit of "forgetting" to pay their bills and it makes it rough to collect. Best thing is to check the Dun and Bradstreet rating of all accounts. If this is not available, check the credit bureau or some other credit source. If you have an account that is good pay but slow, suggest that he pay by the week. This plan is most always successful. Make it known that he can continue his schedule so long as he pays off each week. If this is clearly understood between you, then all you can possibly lose is the last week that he fails or refuses to pay you. It maintains a good cash flow for the station, holds dead-beat accounts at a minimum and everybody is happy including the sponsor because he is not startled at that large bill every month which he probably would balk at paying. Many managers throughout the country use this plan to good advantage.

Section 2

SALES
Advance

THE BIG BAD BULLY

Sometimes an affluent sponsor can be a small person. He's a big sponsor who makes big demands; wants to hog all of the prime time; resents his competition getting any breaks on your station. He throws his weight around. Sad part of this is that he's good pay; his checks don't bounce, but he does make excessive demands. He wants his rate to be a cut below the lowest frequency discount because he does buy in volume. Don't sell your station to one big sponsor. Take it from me, it "ain't worth it." If you let yourself be pushed around by such a person, you're in for a heap of trouble. Before you know it, you've abdicated your position to him and also alienated many other sponsors. If you find that he will not listen to reason; that he can see things only his way; if you've tried every method to be as fair as you can and he still insists upon brow-beating you, then let him go. I say to you that if you have to put yourself into bondage, it's better to get out of the business altogether.

I had this experience. It started in a small way and then grew bigger every month. I suddenly realized that I was catering to Mr. Bully. We went to the mat over his insistence about getting 10 percent less than my lowest frequency discount. I made a decision to stand firm. So, "Mr. Big" cancelled. The co-owners of the station nearly had a fit. But, I went on a selling binge and wound up with more sponsors than I ever had because so much more space was available. My revenues are way up. The Big Man is not on our station. This happened several years ago and I haven't regretted it for one moment. One of the good things that came out of it was that my commercial diet had a better balance. Instead of being top heavy with one kind of product, I was able to include a variety of sponsors. Before I made the decision to let the account go, most people thought that I was a co-owner in his business and that he owned the station. That notion has long since vanished.

IF YOU CAN'T BUDGE IT, BUDGET!

The title of this story telegraphs the theme. If you can't make any headway with a prospective sponsor, get him on a budget. All businesses should have budgets. But, most medium to small sponsors don't practice this. I blame you and me for this. Yes I blame us. I place that blame on us because we are afraid to educate the sponsor to not only establish an advertising budget but to stay on it. It's a rough assignment because people make all kinds of plans, resolutions, etc., but most of them are changed or broken. The very big, blue chip companies establish budgets and usually stay with them. But even those are subject to change. However, here is a little story about "On again, off again Finnegan," a medium-sized appliance dealer who always had the best of intentions but eventually would "get off the air to see whether his advertising was helping him." That has happened to all of us. But this man would start then stop, start again, stop, etc. He confessed to me one day that he really wasn't sure at all about his advertising program. It was too much to keep up with, etc., etc. So I suggested that he accept the formula recommended by his national trade association and use 2.3 percent of his last year's gross sales for advertising. He wasn't even aware of the fact that his trade association had ever recommended that! Anyway, he did allocate that amount of money for all advertising and, of course, I made a bid for and got the lion's share of that budget. It was easy from that time on because we prepared a 12 consecutive month schedule. The chart on page 58 shows the accepted percentages of yearly gross sales used for advertising budgets in most categories.

HOW TO SEQUESTER!

We said "sequester" **not** "siesta." If you siesta, you're asleep on the job; if you sequester, you set apart one thing from another. You ferret out what the sponsor wants by the method of elimination. Here's what I mean. After two years of sponsoring a very good program, our sponsor decided that he wanted a new program. He wanted to reach a different audience. No quarrel with the program, service, or anything else, mind you; he just wanted a change. So we offered the sponsor something new and different and, although it costs him more per month to sponsor it, he paid the freight and everybody was happy. Accordingly, I wrote to the syndicate that we were cancelling the 2-year-old program because the sponsor had selected another one. The syndicator wrote back and suggested that we try to sell the program to another sponsor. It sounded like a good idea so I submitted the program to several prospects but it was turned down.

"It's a hand-me-down. Don't want to take seconds from that sob." (I didn't know there was bad blood between them.) Really, I didn't push it too hard; just submitted it. But, on my third call, I talked to a man who said that he never missed the program; thought it was great but not for his product! "It wouldn't do at all," he said. "Why," I asked. "Because it's an adult program and my product appeals to teenagers," he answered. This was news to me because I thought that the older people were the ones who paid for automobiles. "Really," I said. "Exactly how do you go about selling your cars?" I asked, making like a freshman salesman. "It's true that the payments are made by the parents but the teenagers are the ones who persuade them to buy the cars," said he. "Is that so?" I remarked in wide-eyed amazement. "It does make sense and you've taught me something very valuable." "Si, you ought to know more about what's going on, my friend," said the sponsor and I quickly agreed with him. "Learn something every day," I volunteered. And learn something I did! Because I immediately called a staff meeting and posed the problem. "How do we create a program interesting enough for the teenagers who should be sufficiently impressed with the sponsor's brand of car so that they will influence their parents to make the purchase?" We brainstormed. Ideas galore. We taped the entire session and listened back, picked out the best ideas; sifted; sorted; made rough audition tapes; refined them. At last: The finished product! Now, let's get the best time for this program. Right here, at 4:30 PM. The kids are just out from school, probably at home waiting for supper and just prior to doing their homework. It was a fast moving half-hour program chock-full of music that teeners enjoyed. Adults should like it, too. The sales messages were snappy. Full of zing! We made them sing! It was a great program.

Now, back to the sponsor. We put all of the facts before him; thanked him for giving us the tip about who bought his cars. We went the extra mile in service, prepared this fine 30-minute program. He liked it, and he bought it. Eventually, I found another merchant who like the syndicated program that our 2-year sponsor had vacated. So, we sequestered and we added revenue as a result of our being of service. This is an example of how you can get good information if you recognize it. Instead of arguing that the original program would do the job, we went along with the sponsor who actually told us how to play our hand.

"It is no disgrace to start all over. It is usually an opportunity."

George Mathew Adams.

A LESSON LEARNED FROM JELLYBEANS

There were two candy stores in the same town. The kids bought their jellybeans from one store almost to the exclusion of the other. The jellybeans were priced the same at each store. No-sale-dealer number two was puzzled.

"How come the kids seldom buy my jellybeans, yet they buy in quantity from my competition?" was the big question. Here's the answer: The good jellybean salesman understood child psychology. When a kid asked for 10 cents worth of jellybeans, the confectioner dropped a few on the scale. Then he added some more. Then more and more until the candy came up to the desired weight. The kids appreciated the fact that he added and never took any off the scale.

No-sale dealer number two worked just the opposite. He dumped a pile of jellybeans on the scale and then he took the candy off the scale until he was down to the required weight. The kids thought he was taking candy away from them!

Radio salesmen, learn a lesson from this. Do it in reverse when you make a presentation. Always offer your sales prospect more than you think he'll need. Let him be the one to advise you that the schedule offered is too expensive. Then you can start discarding either sales messages or reducing the number of programs. Work it like this:

"What you're trying to tell me Mr. Sponsor is that a daily newscast for one year is too expensive; OK, how about making it six a week and we'll eliminate Saturdays." The sponsor says that it's still too much. "OK, Mr. Sponsor, let's reduce it to five a week, Monday through Friday."

This kind of selling gets results. If you start with a very small schedule suggestion, you have no ballast to throw out. Use the jellybean lesson in reverse and see whether it doesn't increase your sales.

THE OBJECTION!

Buyer's objections are most necessary in the game of selling. If there were no objections, there would be no salesmen; only order-takers. Ever since my first experience in sales, I am suspicious and alarmed almost at once if a prospective sponsor doesn't offer at least one objection. Here is why I feel that way.

I once called on a busy man. He was courteous, listened intently to what I had to say; agreed with everything. He got up from his desk, put his arm around my shoulder. Told me that I had a great product; said that everybody should use my radio station. He walked me to the door, opened it, shook my hand and said, "Hope you can make some sales today, keep in touch." He smiled politely as he gently closed the door.

The "pushover" had pushed me out of his office with 100 percent buyer agreement to my sales presentation. Hasn't this happened to you? Conversely, haven't you given this treatment to salesmen who have called on you? Now, if my prospect had raised the question of rates or ratings; if he had asked which was a better method of advertising for him, announcements or programs; if he had said that newspaper advertising was more effective; if he had only said something which I could dissolve, I dare say that I could have sold him a schedule. I make a case for objections early in this book because so many salesmen are easily discouraged when they meet a resistant sponsor. Later, we analyze all kinds of objections, all the way from mini to king size, and discuss intelligent ways and means to contend with these objections.

THE RATE CUTTERS

Everybody wants the most for his money; that's the way it is and that's the way it will always be. But, many sponsors want more for their advertising dollars than they are entitled to. The first thing they challenge the salesman with is, "What's your lowest rate?" A salesman who has little confidence in his station or product will offer a "special deal" that is generally off the rate card. He does this because he is hungry for the business and he knows that the station owner or sales manager will "slap him on the wrist" and let it go at that.

You Have One Product To Sell

You have one product and only one product to sell, and if you reduce, alter, change, or tamper with the cost of that product you have put your entire inventory in jeopardy. You not only downgrade your own station and yourself but you make it tough for other stations who are trying to maintain quality control. That is why I make such a point, frequently, that a radio station's first consideration should be good service to his audience, his sponsors, and his community. You must keep quality at its highest at all times so that you can justify your established rate. Remember, you cannot hold a clearance sale, a fire sale, or any other kind of a sale when you are in the business of selling radio advertising.

Operating Costs Plus Profit Equals Rate Card

There are many fixed costs that go into the operation of a radio station. There are unforeseen costs, also, and there must be a fair amount of profit. All of these items should be considered when the rates are created and the rate card should be firm and not subject to any alterations or changes.

One Way To Deal With A Rate Cutter

I dealt with a store that belonged to a large retail chain. When the regional manager of that chain asked me to give him that special "under-the-table rate" that so many other stations had extended, I explained our state of economics this way: "Mr. Manager, you have an advantage that I don't have. You have a multitude of products subject to cost changes, either up or down. If you markdown ten items, you can increase the cost of fifteen items and make more of a profit! Besides, the general public is accustomed to price changes almost every day. You are not bound to stay with a price ad infinitum. But, in radio advertising, we have one piece of merchandise and only one! If we make those alleged "special deals" we're in trouble. Besides, if I had to make deals, I'd rather get out of the business or join another station. When someone offers me a deal, I never know whether I'm getting the best deal. At any rate, no deal is secret or sacrosanct and I refuse to participate in or encourage rate cutting."

This was a bold statement and it hit home because he took a schedule on my rate card. There was a tense moment during this situation, however. That was when he winked at me and suggested that I might not be telling the truth. This infuriated me but I kept my composure. I invited him to call any of my sponsors and get a confirmation. He didn't do this and he was gentlemanly enough to apologize for casting aspersions. Suffice it to say, the rate cutters, shoddy operators, and other elements that demean our great industry, make it tough for the good guys.

WORK WITH THE TOOLS AT HAND

"I hope to learn Spanish so that I'll be able to write a Spanish Opera," said my friend who was taking a course in that subject. At the risk of being impertinent I said, "Why not write the opera in English since you already know that language and then have it translated?" My friend winced. The idea sounded too sound, too pat, and too easy. "Good idea," he eventually mumbled. Of course, the opera was never written in Spanish, English, Sanscrit or any other language.

Don't take the easy, dreamy way out with that "someday I'll do something" bit. Put a target date on the beginning and the end of every project. Before you do this, however, take inventory of the equipment at hand. You probably are well equipped to start the venture. Don't plan to "someday become a salesman when I get enough courage to meet people," or use some other lame excuse. When we hear about a person performing an unusual feat, first thing that comes to mind is that "someday I'd like to do something like that." Well, you can stumble through life in a world of dreams and fantasy and never accomplish a thing. Decide now that you want to become a salesman, that you will become a salesman, and with this determination I will help point the way for you, using the tools at hand.

MORE MARKET STUDY

As this book progesses, we get more sophisticated about market study. For example, there is a bit of homework that is ignored by most salesmen: the business of determining the approximate advertising budget of a sponsor. Sure, it takes time and effort, but it pays off. The problem is least important in the largest markets because the budgets of most advertisers are made known to agencies and representatives. It is more of a problem in medium markets and a whale of a problem in small markets.

Sources of Information

There are several sources from which you can glean the information you need regarding the amount of money spent by consumers for groceries, drugs, furniture, etc. Let's confine our research to just one category: drug stores. Supposing there are seven drug stores in your market. Using round figures, let's also suppose that ten million dollars was spent for drugs, sundries, and other things that drug stores generally sell. First thing to do is search through the newspaper morgue and get a pretty good idea which druggists use the print medium. Be on the alert for handbills, circulars, etc. You can get plenty of these out of the trash cans at the post office. In other words, go to the effort to get an approximate idea which drug stores are addicted to print, then, do a little research to find out the cost of space in those periodicals.

"Shop" the stores to see if there is evidence of radio or TV advertising at the point of purchase. You may see signs such as "as advertised on Radio Station XXXX" or "Channel 11." A pattern will form. You'll get a fairly good idea of advertising medium preferences. You'll also see which stores do most, some, or no advertising. Watch for calendars, almanacs, window displays. All of these devices fall into the category of advertising. With this kind of homework, you'll pretty well be able to tell who the progressive druggists are.

Chain stores are supervised by a complicated chain of command (that's why I think they should **really** be called chain stores) and they have budgets that are assigned to them. The purpose of this research is to see how much each drug store spends for advertising so that you can make plans to get

Industry	%
Automotive Accessories	1.7
Bakery Shops	3.8
Beauty Shops	5.0
Books and Magazines	1.1
Books and Stationery	1.4
Boys Wear	2.4
Candy	0.7
China and Glassware	1.9
Cleaners and Dyers	4.4
Coal and other fuel	0.5
Costume Jewelry	1.8
Dairy and Poultry Products	1.4
Department Stores	5.8
Domestic Floor Coverings	1.5
Draperies, Curtains, Upholstery	1.6
Dresses	2.7
Drug Stores	1.3
Drygoods, General Merchandise	1.6
Household Appliances	2.3
Family Clothing Stores	2.0
Farm Implement Dealers	0.7
Farmers Supply Stores	0.4
Filling Stations	0.7
Floor Covering Stores	2.4
Florists and Nurseries	3.2
Funeral Directors	4.4
Furniture Stores	4.2
Furniture & Home Furnishings	7.3
Garages (repairs)	1.3
Gift Shops	2.3
Girls Wear	2.9

Advertising budget allocations for major industries.

your share of their budgets. Do this kind of research with all prospective sponsors. Believe me, this task is not too easy; it's time consuming, but once you have the hang of it, you have ammunition that really works for you.

MANUFACTURING WHAT YOU SELL

The roll of a broadcast salesman is also that of a manufacturer. After all, what are you selling? Sales

Grocery Stores	0.9
Hardware Stores	2.0
Hardware and Farm Implements	0.9
Hardware and Furniture	1.2
Hosiery	0.7
Hotels	3.0
Housewares, Misc.	2.8
Infants Wear and Furniture	1.6
Jewelry Stores	4.5
Limited Price Variety Store	1.3
Luggage	1.4
Lumber and Building Materials	0.8
Meat Markets	0.8
Mens Wear Stores	3.7
Monument concerns	1.8
Motor Vehicle Dealers	0.9
Notions	1.6
Office Equipment and Supply	2.9
Optometrists	6.3
Paint, Wallpaper, Glass	1.8
Phonograph Record Dealers	3.0
Pictures, Framing, Mirrors	2.2
Shoe Stores	2.9
Restaurants	2.0
Specialty Stores	6.4
Sporting Goods & Cameras	1.5
Sporting Goods Dealers	4.5
Sportswear, Knit Apparel	3.2
Supermarkets	1.5
Tire Dealers	2.5
Toys	2.1

messages, right? The best way to do this is to come prepared with "spec announcements" already taped, or by using the method described earlier, where a "spec announcement" was played on the air while your prospective sponsor listened to it on your portable radio.

    A good salesman should be able to write good copy. Remember, we decided that if an idea originates with you and you describe it to a copywriter, then the copywriter assigns the copy to an announcer, the finished product could well be off course or out of kilter. Of course, if station policy dictates that you must go through the procedure of having the copy written for you and then assigned to an announcer, that's OK. But progress is made by challenging inherited knowledge. I am not advocating that you should start a revolution or become an agitator, but do try to introduce ideas that were possibly considered and abandoned because the sales force lacked the talent or the initiative. Or it could be that management never thought of the idea before.

At any rate your homework also should consist of learning how to write effective commercial sales messages. I can tell you this; there are many stations that **require** salesmen to not only write their own copy but also put it on cartridge or tape. The latter requirement is not always a good idea because the salesman may not be a good announcer and he'll mess up his good idea. He also may not be the best copywriter but he should continue to work at it. If you have the capacity to create good ideas but cannot put them into an acceptable script, then by all means ask for help. If you are able to put your idea into good language but do not have the talent to bring it to life on tape, then again, ask for assistance. The important thing is to be able to determine whether the end result of your creative idea meets with your approval. Become involved. That's the thing to do. Learn every facet from the creation of an idea to the time it hits the air. It may slow down the number of calls that you can make but you'll be getting business on a more permanent basis and that's better than having to chase accounts for renewals.

Y - O - U EQUALS YOU!

At this point let's talk about a real interesting person, namely YOU! How much do you really know about yourself? Have you ever had the courage to **write down** everything you know about yourself? If you want to be an everyday, ordinary "surface" salesman, then you should skip this part of your homework. But, if you want to become a career salesman in radio advertising, then, by all means, start on this project.

When you complete the essay on yourself it'll sound so horrible to you that you'll hide it in a dark, secret place. You'll not want anybody to ever see it. It could be a genuine Jekyll-Hyde treatise because it deals with a real, live, breathing creature...YOU! The reason you should make every effort to catalog your thoughts, attitudes, and habits is to establish a point of comparison. You compare the **real you** with the surface or veneer person whom you pretend to be. That will give you an idea of the contrasts that exist in all people. You'll have more talent to contend with objections from sponsors that may be triggered by personal defects but

THE RADIO SALESMAN'S WEEK

	Monday	Tuesday	Wednesday	Thursday	Friday	Total
Travel						
Waiting for Customers						
Interviews						
"Breaks" (including lunch)						
Desk work						

	Monday	Tuesday	Wednesday	Thursday	Friday
No. of Calls					
Got to Man I wanted					
Future app'ts made					
Presentations to NEW prospects					
Presentations to PRESENT clients					
No. of Sales Made					
$ Value of Sales					
Calls on Prospects with Mgr or SM					
Calls on PRESENT clients with Mgr.					
No. of new or unusual presentations creating interest of enthusiasm on part of prospect.					

After recording your week's activities, check yourself by this list.
1. Am I planning ahead to contact the most PROSPECTS possible?
2. At this rate will I accomplish all I'm capable of this year?
3. Am I applying TOO LITTLE effort to new prospects or preparation?
4. Am I applying TOO MUCH effort on relatively unimportant activities?
5. Does the week's record show that I'm USING MY TIME to the best possible advantage?
6. Am I satisfied with my efforts in each of these phases: Investigation, preparation, pre-approach selling or softening up, approach, presentation, overcoming objections, and closing?

Salesman's time budget form.

blamed on other things. If you work at self-analysis long enough you'll develop a kind of radar system that warns of impending sharp rebukes, sarcasm, or a total rejection of your presentation. It will help you learn how to stop blaming yourself for every failure.

I suggest this assignment with one reservation; that you use it wisely. Don't put all the blame on everybody else. It should provide you with the ability to sift personally inspired rejections from genuine objections to your product. For example, if a sponsor has had a fight with his wife, he is upset, has a "hot head," so to speak. You call on him. You are cool. Heat travels to cold, that's a natural law of thermodynamics. He lets his anger out on you. Not violently, perhaps, but you do know that you are the target of his anger. He'll never tell you the real reason for turning you down. If you are able to ferret out the truth; that he **isn't rejecting your presentation because he doesn't like it; that there is a personal reason of some kind influencing him at the moment,** you can deal with the situation:

"Mr. Jones, perhaps this is not the time to discuss my program suggestion, may I see you again on Tuesday at 4?"

"Mr. Smith, I seem to be visiting you at an inopportune time, may we postpone this meeting until Wednesday at 2?"

Take your leave with a pleasant smile. The sponsor will be relieved that you he doesn't have to deal with you under such trying circumstances. Chances are that you'll have a much better and appreciative audience when you next meet with him.

So, get that "personal-you" chart started now! Don't put it off. Start by listing your **bad, annoying habits,** your quick temper, your lack of consideration for other people, etc. You know what you have or do that is submerged under your skin-deep gilding. Go to it! Do it!

TYPES OF PEOPLE

Sponsors are people. Salesmen are people. People fall into three general classifications: introverts, extroverts and "midiverts." By identifying your prospect you acquire a greater understanding of his buying habits. Your approach should take these personality appeals into account:

A forceful approach appeals to the extrovert.

A smooth, even, presentation satisfies the "midivert." The introvert appreciates a conservative sales approach.

You can recognize the extrovert by his speech which is sharp and colorful. He's usually an optimist. The "midivert's" speech is reasonable, can be smooth to a point of being romantic. The introvert talks softly, slowly, and likes to discuss facts. He can be colorless and is also sceptical more often than not. There are variations to these classifications, of course. Few persons are total types all the time, but their prominent characteristics often dominate most of their actions.

Classify Your Prospects

The only thing that distinguishes one type from the other is that they are different, not that one type is better than the other two. It takes all types to make an interesting civilization. Classify your prospects into one of the three types. Analyze yourself; see which category you fall into. This takes an honest appraisal.

The exercise in type classification is fascinating and rewarding. If you can adjust to your sponsor's type, you have a better chance to make the sale. The big point to remember is to not only avoid a personality conflict but have harmony instead. Then, you have one less problem to overcome, so start classifying your sponsors; classify yourself also; but be honest in your appraisal.

FEAR! HOW TO OVERCOME IT!

Perhaps the biggest enemy you have is yourself. You are afraid of what the sponsor will think of you! That's right, isn't it? Isn't that the reason you hesitate to make certain calls? To the President of the Might Bank? To the Chairman of the Board who sits in the decision making chair? To the man who looks like he's all business, no heart, and no soul? You are afraid not so much of him as you are of yourself and WHAT MR. BIG will do to you. You're afraid that he'll chew you up and spit you out. So you naturally find dozens of reasons to delay making those calls. You rationalize. You agree that "the time is not ripe to make the call," etc., etc.

Refer to your Personal Chart

This is the time to employ your purely personal chart, the one that tells about the real you, not the one that you've doctored up, disguised, and camouflaged. Convince yourself that your prospect also has these deficiencies; that you both are on the same level when the veneer is gone. Then don your best "you," the garments of self-assurance, neat clothing, clean fingernails, and other personals. Get your sales kit in order. Review your programming and station information. Give yourself a shot of self-confidence. Then make your call and concentrate on the man upon whom you are calling. Make him talk to you! Forget yourself and focus your attention upon him and his business. Get him to talk about himself, his business, his problems. You see, if you are paying close attention to him, you cannot think about yourself. You know in advance that you've put on the armor for the meeting and that you are well fortified. So fear leaves you. It drains off. You are not self-conscious.

Keep Eyes and Ears Open

Listen and watch for buying signals. Keep your eye on all of this action and before long you'll wonder why you were ever afraid in the first place. You may not succeed in closing the sale in the very first instant but make an appointment for another call. Then go back to your desk and see whether you have made a first down. You reason thusly: "Let's see, the play started when we were even up."

I succeeded in finding out this much information about Mr. President. He did ask me some questions about me and my station. I not only gave him the information he sought but I also volunteered other information to complement that. I dared to suggest a big budget for his advertising schedule on my station. He took that under consideration. Yes! I did make a first down and even more.

Goal To Go!

Now it's goal to go! So, make your second call. But don't go the other way and act over-confident. Be gentle but firm. Work toward your close. **Ask for the order!** Nine chances out of ten you'll get the order. If there is hesitation about the final decision, review your call with your prospect. "Mr. Jones, you did agree that we could serve you well; that our station was the one that reached your audience. The price is right; unless there is some other question that I haven't answered, why don't you give me the green light to start your schedule tomorrow and get your message to the people right away? What difference will a week make in finalizing your decision? Is there anything else you have to know that we've overlooked discussing? " He'll either ask a few minor questions or take the schedule. He wants to know that you want his business and that's what you came for in the first place, although you didn't let him know that in the beginning because you were paying attention to him! But you knew that's what you wanted and if you leave without his business, you've hurt yourself, added a defeat to your scoreboard.

Keep Cool

Keep cool. Play it cool. If there must be another call, be sure that you make it a definite date, no "see me soon" or words to that effect. Suggest something like this: "Mr. Jones, I hate to see you waste good time by keeping all the good news about your business a secret from our listeners who are prospective customers. So, let's meet next Tuesday at 9:26. AM and finalize this matter. I'll reserve the spaces on our program log. The copy will be ready to go. You'll be the engineer to press the button to start the machinery in motion." Say it not with an air of bravado but with confidence and assurance. You don't become cocky about it. If he has no intention of ever taking the schedule, he'll let you know at that time. If he makes the appointment, then you've got a 99 percent sure bet. It could be that he did want to discuss it with the other board members or his wife or somebody. The main purpose of this sequence is to suggest how not only to work without fear or stage fright but also how to use the situation to make sales.

TOP PRIORITY! GET THE BIG ACCOUNTS FIRST!

Unlike the print medium, a radio station has a limited amount of space to sell. A newspaper can always add more pages when necessary. There is no end to the amount of paid advertising they can accept because of this advantage. More sales, more pages. Therefore, it behooves us broadcast salesmen to utilize our limited amount of time to the best advantage. Along about here I can hear you say "Willing, you're contradicting yourself. A few pages back you sermonized that we are not time salesmen but sales message salesmen!" That's right, I did say that. But we have only a limited amount of time in which to deliver those sales messages. We cannot add additional hours to the prime time segments because that is what The Good Lord ordained.

Time Is Constant

Newspapers and magazines can add pages; we cannot add time! And that's a fact we must accept. So, rather than pursue small, uncertain, time-consuming sponsors first, go after the bigger accounts, then concentrate on the small accounts. Here's where your market research comes in. List your accounts in their order of size and importance. Accounts that will most likely buy bigger schedules; accounts that will pay well and on time. Accounts that will become permanent provided they are not taken for granted and provided that they will be serviced well. Now, I don't advocate demeaning "small" accounts; not at all. I do suggest that you plan your calls in a ratio of three big accounts to one small account. Give each sponsor your full measure of service regardless of size. But, don't utilize more time for the small accounts and take the big accounts for granted.

BE CREATIVE

A good way to get any sponsor interested in your presentation is to create a slogan or theme that will dominate his advertising. This is more difficult to achieve with a big account than a small account because the big account has been established for many years. They probably have a slogan, theme, or personality that has served them well through those years. They expect you to incorporate these into their advertising. But, here's where your ingenuity comes into play. You must be subtle. You must not give them the idea that you have come to reorganize their business or run their shop. You must think; you must create.

In my own experience I used this device and it worked. Yes, it worked with a bank that had been in this town for 95 years. They grew from a small bank into a big bank. They kept pace with progress by installing sophisticated methods and equipment as they became available. As a matter of fact, their slogan had been "Keeping Pace With Progress!" A very good slogan indeed but I was determined to improve that slogan if possible.

The Action Begins

I thought. I prayed. I wrote. I tried. No results. Then I tried again and again. Suddenly, it came to me: "The bank where time turns to trust!" Then I wrote some real action copy using that slogan as the central theme. I made the presentation on a prerecorded tape. The president of the bank read the script while he listened to the taped playback. "That's excellent," he said. "It's about time we made a change and got away from our old theme song." Yes, Mr. President agreed that it was time to make a change and he did. The bank went to a lot of time, trouble, and expense to change their printed material to conform with the radio theme. This account's schedule was increased by three times. It is permanent. It is secure because I went that extra mile to develop something meaningful, something that would give them a new look.

A Slogan Does It Again

Now how about going after another big account! Well known for paying their bills on time and in full. I researched and found that they had a big advertising budget. It required effort to funnel a good deal of that budget into our station's coffers. Let's try again, this time a big automobile repair shop. They did a great volume of business. Reliable mechanics. Dependable and guaranteed service. The name of the account was "Caine's Garage." This was a devil of an assignment but I tackled it. Thought and prayed; tried and failed. That's the process I went through. Yes, I went over it time and again. It had to come! It must come. Yippee! It emerged: "Don't raise cain but call Caine!"
Carefully now Si. Don't get carried away with yourself. Don't rush into Caine's Garage with a naked slogan. Write that action-getting copy. Take your time. Easy does it. Don't get over-anxious. Write, discard. Try again. Refine; refine again. It's looking good. It's looking better. It looks great! Got it! Several themes, three pieces of action-getting sales messages. The presentation. The reaction. Great! "Let me get that slogan on all of my wrecker trucks first," said Mr. Caine. Let me get it on my stationery, on my building, then we'll go to the full route on your station." That was my reward. That's how I go after the big accounts, the ones who dare to accept new ideas. The ones that are big because they think big!

How To Make It Stick

The way to make big accounts stick on a permanent basis is to give them something that will insure permanency. It must stem from your desire to serve first then make a profit as a result of your service. The same goes for any account that you call on. The first priority should be service, then the ultimate result will be profit. If your primary motivation is profit and your secondary objective is service, you're out of sequence. I cannot stress this too much nor too often.

Who Else?

Now, let's see. I succeeded in getting two big accounts. I must get that third big account, then make my call on a small sponsor. How about the other bank in town. They've been here 80 years. They're a good, sound, reliable bank. Research it, Si. Don't rush! think; pray, muse. Discovery: The president of the bank has a set of twins in the high school glee club. How about having the high school glee club make singing commercial jingles to be followed with action getting commercial copy! Yes, how about that?

My meeting with the principal of the school was pleasant. I suggested the idea to him. Before he could object (I **always** anticipate an objection) I said "Mr. Principal let's not upset the amateur standing of the glee club by paying them for their services. Instead, our radio station will make generous contributions to your favorite school projects." Schools, as you know, are always looking for extra income. Band uniforms, instruments for the band; athletic uniforms, etc. You've bought tickets for spaghetti dinners, chicken dinners, pancake affairs, etc. That's the way it always is with schools. They always need more money. So, the idea that I submitted was very acceptable. I employed the talent of the band director to help me write some good jingles for the bank. We featured the bank president's twins. We rehearsed; rehearsed some more. I swore the twins to secrecy. "Let's surprise your dad," I pleaded. The twins were all for it. "Goodness, just think of how proud Dad will be when he hears the finished product," said the twins almost in unison. It worked! Mr. Bank President loved his singing jingles and the subsequent copy. Fortunately, he had some other children who were coming up from the lower grades. This gave us continuity of Family Jingle Singing. Even his wife wanted to get into the act. No need to tell you how happy everybody was, how proud the president was and how many people his wife and her children called on the phone to remind them to listen to the bank's sales messages. We even gave promos like: "Be sure to hear Jon and Billy sing about the ----------Bank at such and such a time." Great stuff. Use it in your own town.

Go After Smaller Accounts Also

OK, so we made it three in a row with the big accounts. Now how about a smaller account? Not **too** small, we want those who will be good pay and appreciate our efforts in their behalf. How about that refrigerator expert, the man who parlayed a one-man shop into quite an operation simply because he was reliable and dependable. He charged more than the smaller shops but his work was worth it because he gave good service. Again I went through the process of prayer, thought, discard, again and again. WOW! It came to me: "Let Stewart do it!" Not too hasty now, Si. Get that good action copy to go along with it. "One good slogan does not a sales message make." But the combination of the slogan with good, action commercial sales messages does do the job!

HOW TO RIGHT MR. WRONG

You can knock yourself out when you try to sell to a "non-decision-maker." Make every effort to see Mr. Right, instead of wasting precious time with Mr. Wrong. Give him the "litmus test"; that's my description of a short presentation that reveals instantly whether he is the buffer between you and Mr. Right. It goes something like this: "Mr. Buffer, you do understand that a decision to use a big budget to advertise on radio is to made. Have you calculated this budget or should we call in the man or men who will help you make a decision?" If he assures you that he is Mr. Right man, then proceed. But, if he hesitates, say, "If you cannot make the final decision, I suggest we hold off until Mr. Right can join us."

In the event you are ushered into Mr. Right's Shadow, the man who is admittedly the Buffer, then you can be real candid. "Mr. Shadow," you say, "I'm happy that you are moving up in this organization. You've taken a great step forward being elevated to be Mr. Right's Assistant. Do you think he would mind if you sit in with us while we discuss your advertising schedule for the year. Sometimes you cannot avoid a confrontation with Mr. Shadow. There are some ground rules you must abide by. Handle this situation like this: "Mr. shadow, we find that every time a story is retold, it loses some flavor. Why don't you let me see Mr. Right and give him the opportunity to hear my proposition along with you. He depends on you to assist him in making final decisions. If he misses any of the details, you can help me fill him in!" This kind of an approach is not to deceive or flatter Mr. Shadow but to help you save precious time with Mr. Shadow who, at best, can only relate a diluted, diminished presentation on your behalf. Remember, if you are sold on your product, **only you can tell it and sell it the way it would be sold!**

SHORT SHOTS

When competing stations start to invade your territory with cut-rate announcements, when the competition knocks you to make a gain for himself, when competitors snap at your heels with gimmicks and deals, stand firm, then walk tall. Don't dignify them by even acknowledging their presence. Sell from a tower of strength; not a well of panic and despair. When the competition is raiding your territory, assume this attitude: "They are selling from desperation; that's why they are cutting their rates, to influence my sponsors against me!"

If you should lose an account or two to the competition because of this shoddy method employed by those barnyard thieves, first get the sponsor to tell you in his own words that your competition did, in fact, offer a better deal. You reply thusly: "Mr. Sponsor, cut rates always means desperation. I wouldn't think of reducing my rates because that means I'd have to reduce the quality of my station accordingly. We don't offer deals to anyone. We serve our hometown sponsors and would never think of raiding our competition's territory." This approach may not get your account back immediately. But if you follow up and follow through with good ideas for schedules; well-thought-out-plans for your erstwhile sponsor, sooner or later he'll be back. You want to know why? Because nine times out of ten your competition will ignore him, smug in the knowledge that he has stolen some of your sponsors. Spoilers seldom enjoy their spoils.

OUR THANKS TO GEORGE N. KAHN

George N. Kahn, a world-wide authority on sales, salesmen and salesmanship, has given me permission to draw from some of his fine published material. We have added comments to his comments that itemize the "10 biggest mistakes a salesman makes."

1. **Rationalizing away sales failures,** blaming everybody and everything for failing to make sales. Instead of blaming third parties or things, look to yourself for the **why** of the failure. Surmise and analyze. Search and explore, then do it some more. Discuss your failure with other salesmen. Level with them; tell them everything that happened. Your approach, presentation, and close. Omit nothing. Out of this analytical laboratory there must emerge the REAL reason for having failed.

2. **Coming back with the same old pitch**: This is like the late-late show. The same old movie; the same old story. Every call that you make should have something new and exciting. If you've been turned down when you offered a schedule of sales messages, then call back with a program audition. If that fails, create a different kind of a program. Make each call different from the last. The same old story, the same old pitch will get you in the ditch and keep you there and the mat will soon have "unwelcome" on it.

3. **Giving up too quickly**: "Faint heart ne'er won fair lady. Pursue the quarry whom you want to marry." That's half the fun of the game. I know a fellow who was madly in love with a fair damsel. He had given up the pursuit because he was turned down twice; on both occasions, his girl had a "headache." "Why do you give up so easily?" I asked. Then I suggested that he renew his quest. He did. They got married. He regretted it. He regretted it because the gal really had headaches; **she had chronic migraine headaches**. I was blamed for encouraging the man to continue the pursuit. Once you are convinced that the game is worthy of your hunt, don't give up until you've landed your prey.

I never encourage a salesman to continue to call on accounts that aren't worth wasting time with. Yes, George and I agree that if the account is worth having, then it's worth making those many calls, each a bit different from the last in order to wrap up the sale. **Don't quit too soon if the sponsor will be a credit to your sales record!**

4. **Don't just be a two-dimensional man**: We've discussed the importance of getting outside interests in your life. "Just working on the job can make you an uninteresting blob." George Kahn suggests that you become a "third-dimensional salesman" and I agree with him. The epitome of culture is to be able to discuss things with a bootblack or with the bank president. Meet each on his own level. Be a storehouse of information. Be interesting; be a good listener. Get off the treadmill; read; travel; develop hobbies; learn something new each month. Your third dimension will gain attention. But, and this is a big but, **don't**, for heaven's sake, **be a know-it-all!** Use your knowledge and information to spice up conversation; it gives you more zest and your calls more meaning. Make life worth living, not only for you but for the people around you. I guess Benjamin Franklin expressed it best for all of us when he said, "Dost thou love life? Then do not squander time because that is the stuff that life is made of."

5. **Spurning available facts and figures:** Times change and you must change with them. The soap companies keep going because they always have a new feature: "Cleaning Power!" "Reserve Cleaning Power," "Grime Buster!" "Green Crystals," "Blue Crystals." Cereals sell because of "more protein," "most protein," "less calories," "more vitamins," "most vitamins." Automobiles sell because of "greater mileage," "greatest mileage." "12,000 mile guarantee," "24,000 mile guarantee."

Package and design is one of the most potent businesses in the world because it provides that frequent new look. And so it must be with you. You must keep in pace with changing times. George and I know that it takes time to consume and digest all of the available material to make us better salesmen. Now I hope that my readers will subscribe to and read all of the available literature that is published about broadcasting; that they will use the facts and figures about their stations to make more effective calls. Don't spurn it, durn it; but read it and learn it!

6. **Ignoring the customer's customers:** Your customer's customers happen to be your listeners. Your station should originate, innovate, create. Your station should make it a business to keep listeners tuned to your frequency. We've discussed this before and George N. Kahn confirms this with his story about a very successful garment salesman who does his own market research. He will find out how a given line or model is moving. If the garment is not too popular, gathering dust on the racks, the salesman seeks suggestions from the retailer for ways and means to improve the line. That's what you've got to do. Make audience surveys. Be sure that when you are advertising for a tractor dealer, the farmers are listening; that the kids are listening when there is something you want them to hear.

Cecil B. DeMille saved the motion picture industry when he discovered that the cameras were stationary and only the actors moved. DeMille said, "If we are to have **moving** pictures, let's get the cameras to move also!" DeMille saved an entire industry on the basis of this one premise. Using the technique of moving the camera, he made pictures that had animation, drama, pathos. No more wooden actors and actresses. So let it be with you.

7. **Flouting the laws of attrition:** Check your sales lists. You'll notice that you have a loss of from 3.5 to 6 percent a year. You must contend with this turnover. Attrition is a law of

nature. Sponsors die. Sponsors retire. Sponsors merge. Sponsors fail. If insurance companies didn't plan ahead with new ways to get new customers; if the telephone company didn't project their plans years into the future to sell more and varied services; if the automobile companies didn't create different models to interest people who liked small cars, medium-sized cars, large autos; if any company didn't make plans to gain new customers to replace the ones who quit their product for any one of a dozen reasons, they'd eventually dry up and blow away. That is why big companies diversify their products. They merge or buy out other companies in unrelated fields simply to have more products to sell to new customers. In broadcasting, you are selling just one item of merchandise and that is advertising!

George Kahn affirms what we have already said and it bears repeating. An advertising man ignored George's admonition to increase his account list; to get accounts other than the three he catered to exclusively. Yes, he ignored the advice and eventually went busted because in less than a year, each of his accounts, adding up to a total of two million dollars worth of billings a year, went out of business. You must have a steady flow of new accounts. Even if you are sold out, you should encourage new accounts. Make plans for them to get on your station in the future because your 100 percent business saturation will soon drop off and you'll have new advertisers to take their place. If you achieve saturation in a small market, then increase your present account's schedules. This has also been mentioned herein. Don't let your lack of ambition make you a victim of attrition!

8. **Forgetting the rest of the team**: We've already discussed the product and the market. If your product isn't good, you have inferior merchandise to sell. So it is a must that you consider the team that makes up the product you are selling. I am talking specifically about the sound of your station. The better the sound, the bigger share of audience you have. With that ammunition it is easier to convince a prospect to buy from you. It makes good sense, as George Kahn so aptly puts it: "A professional salesman should make every effort to keep his sales at a maximum. If business falls off, the jobs of other personnel can be affected. Salary increases could be delayed." I encourage salesmen to make as their primary motive help and service to the customer. If this is achieved, then money will inevitably follow. Elmer Wheeler, that wonderful salesman, said: "Sell the sizzle, not the steak." We can use that as a good example here. "Sell service and

assistance and profits will automatically result." A professional salesman owes it to the team that makes possible the sound he is selling. The more profits that accrue from his salesmanship, the more people the station will be able to employ. More salaries. More income. Better economy. The salesman who operates as a professional wins the respect and full cooperation of the men and women who make up the station's staff.

9. **Overlooking the value of dry-run calls:** George Kahn says, "Rare is the salesman who doesn't at one time or another feel that a change in methods might produce better results." In another part of this book we discuss the importance of simulating sales calls with a close friend. Pretending that he is the sponsor and you the salesman. George Kahn has another idea on that subject. He suggests that you practice your calls on a prospect who figuratively "doesn't count." George Kahn goes on, "Here is the ideal opportunity for the salesman to relax, to almost sit back and watch himself in action. Not being concerned about an order, he can afford to do this."

Show me the musician who doesn't practice and and you'll hear him play off-key more often than not. The baseball player who thinks he can play in the big leagues without spring training will never be a baseball player! We can give example after example of people who want to indulge in daydreams and not convert those daydreams into **do-dreams**! Those are the ones who are left behind. Be a **do-dreamer**! Think first; rehearse next; plan your action then **go into action**. Without "dry-runs" to test your ideas, you can be stepping into water over your head without knowing how to swim.

10. **Ignoring the buying influentials:** George Kahn tells a story about the salesman who finally had the opportunity to make his sales presentation to the company vice president. This man, the salesman thought, would give him that $80,000 order. The salesman accepted the fact that the vice president was the man to be "sold"; accordingly, he focused 99 percent attention directly upon this prospect. The remaining attention consisted of an occasional glance to the third party present. The third party was a gentleman whom the VP had introduced as "one of our plant engineers." The salesman hadn't even caught the engineer's name. Well, to make a long story sad, the VP, at the end of the salesman's presentation, turned to the plant engineer and said: "What do you think, Jim?" The engineer turned thumbs down on the sale. George Kahn knows

this to be a true story because Kahn was the salesman! Kahn sums it up this way: "Any manager pointing out the need to sell the "decision maker" must stress that this requires a carefully balanced approach aimed at selling one man without unselling or offending another. Many times this involves addressing the key decision maker, but with words and ideas that are really aimed at the "influential" who sits by his side. This is a skill, to be sure, that takes a while to acquire, but it is the sort of practice that pays off in profits." We have said as much in different words elsewhere in this book.

I want to thank George Kahn for giving me permission to quote freely from his Booklet: "The 10 Biggest Mistakes Salesmen Make." Kahn would not be considered to be one of the eminent salesmen of our times had he not taken steps to repair his mistakes. I would not be writing this book if I had thrown up my hands and quit whenever I stumbled and fell. It's all right to stub your toe once in a while, but, for heaven's sake, don't break you leg!

CHARACTER

One of the great definitions of character was expounded by J. C. Stallings owner of KEEE Radio, Nacogdoches, Texas, in a talk to NAB members from Los Angeles, Denver and Dallas. Here is what Mr. Stalling said:

We in radio are like the grocer or the druggist. We have an inventory: our music. It represents about 90 percent of our programming. If we do not keep the best known brands, our customers turn to a competitor.

How can a small market station get its music? The answer is so simple: Buy your music! We get a lot of free records, and don't play 90 percent of them. We go for quality instead of quantity. Every album is carefully selected to appeal to **our** audience. We try to stay with the familiar. We do schedule new songs, sparingly, to attract the important young audience and break up the familiar.

Another question is: Does your station just play records, or do you coordinate them into creative programs of entertainment? More to the point: Is your station a "good" station or a "great" station.

I have heard only one great station in my lifetime. I couldn't turn it off. And that is the difference between a good station and a great one. What did they have? The word is character: an intangible something that set them apart from the rest of us. They had music carefully selected and formatted according to tempo, artist, balance of instrumentals and vocals.

Too many stations today let their announcers play off the top of the stack. We believe that to operate a better than good station you have to live with it yourself for several hours a day, and I am not talking about sitting in the front office counting your money! How many hours do you listen to your own station?

Mr. Stallings, we salute you for your contribution to broadcasting and thank you for letting us share your views.

SKIRMISH!

Shakespeare said it well:

"Sweet are the uses of adversity, which, like the toad, ugly and venomous, wears yet precious jewels in his head."

The last man to hear about his wife "running around" is the wife's husband. I accidentally learned that my out-of-town competition was raiding my hometown. I guess that I was "coasting" for a while. Business was good. I was making calls, creating ideas, selling sales messages and programs. But, I wasn't paying attention to my neighboring stations.

We had a gentleman's agreement: "You stay out of my territory and I'll stay out of yours." But things change. Ownership changes. New managers, salesmen. The old agreements are not binding upon those new owners and salesmen. I learned about this invasion in a casual manner. "Si" said one of my sponsors "Did you know that Station ——— is under new ownership?" "I heard that someone was buying it, but that's all I know," was my answer. "Well, the station was sold and the new owner called on me and did he offer me a deal!" "He did?" I said in a stronger tone. "Tell me about it." The sponsor softened his voice. "You know that I'm not interested in advertising on that station, but I know for a fact that (and he mentioned three of my good sponsors) are planning to switch from your station to the other one." "Who are they?" I fairly gasped. He told me. I thanked him. I tuned to the other station and listened. It was true! Within an hour, I heard announcements from those three sponsors.

Counterattack!

There I was, the man who preached about the importance of being aware of all things at all times. A raid had taken place and I didn't even know about! It was comforting for the time being, at least, to know that those accounts had not cancelled their schedules with me. "Woe is me, what to do?" Perplexing indeed. I called on one of the sponsors. It was a service call; change of copy and all that. "Nothing new, I've been busy. Tell you what, why don't I take a little break, then get back in touch with you." That, from the mouth of one of my good sponsors. "Anything wrong?" I asked. "Oh no, nothing, just thought I'd take a break for awhile." I summoned courage, "Mr. Jones, level with me! It's because you're on the other station, isn't it?" "If you really want to know, yes, that's the reason," was his answer. "Might as well give me the whole story, Mr. Jones, from start to finish. Why? Why the switch???"

"OK, I'll level with you. It's because the other station covers this area as well as yours. Their rates are lower. They play better music (pause) do you want to hear more?" "Yes! I want the entire story," I said emphatically. "OK, you asked for it so here goes. The other station puts you in the shade. They have lower rates, better programming and they can bring customers to me from their territory!"

I was happy that I had the courage to ask for the whole story because the facts were not true! We had just subscribed to a major rating service and we were so far out in front of the other station that I never presented it to anyone except our national rep, because it would look "fixed." I calmed down because I knew that the truth was on my side. "Did the other station prove these things?" I asked. "No, not exactly. But I heard enough to convince me." "What did you hear?" was my next question.

The sponsor answered the question just as he would have had he been a witness at a jury trial. He said, "The owner of the new station invited me to turn on some car radios that were parked on my lot; they were all tuned to his station. We listened to about 12 of them and then suddenly, I thought I could be accused of stealing from cars on my own lot, no less, so I called it quits."

Innocent Victim

I was the victim of circumstantial evidence, but I decided not to try to refute it. I started another probe. "About his lower rates; may I ask just how much lower?" "Forty percent lower than yours," he answered.

This was my cue to think fast. "Now, Mr. Jones, if his station is so much better than mine, **why are his rates lower than mine?**" I went on, "Seems to me that your better merchandise commands higher prices, so why didn't that idea occur to you when you considered his station to be superior to mine?" It was a pointed question and certainly stimulated some thought. "Don't know," he said. "Did he show you the latest ratings?" I asked. "No" was his short reply. "Then let me show you," I said as I reached into my briefcase. "Here is the latest; our station has the major share of audience in every time period. Here is the other station, barely 1.4 percent and mostly teenagers." I rested my case. He looked at me rather sheepishly. "I signed a contract and I've got to see it through, but I'll be back. Anyway, it's good to change up once in a while. See you soon." He said that as he busied himself with some cartons that had to be opened. "Thank you, Mr. Jones, I'll be in touch." I said as I walked out.

Don't Panic

The fresh air was good but I was beginning to learn the importance of "victory forged in the crucible of despair," despair that could be turned into victory if I handled it right. Not panic; not defeat; just good old common horse sense. A better product should command a higher price tag. Why, therefore, was this allegedly better station charging less than our station? Deception, chicanery, that's why! Those radio dials were fixed by the owner of the new station. Just enough convincing circumstantial evidence to prove his point. I thought that this would eventually occur to Mr. Jones. But I wasn't taking any chances.

Team Work

I held a staff meeting and presented the facts. My staff is loyal; they feel the loss of a sponsor as keenly as I, so this called for strategy. We had a brainstorm meeting and out of it came good ideas, great suggestions for station promotions. Let's crow about our latest rating on the air!

We created real action-getting sales messages for Jones and for the other sponsors who had gone to the competition. I put Jones' announcements in the "hold" bin and visited the other two sponsors who were on the other station, but this time I played it dumb; just played the announcements for them and told them about our newest promotion ideas; the improved sound that we had planned; the increased service, just like I didn't know these accounts had made the switch. Then, much to my surprise, one of the sponsors volunteered that he had signed a contract with the other station but regretted his decision in the light of these new plans we had for our station. He said that those twelve radios tuned to the other station had convinced him that everybody was listening to that station. I showed him the rating. He suspected skulduggery also. He cancelled the schedule on the opposition's station and continued on my station without interruption.

Victory!

Now to sponsor number three. Similar approach; same reply different variation. We talked; reasoned. He also saw through the scheme of the other station. As a result, he continued his schedule on my station and cancelled the other station's schedule.

There's a lesson to be learned from this episode. First, if you speak the truth and practice it, you can't go wrong. Second, the very fact that you know your product; know the facts and are familiar with your marketplace, you can take your time in making decisions. You can walk tall; think big; never panic and chew your cud several times before taking action. Actually, the efforts of the other station to sink our ship didn't let up. This was very good because it kept us on our toes; reminded us that we were off quard; asleep at the switch. We had surcumbed to the very indifference that I caution you about throughout this manual.

You see, it did happen to me and I want you to profit from my experience. "Eternal vigilance is the price of liberty." We get our automobiles checked periodically; we paint our homes to preserve the wood; we keep tabs of many things, don't we? Why not, then, keep a sharp eye for erosion of your station. Why let it fall prey to spoilers and marauders who would weaken your station's stature and structure by **foul** means or FOUL! I will compete with any salesman in any market but the game must be played honorably. If he beats me fair and square, my hat is off to him. But if he uses illegal, shoddy tactics, he'd better be sure of what he's doing because the truth will eventually overwhelm him.

Section 3

SALES
Lead

MANNERISMS

All of us have mannerisms; good ones; medium-sized, bothersome, pleasant. You name it and we've got it. This may be off the subject but I know a woman who divorced her husband after 10 years of marriage because of one habit that he had. He walked around the house barefooted. This woman never told him how much it annoyed her. They didn't discuss this during their courtship (no market research). He never took the hint in spite of the ten pairs of houseshoes that he had (she bought him a new pair for every anniversary which he never wore). The trouble here: no communications were ever established on that one subject. Her nerves were frazzled; his feet were comfortable; but this combination resulted in a blow-up and then divorce. I mention this here because you should be aware of some of the more familiar mannerisms that annoy and some of the minor ones that irritate and ring up "No Sale Today!" Here are some of them:

Handshakes

It is generally believed that a handshake is in order sometime at the beginning of a meeting between two or more people. Some people don't like to shake hands for personal reasons. Sweaty palms, poor grip, tight grip, sore fingers, germs, etc. They just don't shake hands, but it doesn't mean that they are not cordial or friendly. I always wait for a person to extend his hand first, especially a sponsor.

Handshakes originated way back when knighthood was in flower. Handshaking developed because it indicated that there were no hidden weapons in the palm, that the meeting between or among people would be free from weaponry. It's a carryover from those days and accepted by most people as standard contemporary procedure. If possible, find out in advance of your meeting what your prospect's attitude is toward handshaking.

Variegated Varieties

Combing hair: This is sometimes a subconscious habit that salesmen have during a presentation. Don't do it! If this happens to be one of your habits, simply be sure that you don't have a comb along when you make your call.

Chewing gum: A good thing to do except when you are making a presentation.

Smoking: Lots of pros and cons on this one. A safe rule of thumb is don't smoke while talking to your sponsor. If he smokes, then you may smoke also. But if he doesn't light up, you refrain from smoking. It may offend him. Besides, it's a distraction; you must reach for your cigarette; light it; be sure you have an ashtray, etc. My advice is don't smoke while in the presence of a sponsor.

Fidgeting: This takes practice before the interview. Learn to sit in one position. Keep your hands still, unles you have use for them. Don't pick your nails or twiddle your thumbs. These are nervous betrayals. Makes your sponsor think you are ill at ease and he becomes uncomfortable.

Smiling: Don't frown but don't keep a perpetual smile on your face. Practice before the mirror; look pleasant; a "pasted-on smile" looks just like what it is. On the subject of frowning, I mean don't refrain from frowning all the time; sometimes a frown is good for a dramatic touch.

Doodling: Your main job is to pay attention to your sponsor. If you indulge in an extra activity like doodling, it's distracting to him; shows that he is not your main interest. Don't doodle it!

More Don'ts & Do's

Here are some don'ts. Don't bite your nails; don't click your teeth; don't pick your nose; don't pick your teeth. Here are some do's: Do see the dentist regularly and be sure that you are free of bad breath. Do have clean fingernails and ears. Do be sure that your collar doesn't tell the secret about your dandruff. Remove your hat and coat during the call. If you are sure that the sponsor has enough time to spare for a complete interview or presentation, then be comfortable. Removing your coat (I don't mean jacket) shows that you plan to stay for as long as it takes to complete the business at hand.

Here's another don't, while I'm at it! Don't overstay your visit. Leave as quickly as possible after your business is finished. Don't linger! Get the schedule, pass the time of day in the next few minutes and then go! This shows that you respect the sponsor's time and also indicates that you are a salesman who puts a value on your own time. But, for heaven's sake, don't disappear abruptly after you get the sponsor's account. This should be practiced before making the call.

Your exit should be fluid and with grace, just like your entrance. Don't falter in your footsteps, walk with certainty. Don't mumble; be audible. Speak with authority but don't shout. All of these mannerisms can be dealt with if you practice with someone who will be honest enough to give you critiques; practice in front of a mirror; practice before you make your call. We have suggested the more prominent irritations and good points. It's up to you to make the proper adjustments to polish yourself into the most presentable "presentor." Oh yes, one other thing: Keep your sense of humor! Don't be a comedian but be pleasant. Don't be a clown but learn to laugh at other people's jokes.

"Be of good cheer, my friend"
Wm. Shakespeare

CLOSING THE SALE

We have discussed many phases of sales presentations. There is one part of this project that stumps most salesmen. It is closing the sale! Not knowing when to close; not being alert to buying signals; being timid; being arrogant; being too talkative; over-selling; under-selling. Oh, there are so many reasons why so many salesmen come to the brink of closing the sale and then fail to do so. In the following pages, we will examine the more prominent reasons for this failure.

Timidity

The neophyte dreads the time when he must ask for the order. He's timid, inexperienced, afraid. So to the beginner, I suggest that you practice your closing with someone whom you know. Great boxers use sparring partners, so you get yourself a sparring partner and pretend that he's your sponsor and don't spare the punches. If you have enough facts to support your reasons for the sponsor to buy from you, then you should consider any objection insignificant. If the preponderance of your presentation is favorable to the sponsor, you should be able to clear up any objections. Let me illustrate.

You've intelligently presented your station for its audience acceptability; you've pointed with pride to the many success stories you have in your sales kit. All of the evidence has been presented and accepted by the sponsor, then whammo! you have a head-on collision with an objection. That's great! Remember, we said that seldom if ever, is it possible to make a sale when there are no objections! OK, let's suppose that the objection shapes up to be your rates. "Too high," says the sponsor. "Higher than what?" should be your question. "Higher than Station" says the sponsor. You never argue this point but you agree because, after all, your rates are higher than the other station, so the sponsor has stated a true fact. Instead you qualify the reason for the higher rate. "Yes Mr. Sponsor, our rates are higher than Station B. Station B is a good radio station. They know their business and so do we. Our rates are established to give the finest service, best quality of sound, and we have a reasonable markup to make a fair profit. If we were to reduce our rates to meet the competition, then we'd have to reduce our quality and service and you wouldn't want us to do that, would you Mr. Sponsor?

If the sponsor has agreed with you on all of these points, up to the objection of your rates, then he must reaffirm his agreement. He can hardly say that your station is no better than the other station; that is, if you've made your presentation so palatable and honest that he honestly agreed with you up to his objection. There you see, you've gotten a 90 percent endorsement of your station; the other 10 percent is to make him understand that your rates are justified. Remember this: If you've won 90 percent of the game, why lose the entire game because of only 10 percent? Your timidity must be replaced with confidence in your rates. Don't argue! Don't fly off the handle! Don't retreat into your shell! But do qualify your rates by briefly repeating the advantages a sponsor has when he advertises on your station.

Remember what La Rochefoucauld so wisely said: "True eloquence consists in saying all that is necessary and **nothing but what is necessary.**" Stay with the facts. Don't introduce new evidence because you've had approval already. Unless the sponsor has deliberately "yessed" you down the line and was waiting to explode his "too-high bombshell" to make you lose the sale, you can win the game by restating your case briefly to refresh your sponsor's memory. If he booby-trapped you deliberately because he had no intention of buying in the first place, then you've encountered one of the minority who cannot or will not be sold. But, if your prospect is in the market for your product, he will agree with your rates being what they are because you have qualified them!

Study the Prospect's Weakness

A good actor can play the same role with enough variations to please most audiences. He knows that a New York audience is different than one in Boston. When he is playing in San Francisco, he must play his part differently than in New Orleans. This is called poetic license. The dialogue is the same, but is spoken differently. The business of the play is the same but is acted differently to suit the mood and tempo of the audience. The actor's latitude must match the audience's attitude.

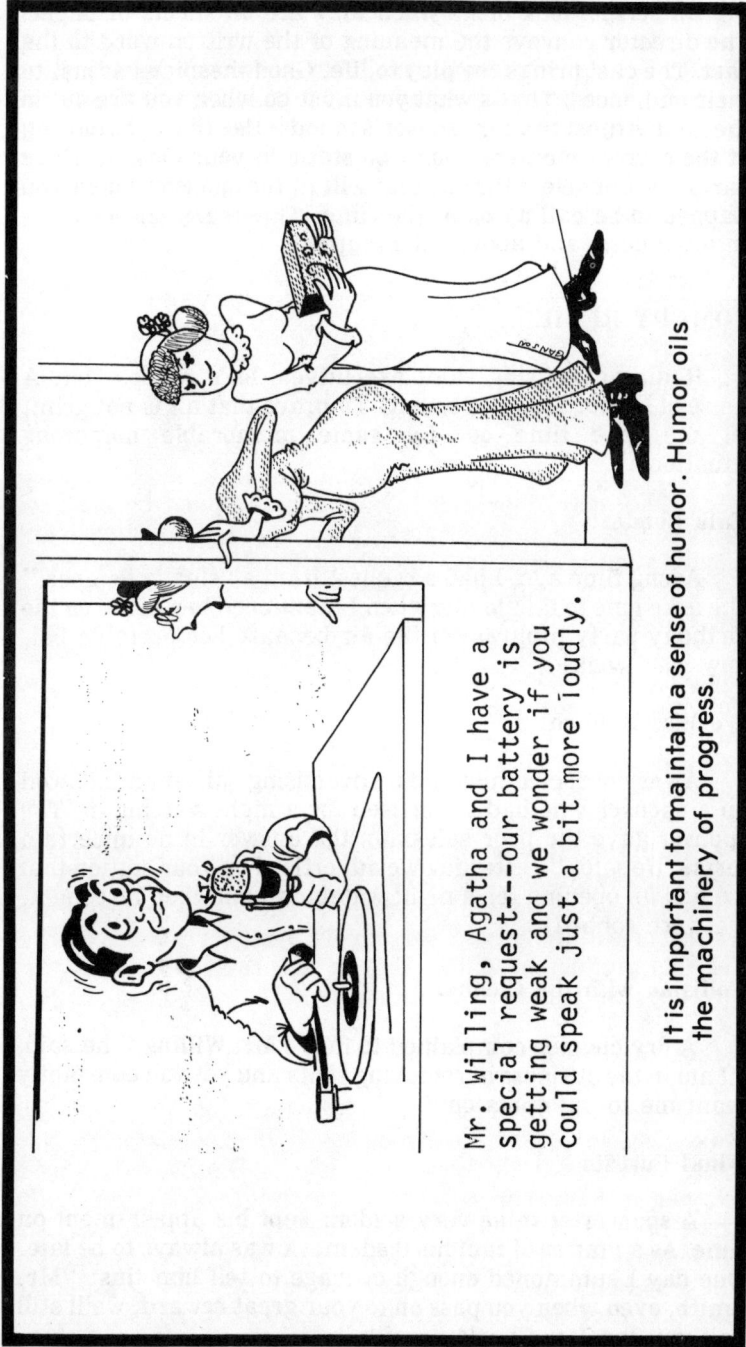

All scripts look bleak when they are on sheets of paper. The director conveys the meaning of the written word to the cast. The cast brings the play to life. Good thespians adjust to their audiences. That's what you must do when you are out in the field. Adjust to your sponsor's moods. Use the right closing at the correct moment. Don't be static in your closing. Have variables but select the one that will fit the sponsor whom you happen to be calling on at the time. This takes observation; intuitiveness, and above all **practice!**

COMEDY RELIEF

Radio advertising sales executives, let's relax a bit. A sense of humor is so important! To prove that all is not grim, let me take time out for some memorable humorous situations.

Talk Louder!

A long time ago, I had a request from a "steady listener." She asked me to talk **louder** when I mentioned her name on the birthday party program of the air because her portable battery was weak!

We Wuz Robbed!

A very conscientious radio advertising salesman followed up a sponsor who had advertised for a night-watchman. The sponsor gave the poor salesman the answer in no uncertain terms. He said, "Yesterday we advertised on your station that we had an opening for a night watchman and then last night, we were robbed!

Collision with the Cleaner

A dry cleaner complained to me: "Mr. Willing," he said, "I am in the business of removing spots and yet you constantly want me to put spots on."

Final Curtain

A sponsor of mine very seldom kept his appointment on time. As a matter of fact his trademark was always to be late. One day I summoned enough courage to tell him this: "Mr. Smith, even when you pass on to your great reward, we'll still call you the **late** Charley Smith."

A Poor Finish

It took a great deal of effort but I finally convinced the restaurant owner to advertise that his restaurant was completely air conditioned. He took a limited amount of announcements. One of my announcers ended one of the announcements like this: "Remember, Kelly's Restaurant is completely air conditioned; now you can die in comfort."

USE STRATEGY NOT DECEPTION

Although a prospective sponsor may say that he is not interested in advertising he most certainly doesn't mean exactly that. What he is trying to tell you is that he is not interested in certain kinds of advertising. First of all, advertising is just as important to any business as an insurance policy. An insurance policy protects against loss in the event of fire, theft, etc. Advertising not only protects against loss of customers but also increases the customer count.

Of course, we're talking about responsible businesses and businessmen; not the small, non-progressive man whom you will not call on anyway. If you accept the fact that attrition and erosion take a toll of customers every year from every business, then you are well on your way to closing more sales, because this is one of the tools you will use in your strategy to close sales. Another mighty important sales tool is your honest conviction that your product is salable. Unless you yourself believe these two facts, I cannot do a thing to help you close sales. But, if you do believe, then I will suggest how to employ those beliefs in the delicate art of being a strategist. Here's how:

Prospect: "Mr. Salesman, I do not believe in advertising."

You: "Mr. Prospect, why don't you believe in advertising."

Prospect: "No special reason, I just don't have any faith in it."

You: "Mr. Prospect, your lack of faith in advertising must be due to one of two reasons: One is that you don't believe that your product, service, etc. is worth very much; the other is that you are not sold on my radio station. Please tell me which it is." The prospect must select one of the two as a reason for not wanting to advertise and he will never offer the first as the reason. You know that he knows that he is in business to make money. Therefore, he believes in his product or service. The

WHY?

Because I failed to:
1. Investigate before the call.
2. Prepare facts and information.
3. Get prospect's attention.
4. Give good reasons to buy.
5. Overcome stall or objection:
   - A. Rate
   - B. Competition
   - C. Consult Associate
   - D. Previous dissatisfaction
   - E. Can't afford it
   - F. Other

Use trial closings with confidence.

Every salesman loses sales. The professional broadcast salesman understands why he does. You can analyze your own interviews and find your pattern of losses. Then do what's necessary to improve your weak points. Just check the appropriate box after every lost sale.

The Power Technique
NEIL TERRELL   2724 Mailan Drive   Nashville, Tennessee 37206

Neil Terrell suggests keeping a record of sales failures as a means of determining why.

only reason he can give you is that he doesn't care sufficiently about your radio station.

At this point, if you are sold on the merits of your station, you can communicate this faith to him. Just telling him that you have a good medium of advertising is not enough. Coverage maps and rate cards serve a purpose but not a sufficient purpose. Ideas! That's what you need. You must be armed with ideas! Action copy! Attention-getting programs! We've already mentioned this bill of fare.

The point we are trying to make here is to ferret out the prospect's objection to using your station and then demolish that objection with a barrage of ideas that should be tailor-made for that sponsor.

Obviously, all of this must be prepared before your meeting with the prospect, not during or after the meeting. The planning of your call should consume more time than the call itself. When you make your call, you should already have several avenues of strategy in your sales kit. Deception on your part may make the sale but it will be a one-time only sale. Honest strategy will insure not only a sale but subsequent ones also. Your prospect may not be fully aware of, nor will he accept the fact, that he loses customers every year. It's up to you to bring this into clear focus.

"Mr. Prospect, there is a natural law of customer loss that takes place in every business. Our radio station can help you to not only keep a perpetual customer count but also increase your customer count.

Here's where we draw the line between strategy and deception. Notice that I used the expression "our radio station can HELP you to do this and so." That's all you can promise your prospect; you cannot offer a firm, hard and fast guarantee that your station will produce a specified number of new customers. If your ideas, copy, programming, etc. are good enough, you probably will achieve desirable results. That's where your talent comes in. In other words, a full measure of earnest assistance as compared to an empty promise! That's why "hot-shot" salesmen are fly-by-nights and I am addressing my self to you, the honest salesman.

HOW TO BEST LACK OF INTEREST

Tell-tale signs of a lack of interest in your presentation are: Fiddling with things on the desk; glancing around the room; yawning, etc. I may be insulting your intelligence, but the purpose of this narration is to consider how to combat this lack of interest on your prospect's part. Just to suggest that you be interesting is not enough. To be interesting and command attention, you must have items of interest. A bland, unimaginative presentation is boring and is conductive to a lack of interest.

Practice how to use your voice. Make it palatable, listenable. Learn how to use production pauses in your talk. Get dramatic on occasion. Prod your prospect into talking to you and give him your undivided attention. Give a brief resume of what he said just to show that you were not only listening but that you also heard and understood what he said. We've reviewed this before, but because it is so important, we think it deserves several mentions throughout the book.

INERTIA

Resistance to change is not endemic to sponsors; it is universal. You and I resist change, We get into habits. We must be convinced that a proposed change is necessary or that it will be a change for the better. Many times it becomes more of an effort not to make a change. For example, when the great machine revolution was taking place in farming, the 40-acre farmer stubbornly clung to his belief that "what was good enough for my father is good enough for me." He plowed with a mule while his neighbor was using a tractor. The stubborn farmer broadcast his seed by hand while his neighbor was using a mechanical planter and so on.

One of the great actors of all times resisted making talking motion pictures because he had amassed millions in the silent era. But, even he found out that it was necessary to make a talking picture because customers simply would not go to see a silent movie.

A good salesman told me this story and it's true. He called on a prospective sponsor one day. The man told him rather succinctly that "nobody listens to radio, not even I." Sitting on a shelf was a portable radio. My friend (the salesman) reached up, took the radio, threw it on the ground, stomped on it, broke it into pieces. He calmly sat down and said, "Mr. Sponsor, now that we've disposed of the radio, let's talk about getting more customers in your store by means of advertising." It worked! You must show why change is necessary if you encounter a sponsor who should be advertising. If dust is gathering on his merchandise, suggest that he get out of business or else advertise with you in an effort to get customers. If cost is a factor (your rates), show him why it is more costly not to advertise.

THE EMOTIONAL BULLY

No matter which market you are selling in, you are bound to find the sponsor who gets his feelings hurt because of the slightest provocation. He'll let his feelings be known to you by one of several methods. "How come I always hear my competition's ads and never my own?" or, "Why is it that so and so always gets prime time?" or, "How come you didn't offer me your football games?" or any of a dozen "How comes?" You've got to expect this in each and every market. Whether or not their feelings are actually hurt, these people will resort to persuasion through the medium of emotion.

The best way to handle this kind of sponsor (that is, if you want his business badly enough) is to let him blow off his steam. Be a good listener. Don't argue! Don't refute! After you have heard his harrangue, be sympathetic. Agree that he probably has a genuine complaint. Rectify that complaint by offering him choice programs, availabilities, etc. Go overboard to cater to his every whim. Chances are that he'll retreat from his position. He'll turn down every offer. He'll stand on his dignity. Let him stew in his self-made misery. Give him first refusal rights on all the goodies as they become available. Sooner or later he'll come around. All he was doing was reverting to his childhood when he counted the strawberries in his plate and demanded that he be given as much or more than his older brother or sister. His mother either would comply or deny that there was discrimination. "The grass in the other pasture looks greener" pretty well sums up the attitude of the emotional bully. He's not sure of his own talent; he has a bit of paranoia in his personality.

I mention this kind of character only to alert you to his existence and how to either decide to contend with him or not have anything to do with him. It's up to you to make that choice.

THE FALSE OBJECTION

This is such an important subject that it must be reviewed time and again. Answer this question and you'll quickly see why I make such an issue of the false objection! Here is the question: "If the prospect throws up a smoke-screen of false objections and you fail to isolate the real objection, aren't you battling a ghost? Let us suppose that the reason given for not "advertising at this time is because people have no money so they aren't going to buy no matter what I advertise." You counter with "Yes, but as long as your doors are open for business, you should invite people to trade with you; you must make a bid for your share of customers."

If this doesn't do the job, do some more ferreting. "Mr. Sponsor, if, as you say, there just is no spendable income at this time, why don't you close your doors and take a vacation?" Sarcastic as it may sound, it will show the sponsor that his reasoning is fallacious. "Can't do that," he'll say. Don't pursue the point any further; instead, begin to isolate the real objection. "OK, I agree with you," you say, and then, "Mr. Sponsor, if you cannot afford to close your doors temporarily until the economy improves, why do you hesitate to advertise to get your fair share of the money that is available?" That will produce results!

"Well, I would advertise only I didn't like the way your station handled my copy." Or, "You promised to give me an availability to the local news last month and I heard my spot in a musical program." The real objection will emerge and then you can demolish it by admitting your mistakes in the past; promising better performance in the future. But, if you don't isolate the genuine objection, you've been shadow-boxing and you can't win a battle with a shadow.

FACT! A NEGATIVE AND A POSITIVE MUST PRODUCE A CHARGE!

If you accept your prospect's negative attitude without a positive approach you and your family will starve because you'll never make a sale. You must believe the above statement or else give up as a salesman. That is the stark, naked truth. Let's look at it another way. Unless and until you learn to overcome negativism, not only in your sponsor but also in yourself, you cannot make a sale. Try as you might, you cannot produce electricity without a negative and a positive. Try as you might, you cannot produce a sale if you and your sponsor take negative attitudes.

Did I hurt your feelings? Did I frighten you? If I did, I am glad because that is the jolt you need to either get you into sales with both feet or else get you out looking for other fields of endeavor. Let's explore the several reasons why a prospect will say "no!" to your presentation. The most prominent are:

1. Lack of interest in your product

2. He wants to be the boss; resents anybody suggesting things to him

3. Resistance to change

4. He got stung before by unscrupulous salesmen

5. He automatically dislikes salesmen

6. He hates to make decisions regarding spending of money

7. He is convinced that he is doing as well as he can and advertising will only add to his overhead.

8. He's a creature of habit. "Been using a quarter page ad for a million years; that's all I need."

Instead of going into detail about each and every objection mentioned, let me tell you a a true story. You can pick out the negatives and the positives for yourself.

The Farmer and His Dog

A farmer owned a dog, a faithful animal that was considered part of the farmer's family. He was loyal, obedient, and gentle. Yet, he could be vicious when the occasion called for it. Prowlers knew better than to trespass on this man's farm because of the dog. Children knew they were safe because of the dog. Yes, the dog was a lovable animal because of his many splendid attributes.

It came to pass that the farmer decided to move to the big city because he was suffering from all kinds of aches and pains. The doctor advised him to take a job in the city that wouldn't be as strenuous as farming. But, what about the dog? No apartment owner would allow such a big animal in an apartment. So the farmer reluctantly decided to give his dog to some other farmer who would take good care of him and would give the former owner visiting privileges.

He offered the dog to his neighbor but was turned down. The reason for the refusal was this: "John, thanks for asking me to take Fido off your hands, but I just have no use for a dog." The owner of the dog was chagrined because his neighbor refused to accept his offer. The farmer went back to his house and sulked about the refusal. Couldn't understand why anybody in his right mind would refuse to take such a splendid animal, for FREE, no less!

Almost the very next day, the farmer was visited by a good friend who also happened to be a good salesman. When the salesman heard about the dog, he decided to do something about it. The salesman visited the man who had turned down the dog. "Nice place you have here," he commented as he was being given a tour of the farm. He glanced at the huge grain storage bins and said, "My goodness what a tempting treat for rats and field mice." The farmer agreed that it certainly was a problem keeping out the marauding rodents. They went on. "A wonderful flock of sheep you have; how do you manage to protect them from invading wolves, hawks, and weasels?" "That's a big problem, too," answered the farmer. "Are you a sound sleeper?" inquired the salesman. "Sure am," replied the farmer. "What if you have a fire? How would you know about that in your sound sleep?" quizzed the salesman. "Don't know; never thought about it," answered the now concerned farmer. "You sure have problems," said the salesman. "Guess I do, but what can I do about them?" was the worried question.

The salesman took his time. "I think I can provide the answer to most of these problems but it may cost you some money." "How much?" was the immediate response. "Waaaal, let's see," said the salesman, "How much value do you put on your grain, livestock, **your life, the lives of your family,** your home, etc.?" "Gosh, there's no telling; can't begin to give you an estimate," answered the farmer. "Would you say about $300?" "Three hundred dollars!" exclaimed the farmer. "You must be kidding!" The salesman feigned ignorance. "Do you mean my estimate is too high?" he asked casually. "Too high! No, dern it, it's too low, that's what it is!" asserted the exasperated farmer. "Well then, what is **your** estimate pursued the salesman. "Can't tell you; there is no way that I can put a value on all that you've mentioned. But tell me, how can you provide the protection that you have in mind anyway?" asked the worried farmer.

The salesman side-stepped this question by staring into space. "Just give me a few minutes to work this out," he said as he busied himself with paper and pencil. The silence was deafening. The farmer waited. He was anxious. The salesman took advantage of this long production pause, then he finally looked up and drawled. "Let's see now, I estimate your real property to amount to about $40,000; that is, for your cattle and grain. Your house about $25,000; the lives of you and your family are priceless; really, I cannot tell you just how much they are worth. But anyway, here is what I suggest: "First, get some good watch dogs, dogs that are trained to attack predators like wolves, weasels, etc., dogs that will bark at the first sign of smoke or fire, dogs that will attack rats. Also, get some real good insurance that will cover your losses just in case you don't respond to the dog's barking or just in case somebody decides to poison your dogs or shoot 'em."

That's what the salesman suggested. The result was that he sold the dog to the farmer that the farmer once rejected. He put a price tag of three hundred dollars on that dog. He also sold several other dogs to the farmer at various prices, along with a very good insurance policy.

KEEP YOUR TEMPER; NO ONE ELSE WANTS IT!

True, we are discussing various ways to close a sale, but how about after the close? Can we afford to lose an account that we worked so hard to get in the first place. Keeping an account after the close is most necessary. Many an account has been lost because of quick tempers. Sometimes we react to a situation by flaring up; losing our cool, etc. Let me illustrate how I handled a sponsor who took me months to get. This man was generally regarded as "peculiar." He had a thriving business in spite of himself. His customers didn't especially care for him as much as they did for his product. It was because of this that it took me so long to "land" him.

It was a challenge to me, and after walking on eggshells with hat in hand, presenting new ideas with each call, I finally struck his Achille's Heel and he bought a nice schedule. We treated him with kid gloves, gave him every ounce of care and attention. Mind you now, this was not done in an atmosphere of servitude; service was more like it. Well, to make a long story more interesting, I had an unexpected collision with this man. It happened at our local chamber of commerce. There I was, seated at the table, surrounded with sponsors whose billings amounted to several thousand dollars a month. Seated across from me was this dissident man. Appropos of nothing at all he proclaimed in a loud, clear voice: "Si, I'm thinking of switching my advertising to Station K---- because their kind of programming reaches my customers best. I had to make a split-second decision. Should I challenge him on the spot? Should I table what he said until I could refut his allegations? Make a scene in the presence of thousands of dollars worth of advertisers.

Easy Does It

My adrenaline started to flow immediately. I imagined that all eyes were upon me. But I reasoned (all in that wink of an eye) that people knew the man for what he was. Also, I remembered that a good lawyer once asked the defendant when he last beat up his wife. The implication was there. If you attempt to deny it, you acknowledge its presence. Yes, this admixture of emotion, reasoning, and sudden attack overwhelmed me in the twinkling of an eye and a reaction was inevitable. So, in a calm voice I said, "Mr. Jones, perhaps you have a more recent survey than the one which we just paid good money to get; may we compare demographics first thing tomorrow morning?" I smiled when I said it even though I was boiling inside. This response only added fuel to fire. "I don't need a professional survey," exclaimed the tactless sponsor, "I just listen to the portable radios carried around by the teenagers who come into my store; they are all tuned to that other station." Now, how do you get out of that one?

Time To Firm Up

Firm up! That's what you do and here's how! "Mr. Jones, many of your customers are my neighbors. It is inevitable that they discuss items of local interest, such as the cost of merchandise in this town as compared to the cost of the same merchandise in the big city about forty miles away. Many of them insist that most merchants here charge more than the chain stores do in the city.

This is idle chatter because we compare your prices as advertised on my station with the ads in the metropolitan daily newspapers. There are variances. But, when I consider the cost of making a trip all that distance to buy a few things that may be less that you charge, I find that I'm losing money. Besides, we shop at home! I know that you appreciate our efforts to have our local citizens shop at home also. If you advertise on an out-of-town station you are, in effect, indicating that you endorse the policy of spending money out of town. But that's not here nor there; let's get together in the morning and compare facts and figures, OK?"

Keep Calm

That was oil poured on a troubled sea. One of the sponsors sitting next to me gave me a knowing wink and I knew that I had scored a good point. The sponsor continued his schedule on my station and nothing more was done or said about the incident. Here is a classic example of how reason replaced an ugly temper and how I avoided a head-on collision in an arena with more than 75 percent of my sponsors as spectators.

Sudden Shocks Are Killers

I respectfully suggest that you learn to expend energy in proportion to the work to be done. A quick flare-up of temper is very enervating and, in many cases, out of proportion to the job that is to be accomplished. First of all, an uncontrollable temper blows out the lamp of the mind. Secondly, you put yourself on display as a person who loses control.

Don't retreat; stand firm, and above all be armed with

enough discipline to contend with the unexpected. An overbearing, arrogant attitude invites trouble. Act respectable and you will be respected. Keep your mind supple; anticipate the unexpected by actually simulating situations such as I described. You supply yourself with an antidote against shock that comes unexpectedly. Electricians say it isn't the amount of amperes that kills; it's the unexpected shock of electricity that knocks you out. This is true up to a certain point. We're not talking about a man who is being strapped to the electric chair.

NEEDS AND WANTS

Needs and wants are related and yet totally different. A person who is freezing **wants** some heat. A person who still does her washing by hand **needs** a washing machine. It's up to you to not only recognize the difference between needs and wants but also use this knowledge to your advantage. A businessman **wants** to make money, yet that same businessman **needs** an advertising program to help him make the money that he wants. If he's just chugging along, making some profit, it's up to you to point out the **need** for making substantial profit to get him out of the marginal operator category. If no effort is made to improve his profit picture, that profit can be erroded by increasing costs. Therefore, you must be subtle enough to point out the difference between his **needs** and his **wants** and show him how you can help him.

The unfortunate part of this situation is that often a person doesn't realize what his needs are! For years people needed electric knives. They knew that somehow the performance of carving the Sunday turkey could be improved. Then, when electric knives came into being, those Sunday turkey carvers realized that those electric knives were **needed** all along. Just take a few minutes and think of your own reaction to needs and wants. Your wife's dishpan hands, then your recognizing the need for an electric dishwasher. The dishwasher was brought to your attention through the medium of advertising. Spend the next few minutes thinking over what we are trying to tell you, and the point will emerge like a picture being devloped in a dark room.

COMBATTING INDECISION

There are many factors that contribute to a sponsor's indecision to advertise on your station. Let's select one at random: "It's too early to advertise my farm equipment. Think I'll wait for the weather to get right and then advertise."

What the sponsor is really telling you is that he is not sure whether his prospects are in a buying mood. Therefore, he wants to wait and see what changes the weather will bring. You make up the sponsor's mind for him by suggesting that because farmers cannot be in the field now, they have a better chance of listening to your station. This being the case, your sponsor's messages about his tractors, farm equipment, etc., should be given at this time so that the farmers can be motivated to buy during the slack season and avoid the rush later on.

In this case the sponsor can point out these advantages in his sales messages: 1. Buy now and be ready to go when the weather clears. 2. Delivery can be arranged faster because it is off season. 3. The farmer has more leisure time to use profitably by advance preparation. And on and on we can go.

It's up to you, Mr. Salesman, to prod the sponsor into action now! You must stress the point that the sponsor's obligation is to remind the farmer about his own needs. Of course, the best way to do this is with a schedule of action-getting, thought-provoking sales messages on your radio station! This applies to all sponsors who put you off because "the time isn't ripe to advertise."

ENTHUSIASM

Without enthusiasm, you're not going to succeed in sales. Now I don't mean that you should prance around all day, slap people on the back, tell 'em how wonderful the weather is when it's snowing like mad. Nothing of that kind, at all. Gilbert & Sullivan expressed it pretty well with: "Things are seldom what they seem, skimmed milk masquarades like cream, etc." If you are sold on your product, if you are satisfied that you can make a good presentation that will be honest, intermingled with a positive attitude, laced with good ideas and how they might help your sponsor, you've got the basic ingredients for being enthusiastic. Compare this with the Doubting Thomas kind of salesman who tells his troubles to his prospects, and you can quickly distinguish between the two. Some people never waste a smile; some have no frequency response, and still others run the gamut of emotion from A to B. (Thanks to Dorothy Parker for this wonderful description of a non-enthusiast.)

Be A Realist

Being a realist is also part of enthusiasm. I can best illustrate this with the story of three men who invested in the same stock. They each bought 100 shares on the same day, at the same price from the same stock broker. One man said, "I'm going to make a killing with this stock; it's low now but the future is wonderful for my investment." The second man had the same idea but didn't quite trust his judgment. The third man bought in the same quantity and said "The stock is low now, and when it reaches a certain price I'm going to sell it and make a modest profit." Time passed. The stock rose in value. When it reached the price expected by the third man, he sold and was happy with his modest profit. The second man sold his shares when he thought that the stock had reached its maximum level of performance. The first man held his shares. Then, suddenly, the company that had issued the stock struck oil and the value of the stock zoomed to dizzying heights. Here was the reaction of each man and how we illustrate vividly what we mean by being a realist:

The third man remained content with his modest profit because that is what he had planned on. He had no regrets because he didn't hold onto his stock. He had reinvested his profit and had earned money from that source. He was a realist because he set a goal and acted according to plan. He was satisfied.

Man number two regretted that he didn't hold his stock longer. "If I had just held on to that blankety blank stock, I'd be in good shape today," was his complaint. Even though he made more money than man number three, he was miserable because he didn't wait for "the kill."

Investor number one was even more miserable than investor number two because he had bought such a small quantity of the stock. "Why didn't I buy a thousand shares when the stock was so cheap?" he moaned. He was indeed an unhappy man. So you see, realism is a part of enthusiasm. Set your sights on a goal; be enthusiastic about reaching that goal; anticipate disappointments on the way; be prepared to contend with setbacks. Enthusiasm contains all of these ingredients, so I suggest that you start preparing yourself a good recipe of attitudes that should make you enthusiastic and a realist at the same time, as well as a better radio sales account executive!

OF TIME AND TIMING AND SQUELCHING PEOPLE

Next to your health, the most precious thing you have is time. Time evaporates. It flies! Tempus does fugit! And time doubles in value when you use it wisely. Oddly enough, this most precious commodity is doled out to each one of us in the same measure. Whether you be emperor of the world or lord of your estate or a lowly serf, you are given time in equal amounts. Of course, I don't mean that we all live to be the same age, but while we are alive, the seconds, minutes, hours, days and years pass for each of us at the same rate of speed. Because it is free, we tend to squander it; that goes for most anything that is given to us without any charge. I implore you to use your time wisely.

Timing And Squelching

Timing is important, too; timing your sales call. Do you watch for a buying signal? Or, are you a "squelcher?" Do you deflate people's egos? Do you puncture balloons? Do you treat people like this? Like the story about an advertising executive and his sweet copywriter. This sweet gal was asked to hand-letter a parchment scroll proclaiming the advantages of doing business with the independent insurance agents. The scroll read:

"WE, THE INDEPENDENT AGENTS, DECLARE THIS TO BE OUR POLICY:

1. We represent YOU and not the insurance companies.
2. We select the insurance company that is RIGHT FOR YOU!
3. We settle claims in your best interests.
4. We are INDEPENDENT insurance agents and can stay in business because of the policies that YOU buy from US!
5. Our best policy is to give YOU prompt, fair service.

Signed (Several names)

Three months passed. Our sweet gal completed the scroll. It was a beautiful job and she was proud of her work. Every flourish in place; not a blemish. "Ah," she said, "this is my crowning achievment. Now I'll present it to my boss."

So, she presented it to her boss. While he looked it over very carefully, she quivered with excitement. These thoughts ran through her mind as she stood in his presence: "He hasn't moved a muscle in his face. Could he be so taken in with this perfect job that he is transfixed with complete satisfaction?"

Then, five minutes later, she thought, "No reaction yet! Wonder what's wrong?" A few minutes later, "I can't stand this suspense. I must know his reaction. It seems like an eternity."

The gal summoned up courage; she cleared her throat and said rather timidly, "Well, Mr. Jones, what do you think?" "Think?" he blurted. "Mrs. Smith, you forgot to dot this I!" Mrs. Smith's balloon was punctured. She was crestfallen. Imagine, three months of hard work to complete a hand-lettered parchment scroll. Her very best effort. Every flourish in place; not a word missing. But the boss caught the only error and that was his appraisal of her best effort!

As a salesman, do you do this? Do you squelch people? Do you deflate egos? Do you make yourself unpopular because your timing is bad? Because your enthusiasm doesn't enthuse? Remember, use your time profitably and time your timing perfectly. Be constructive, not destructive! Avoid hurting people's feelings! Sponsors will like you and the result will be bigger and better sales in radio advertising.

PERSONAL STANDARDS

This is a true story about an Englishman. He was lost in the jungle and was the object of a big manhunt. After days of searching, he was finally located deep in the wilds of the jungle. The people who found him were happy and perplexed almost all at one time. They were happy because they found the man and perplexed because he was seated at a campfire, dressed in a neat suit, clean shaven, a napkin on his lap. He had silverware neatly arranged next to clean china. The scene was indeed out of keeping with the environment. After a few moments of elation, one of the searchers asked this English gentleman why he was so neatly dressed and had such an elaborate table set in the wilds of the Jungle. His reply was short and simple: "Because," said the Englishman, "tonight I am dining with God."

The man had a set of values, and not even being out of touch with civilization would make him deviate. The story has a lot of meaning. It is easy to follow the lines of least resistance. It is easy to blame circumstances for misbehavior. It is easy to rationalize. It is easy to let down your guard when no one is looking. But, it is real tough to maintain your standards under these conditions. My advice is to work for a station that runs a clean shop, a station that serves the people. Service first, profit next. That's the order of business at the stations that I own. How about yours?

REAL LIFE DRAMA

This a true story and it illustrates clearly the frequent catastrophic result of inadequate communications. It concerns three teenaged girls, a poorly worded note, and a near-suicide. Names are ficticious; events are true.

Susie and Mary had a falling out. They had been close friends, but a disagreement about an inconsequential matter flared up and "they were not talking to each other." This is an everyday occurrence.

Along came teenage girl number three. Her name is Jane. Jane wrote a note to Susie: "What do you think of Mary now?" Susie, although not on speaking terms with Mary, still felt a strong bond of friendship. She answered Jane's note like this: "I hate Mary the same way that her parents hate her." (At this point, let me explain that Mary is an adopted child and never did feel 100 percent certain that her parents loved her as if she had been born by her adoptive mother. Also important to the story is the fact that neither Jane nor Susie knew that Mary was an adopted child.)

Now, Jane had some damning facts about Mary; namely that Mary's parents hated her. Pretty soon, one of Mary's protective friends said to Mary, "I heard that your parents hate you." This startled Mary because it seemed to confirm her suspicion that her parents never did really love her. She attempted suicide but it was thwarted.

After some prodding, she blurted out the reason for her attempted suicide. Mary's mother summoned the mothers of Susie and Jane, and after a bit of interrogation the truth emerged. What Susie really wanted to say was that she **loved** Mary in the same fashion that Mary's parents did. The only trouble was that she chose the wrong word, and it became a lethal weapon when it was put into writing and exhibited by Jane. As radio salesmen, we are in the communications business. A careless word or a hastily written letter can cause a disastrous chain reaction. It can sometimes be fatal.

JOIN THE FIVE PERCENT

Earl Nightingale estimates that only about five percent of the people in this world actually plan their future. This five percent also has a unique quality that is lacking in so many of us: **They are considerate of other people.** It costs no money to join the successful five percent. Resolve now that you'll become a member of this successful minority group and learn a lesson from the following experience:

A friend of mine asked me to get some important information. I went to a great deal of time, effort, and trouble to get the facts. I called him long distance because he said that he needed the information in a hurry. Much to my surprise and chagrin he said, "Just a minute, please, while I get a pencil." There was a 2-minute waiting period. Then he said "Oops! I have the pencil but no paper. More waiting (at my personal expense). To finish this aggravating experience, the charge for the phone call was considerable, all because this man didn't think in terms of being considerate; because he wasn't ready for action.

Such an experience may sound trivial to you, but it is all important. Earl Nightingale's formula for success calls for planning a goal and being considerate of the people you meet on your way up. Many are called but few are chosen! And you can be among the few who are chosen IF you work at it!

SURVEYS

I have reams of unsolicited letters from listeners, commercial accounts, and non-commercial accounts (churches, civic clubs, governmental agencies, etc.) that give proof of our acceptance in the community. Yet, when we were trying to get one of the better station reps to represent us on a national basis, they insisted that we go to the expense of a professional survey. I was overjoyed with the results. We were so far out in front of the competition that I was reluctant to use these figures for fear that someone would suspect the results were "fixed" in our favor, simply because we paid so much money for the survey.

To circumvent the "fixed" charge I ran a contest. I asked listeners to write, in a hundred words or less, why they liked or disliked our station. I paid one dollar each for every letter received, regardless of the contents. Out of all the letters, we would pay $100 for the best letter telling what they liked about us and $100 for the best letter telling us what they disliked about us. We also would pay one hundred dollars for the letter giving us the most constructive criticism.

The contest ran for one month and the response was phenomenal! We had letters scrawled on lined tablet paper (neatness didn't count); we had beautiful letters on expensive stationary; letters of all kinds from all walks of life. Hundreds of them. Good, bad, indifferent. It nearly broke us, but we paid off one dollar for each letter (one to the customer; we didn't pay more than one dollar to each of the several writers who sent in more than one letter). Then, we asked three out-of-town people to judge the letters. We carefully described what we were after.

The judges pondered, read, re-read, and finally came up with the three winners and we paid them off. Boy, did we pay out a lot of money, more than the expensive professional survey cost us. But we did get a good analysis of our station and we did find what people disliked, liked, and wanted us to do. One of the things that was worth the price of the contest was the suggestion that we put more humor on the air. "Don't be comedians but supply funny quirks in the news. After all, the news is so grim, filled with war, hate, and riots. Somewhere in this world there is a chuckle, a laugh; let us share in that bit of humor," the letter read. The same letter also suggested humorous records and listed them. We bought the humor records and played them, much to our listeners' delight. Now, humor is a must on our station. Again, I say that we don't have comedians but we do present humor to offset the grim realities of everyday news.

EFFECTIVE USE OF AUDIENCE SURVEYS

There are many great stations in our land and they all enjoy excellent ratings. We could fill this book with samples of brochures that use audience surveys to their greatest advantage. However, we have selected Radio KRTN in Wichita Falls, Texas, to illustrate how dynamic an audience survey presentation can be. It is information like this that makes it easier for a salesman to make bigger and better sales. Regional and national representatives love this kind of sales ammunition.

Surveys are expensive and there is never a guarantee that you'll be the number one station even when you pay for the survey. Also, a survey in and of itself is not enough to make the sale; it is only a sales tool. New, bright, fresh ideas must be used to make sales. Surveys, coverage maps, and rate cards only augment the ideas you present. These devices are complementary and could result in your sales manager being complimentary if you use them correctly. Remember, the route to bigger and better sales is to have an admixture of motivating new ideas plus an arsenal of satisfied customer endorsements, good audience survey ratings, and a realistic rate card.

This is 1290 COUNTRY KTRN

KTRN's 5,000 Watt signal on 1290 KCS. in the nation's highest soil conductivity area, blankets the Wichita Falls, Lawton trade area with .5 Millivolts of signal strength or MORE.

KTRN serves ALL of TEXOMA

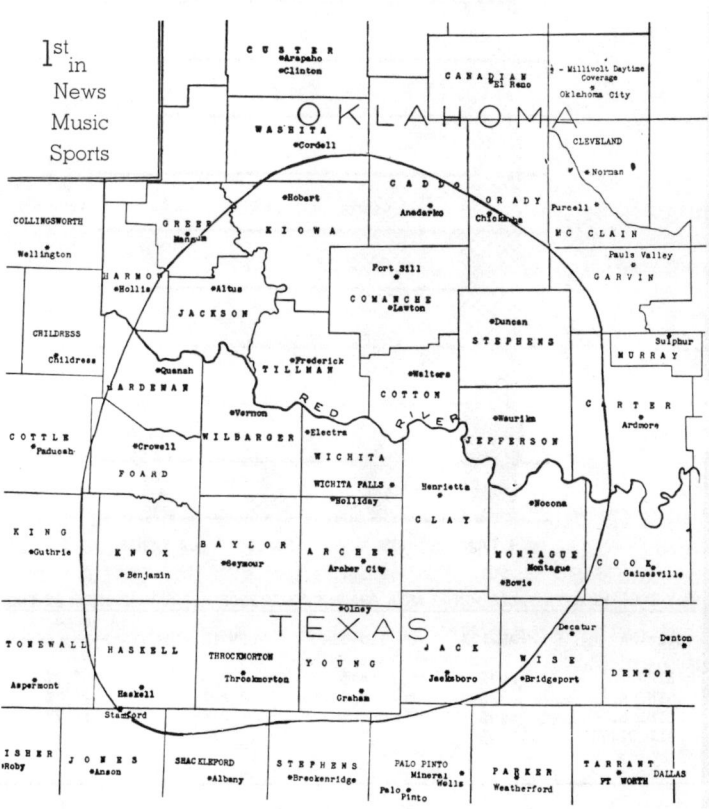

And...Where KTRN Goes...SO GO YOUR CUSTOMERS! ▶▶▶▶▶▶▶▶

KTRN's brochure begins with a coverage map.

KTRN corners more of your customers and prospects than your firm does* and more than any other station!

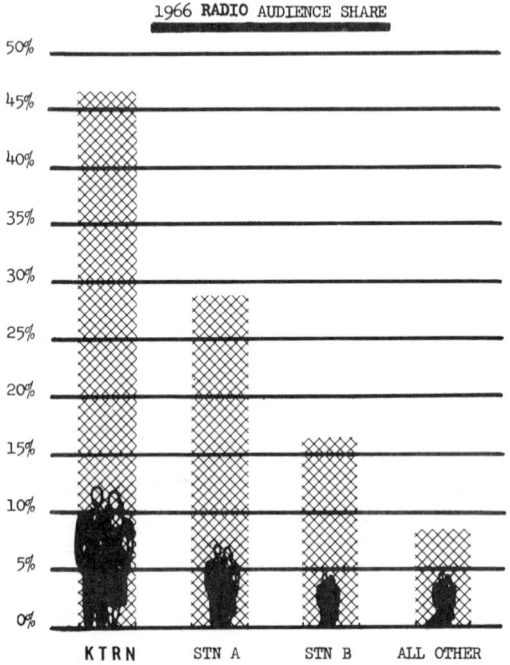

1966 **RADIO** AUDIENCE SHARE

MAY 1966 WICHITA FALLS METRO AREA SHARE OF AUDIENCE M-F 6AM-12 MID. BY PULSE

Station	6AM-12N	12N-6PM	6PM-12 MID.	Average of these shares
KTRN	44%	44%	52%	46.7%
STN. A.	33%	33%	20%	28.7%
STN. B.	19%	9%	22%	16.7%
ALL OTHER	5%	13%	7%	8.3%

*Unless your's is a public utility firm!

This page illustrates audience shares by time period.

KTRN is HABIT FORMING too!
AN <u>AMAZING</u> Decade OF Dominance!

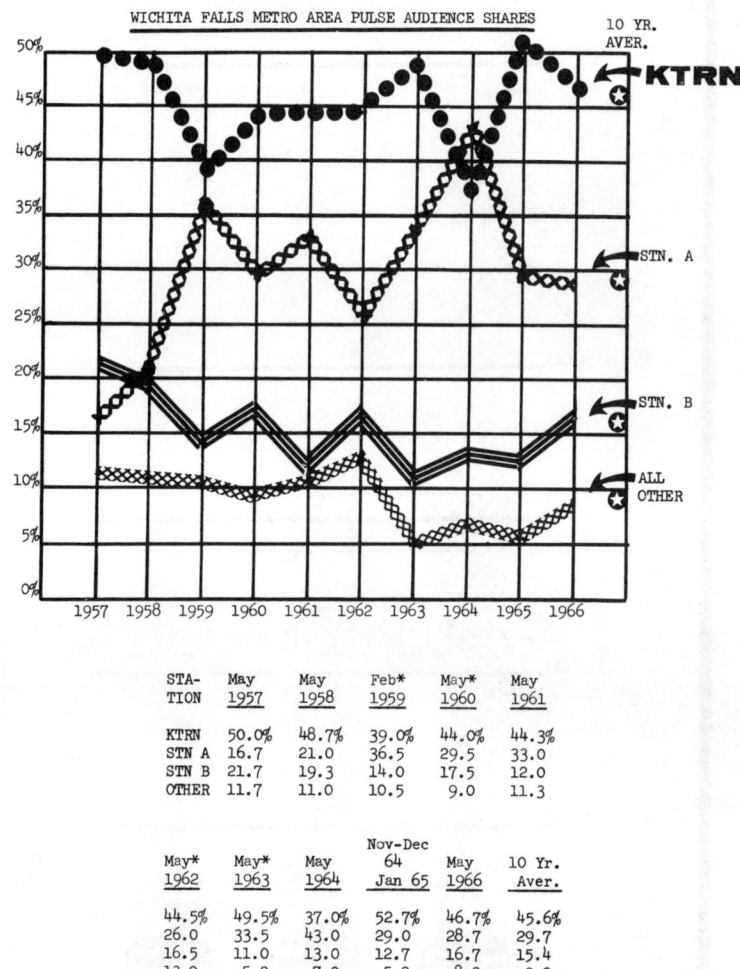

STATION	May 1957	May 1958	Feb* 1959	May* 1960	May 1961
KTRN	50.0%	48.7%	39.0%	44.0%	44.3%
STN A	16.7	21.0	36.5	29.5	33.0
STN B	21.7	19.3	14.0	17.5	12.0
OTHER	11.7	11.0	10.5	9.0	11.3

May* 1962	May* 1963	May 1964	Nov-Dec 64 Jan 65	May 1966	10 Yr. Aver.
44.5%	49.5%	37.0%	52.7%	46.7%	45.6%
26.0	33.5	43.0	29.0	28.7	29.7
16.5	11.0	13.0	12.7	16.7	15.4
13.0	5.0	7.0	5.3	8.3	9.2

KTRN's brochure makes use of the audience figures for an entire decade.

Let's Be **MORE SPECIFIC**
(and count the homes delivered at any given time)

MAY 1966   WICHITA FALLS METRO AREA PULSE

Average Homes Delivered Per Quarter Hour
6:00 AM To Midnight M-F

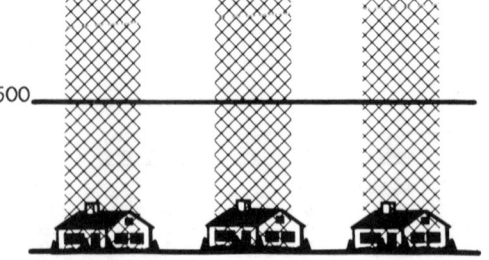

Data showing the home count.

KTRN dominates PENETRATION too

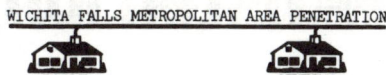

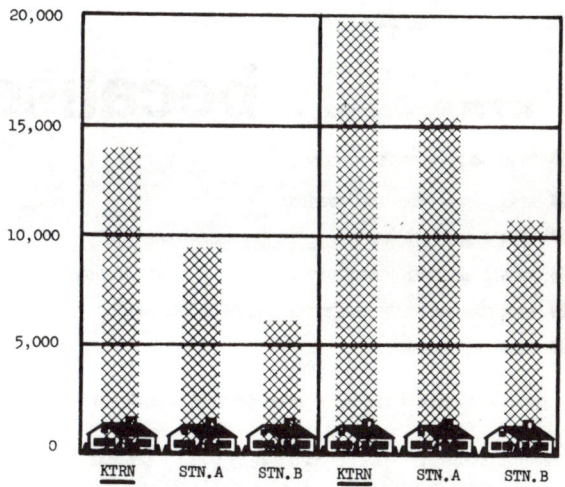

Daily and weekly penetration figures.

KTRN HOMES listen longer

- Nearly one Hour Longer Daily than any other Wichita Falls Station's homes.
- Nearly six Hours Longer each week!
- 38 (eight hour) Days Longer each YEAR!

KTRN HOMES LISTEN LONGER because:

- KTRN DELIVERS SUPERIOR NEWS!
- KTRN OFFERS MORE INFORMATION!
- KTRN'S CONTESTS ARE FOR LISTENERS NOT ADVERTISERS!
- KTRN'S BALANCED MUSICAL FORMAT APPEALS TO ALL AGE GROUPS!
- KTRN HAS SOMETHING FOR EVERY MEMBER OF THE FAMILY!
- KTRN IS DIFFERENT!

The Facts: (Pulse Wichita Falls Metro Area May 1966, 6am-Mid.)

	KTRN	STN. A.	STN. B.
Weekly Hours of Listening:	518,742	321,300	174,258
No. Metro Homes Penetrated Weekly:	19,600	15,600	11,100
Weekly Hours Per Home	26.46	20.60	15.70
Daily Hours of Listening per Home:	3 Hrs, 47 Min.	2 Hrs, 56 Min.	2 Hrs, 14 Min.

Your CAMPAIGN will be 29% More EFFECTIVE per HOME on KTRN than on any other Station!

Your MESSAGE has a 29% BETTER CHANCE to be heard in a KTRN HOME

Breakdown of KTRN's penetration.

THE SAVING ON KTRN IS A COLD STATISTICAL ADVANTAGE

There's More..........on KTRN you get...............

1 Far superior believability for your message. The cornerstone for KTRN's believability is it's accurate news, unequalled anywhere in the Southwest, year after year.

2 Constant attention by listeners for your message. Ask your KTRN Representative to explain why a noisy station is "background Commercial Radio" just as FM is "Background Radio". And why Radios tuned to KTRN are tuned up LOUDER.

3 No competition for your message from Station promotion and contests. Ask your KTRN Representative to explain.

4 Pre-Conditioned Reaction to your Message. Ask your KTRN Representative to explain.

5 Proper Separation for your Message from Competitors.

6 Most Buyers of Acquisitive Age.

7 The listeners who'll soon be homemakers are your best prospects by far!

8 SUPERIOR Air Salesmen, Experienced in Big Market Radio..... Oklahoma City, Tulsa, West Coast, Etc.

9 And Much More............Too Much to Detail Here!

List of advertiser advantages provides the salesman with many "talking" points.

Dominance of **Adults** TOO

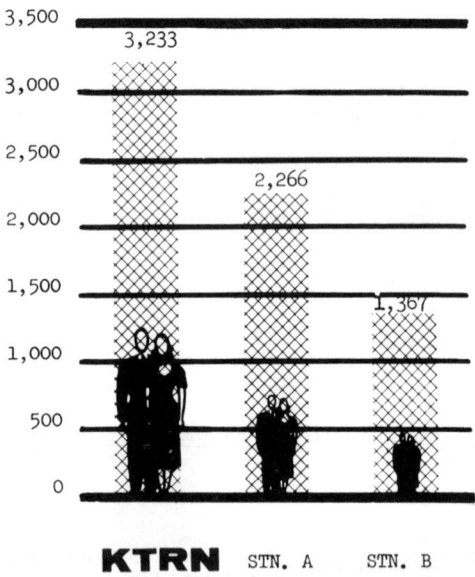

AVERAGE NUMBER OF ADULTS PER QUARTER HOUR

Wichita Falls Metro Area Pulse, M-F 6AM-Mid, May, 1966

KTRN DELIVERS ALMOST AS MANY ADULTS AS
ALL OTHER WICHITA FALLS STATIONS
COMBINED

Audience makeup statistics presented in an easy-to-understand way.

PROMOTING YOUR STATION!

A good radio station will backstop the efforts of its sales team with good promotions on the air and in other media. The best theme of any promotional program is to show progress. Just to say that you've been doing business from the same stand for one hundred years is not enough. What's New???? That's the big item of interest.

A mistaken notion in many radio stations is that if you use the print medium in any form, you are giving aid and comfort to your competition. That is narrow thinking. Let's fact it, no radio station reaches all of the people. It is important that your

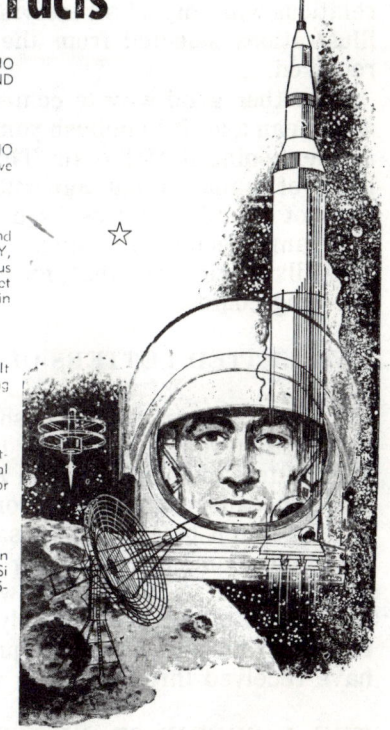

Down To Earth Facts

Mr. Advertiser, you tell your message on RADIO KMAR for LESS than ONE CENT PER THOUSAND LISTENERS.

FACT
Mr. Advertiser when you advertise on RADIO KMAR, WE DO ALL THE WORK! You do not have to spend valuable time laying out your ad.

FACT
KMAR listeners INVITE us into their homes and cars. According to latest MEDIASTAT SURVEY, over 11,000 adults and 1,300 Teenagers listen to us daily IN FRANKLIN PARISH ALONE! This does not include the hundreds of people who listen to us in THEIR CARS!

FACT
KMAR advertising is flexible. No typesetting. It takes just a few minues to change your adverising copy if necessary.

FACT
Since listeners tune to KMAR, that indicates listener endorsement of our programs and commercial advertising. Listeners SHOP KMAR RADIO for things to buy and places to buy them.

FACT
Continuous advertising on RADIO KMAR results in CUMULATIVE GAINS for our sponsors. Call Si Willing at 435-5644 or Murray Shoemaker at 435-5141 FOR THE KMAR ADVERTISING STORY!

KMAR
Winnsboro, Louisiana

KMAR ad stressing the flexibility of radio advertising, aimed at advertisers and listeners. It implies that the print medium is rigid and emphasises the economy of radio.

station be advertised and promoted in newspapers and magazines as well as on the air. Other methods of station promotion include roadside billboards, state maps showing the location and frequencies of radio stations in every city and town; these are distributed to tourists by hotels and motels.

There are scores of ways to promote your radio station and we say again, **good** station promotion attracts listeners; the more listeners, the better the station's rating. You know the rest, the better rating your station can have, the easier it becomes for you as a sales representative to make sales to your sponsors. We illustrate just a few samples of meaningful, progressive advertising.

PUBLIC RELATIONS

Another way to promote your station is to maintain good relations with important individuals. Examples appear in the illustrations selected from the many letters that we have received.

Another good way to cement good relations with people who mean a lot is to publish your appreciation in print as well as mentioning it on the air. This is illustrated with the open letter of thanks to our agricultural experts. Also notice the copy of an ad that was used to convert our listeners into program directors. This ad also did a bit of merchandising for Pet Milk. Notice, too, that, for good measure, we conducted a guessing contest.

UNSOLICITED LETTERS OF TESTIMONIAL

Next to hearing the cash register ring, the greatest satisfaction you can have is to get complimentary letters. Such letters are valuable and make your job as a salesman easier because they show prior endorsement.

We said it before and we say it again. It takes the entire staff, the team, to make your station so wonderful that unsolicited letters of testimonial will arrive frequently enough to enable you to keep your supply fresh and clean. Selected at random from our vast file are just a few of the many letters we have received throughout the years.

THE DIFFERENCE BETWEEN PUBLICITY AND ADVERTISING

Advertising is intended to create sales for your sponsors. Advertising is bought and paid for. You earn your salary or commission from the advertising that you sell.

LOUISIANA

Louisiana Association of Broadcasters and Louisiana Motor Hotel Association brochure listing stations in each community. It also contains a list of motels plus special events of interest to travelers.

FOR 12 BIG YEARS

Many thanks to our listeners and sponsors for making possible our twelfth year of continuous broadcasting. In 1957 we had one control room, a small staff and tender, uncertain roots. Today, we have two control rooms, we have more than doubled our personnel, we are installing our FM station (KCRF) 95.5 MHZ in order to give nightime service, and our once-tender roots have grown strong and deep in community service. We pledge to continue our efforts to keeep pace with the growth of our fine community.

The Staff and Management of Radio KMAR

K M A R

Si Willing, Gen. Mgr.

Anniversary ad serves several purposes.

Publicity is another thing. Publicity is any information that brings a person, place, or thing to the attention of the public. Publicity stories generally go into newscasts and are devoid of all advertising. The difference between advertising and publicity is a debatable subject. Some stations insist that any mention of a profit-making company is advertising. They also say this kind of public mention should be paid for. Because this is such a "fielder's choice" decision to make, I will give you my own interpretation:

If a sponsor is celebrating an anniversary and is holding open house for the public, this can go into the news as a publicity story. If that sponsor wants to make sure that the open house is well attended, he must then pay for all sales messages to that effect. Each time an invitation to the public is broadcast, it should be considered to be a commercial message. Illustrated are several typical publicity releases.

DEAR LISTENER:

We Are Proceeding With The Installation Of Our FM Station As The Weather Permits. In The Meanwhile, We Would Appreciate Hearing From You By Letter, Suggesting The Kind Of Programming You Would Like On Our FM Station. Our FM Station Will Simulcast With Our AM Station During The Daylight Hours And Then Continue Operation Until 11 P.M. After We Sign Off The AM Station. We Welcome Your Programming Suggestions. Please Write To KMAR, Winnsboro, La. 71295.

SINCERELY,
SI WILLING, Gen. Mgr.

RADIO KMAR

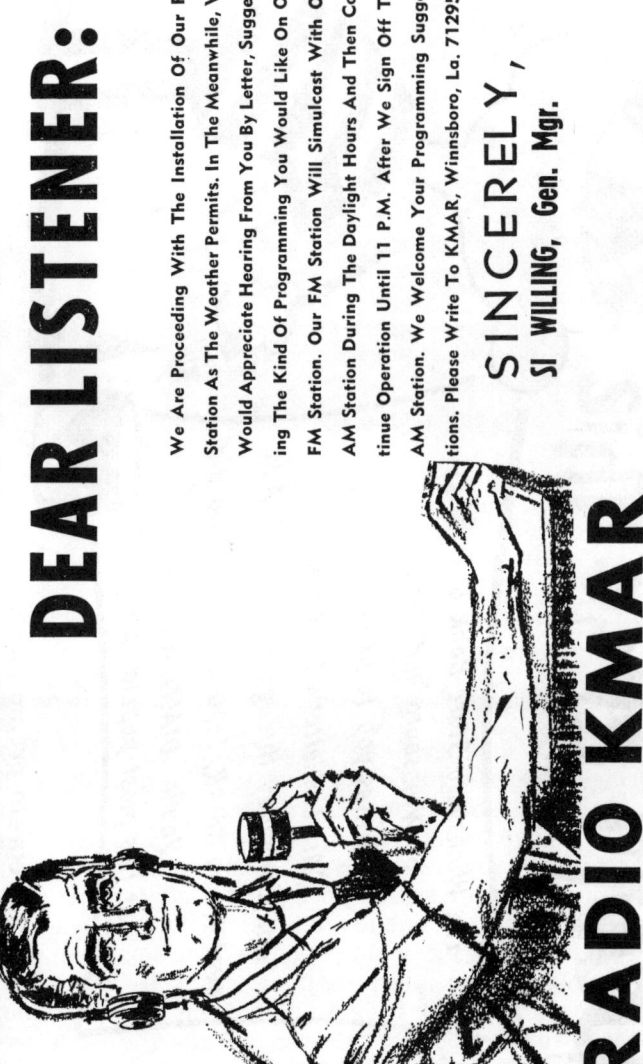

Ad keeping listeners posted on FM construction.

Program promo piece.

Newspaper ad points out to listeners that radio programs are free. They also stressed the variety of KMAR's programming.

United States Senate
COMMITTEE ON
AGRICULTURE AND FORESTRY

November 3, 1965

Mr. Si Willing, President
 and General Manager
KMAR
Box 312
Winnsboro, Louisiana

Dear Mr. Willing:

    Senator Ellender is now beginning his annual tour of Louisiana. Although his itinerary is as yet incomplete, he has scheduled several speaking engagements and plans to spend some time in visiting every Parish. Accordingly, he has asked me to let you know that he hopes to see you during the coming weeks, and that he will be available for news interviews and comment upon his arrival in each area.

    With kindest regards and best wishes, I am

                  Sincerely yours,

                    C. B. MORRISON
                    Assistant to Senator Ellender

CBM: B

Response to an invitation extended to a U.S. senator.

State of Louisiana
EXECUTIVE DEPARTMENT
Baton Rouge

JOHN J. MCKEITHEN
GOVERNOR

March 19, 1968

Mr. S. J. Willing
KMAR
Lone Cedar Road
Winnsboro, La. 71295

Dear Mr. Willing:

I would very much like you to be my guest at a "Louisiana Made" luncheon at 12 o'clock noon, Thursday, April 4, in the Grand Salon in the Royal Orleans Hotel in New Orleans.

The luncheon will truly be Louisiana made, featuring many of the famous foods of our great State.

This gathering will officially open the month long "Louisiana Made", State Pride/Statewide, campaign. I believe you will find it well worth attending.

I look forward to seeing you there.

Sincerely,

John J. McKeithen
Governor

Reply card enclosed

Invitation from the governor.

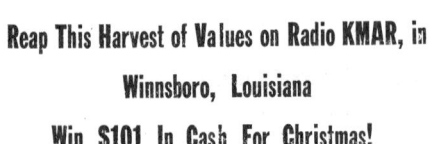

Contest promo ad.

Making The Best of Every Opportunity

Here's how we made some money by tying in with the National Rifle Association's public service promotion. We sold Smith's Sporting Goods Store on the idea of a big shooting match on a local level. "Show me a sample of your copy and I just might buy the idea," said Mr. Smith. This is the sample copy that sold the idea:

Sportsmen, get the lead; take a bead on the final tryouts for the selection of the U.S. World Moving Target Team. Register now for the BIG SHOOT OUT to be held at SMITH'S FARM this Sunday. Register at SMITH'S SPORTING GOODS STORE in Winnsboro. No charge, no obligation, no purchase necessary, just register. Use your own rifle and ammunition for the BIG SHOOT OUT. If you need more supplies, shop

SMITH'S SPORTING GOODS STORE first! The BIG SHOOT OUT will be supervised by the Sheriff and his deputies. Don't wait, but register TODAY at SMITH'S SPORTING GOODS STORE in Winnsboro to enter the BIG SHOOT OUT this Sunday at SMITH'S FARM. No obligation or entry fee BUT if you need a rifle or ammunition shop SMITH'S FIRST. SMITH'S SPORTING GOODS STORE, THE LARGEST IN THE SOUTH, located in Winnsboro, La.

Mr. Smith bought the idea and the Shoot Out went over with a bang!

If you are alert, you'll find dozens of opportunities to make extra sales. This tie-in with a non-commercial publicity notice is just one example! You can do it! But, you must look for and recognize every opportunity that presents itself.

Disguised Commercial Announcements

Many of the big Blue Chip Companies create interesting, entertaining programs and commercial announcements that proclaim their products or services. They contact radio stations and advise those stations that it will be perfectly all right to broadcast those programs or sales messages on a "Public Service Basis."

Usually, such handouts are commercial programs or commercial messages disguised as public service. Many stations welcome these well produced programs because they add prestige to the station but produce no revenue. We never accept this kind of propaganda. We simply send our rate card to the producers of such programs, advising them that we will use the program material or commercials **provided** it is paid for on our commercial rate card. Why take up valuable space on your limited daily program log with commercial programs that are not paid for! Isn't a better idea to let you, as the station's sales representative, bring in revenue producing advertising? The accompanying examples of commercials disguised as public service illustrate the nature of such material.

BORDERLINE SALES PROMOTIONS

We offer a couple of exhibits that might be classified as a combination of commercial-public service promotions. Some radio stations may use them in their entirety; other stations might eliminate any reference to the commercial name mentioned therein.

SERVING THE COTTON CAPITAL AND LIVESTOCK CENTER OF LOUISIANA

SI WILLING
PRESIDENT

PHONE: (318) 435-5141 - 435-5644 P. O. BOX 312
WINNSBORO, LOUISIANA
ZIP 71295

KMAR's policy is to go the second mile in service. We make a continuous effort to determine the program needs of our community. Will you help us to keep the quality of programming at it's highest level by taking the time to answer the following questions and returning in the self addressed envelope?

1. Do you prefer (more less none) country and western music?

2. Would you like (more less none) rock and roll music?

3. Would you request (more less none) popular music; (none some) classical music?

4. Do you suggest that we (do don't) editoralize?

5. Does KMAR give (not enough enough too much) local, regional, national and international news?

6. Do you think there are (not enough enough too many) agricultural programs?

7. Does KMAR have (not enough enough too many) religious programs?

8. Please give us your opinion, in the following space, of HOW we can best serve the needs of our community:

We deeply appreciate your suggestions.

Thank you.

Sincerely,
Radio KMAR

Si Willing

Sample questionnaire sent to 100 industry leaders.

May 21, 1957

Mr. Si Willing
Radio Station KMAR
Winnsboro, Louisiana

Dear Si:

I just heard your summary of the Town Council meeting. This is the first time I have ever heard of this, but it brought me up to date. I was especially interested in the parking situation at the Little Boys League games. We own about one and one half acres just north of the tennis court; and, we would be happy to let the Town place signs there designating this as a parking area.

Sincerely,

J. W. McLEMORE, JR.
MCLEMORE'S JITNEY JUNGLE

jwm/sb
cc: Town of Winnsboro

Advertisers appreciate public service and coverage of local events.

FRANKLIN STATE BANK & TRUST CO.

WINNSBORO, LOUISIANA 71295

January 30, 1969

Mr. S. J. Willing
Radio Station KMAR
Winnsboro, Louisiana

Dear Si,

Often times we neglect to tell people how we appreciate the good job that they are doing. I just happened to remember that I had let sometime pass since I told you that I appreciate you and KMAR for the fine job that you are doing for Winnsboro and Franklin Parish. If we had more such Citizens it would be a much better place to live.

Thanks again for a job well done.

Sincerely,

Emmett E. Richardson

Letters from advertisers make potent sales ammunition.

JUNIOR CHAMBER OF COMMERCE OF WINNSBORO, LOUISIANA
POST OFFICE BOX 655

January 3, 1958

Radio KMAR
Winnsboro, La.

Dear KMAR:

    We, the Winnsboro Jaycees, were proud to receive your letter dated, December 2, 1957. We are pleased with your fine cooperation and help which you have rendered to us during the time that you have been serving Winnsboro and Franklin Parish.

    We feel that we are a better organization because of your help. KMAR, we feel, is one of our most prized possessions. KMAR's worth is measurable only in the hearts of every person in its listening range.

    We appreciate your interest in our organization and your invoice to us marked PAID IN FULL.

    As you know, we are an action organization of young men dedicated to the betterment and progress of our community and in the development of leaders for our community. Therefore, we are open to any suggestions that you may have which would lead to our fulfillment of this duty.

    Again, we say your services to us, to other organizations, and to Winnsboro and Franklin Parish are invaluable.

Sincerely,

Barney B. Cottingham, Pres.
Winnsboro Junior Chamber
of Commerce

This letter from the Jaycees is a testament in a nutshell.

FRANKLIN PARISH LIBRARY
WINNSBORO, LOUISIANA

May 16, 1959

Mr. Si Willing
Radio Station KMAR
Lone Cedar Road
Winnsboro, Louisiana

Dear Mr. Willing:

    Thank you very much for the free publicity that you gave the Library yesterday afternoon. I listened to the program and was delighted to hear all you had to say.

                          Sincerely yours,

                          Mrs Geo. V. Cotton
                          Mrs. George V. Cotton
                          Parish Librarian

EC:LMT

KMAR's public service ranges far and wide, thus strengthening the station's image in the community.

REGIONAL CITIZENS EDUCATION MEETING SCHEDULED

The Lincoln Parish Citizens Committee for Quality Education has announced plans for a regional meeting to be held at the Ruston High School Gymnasium at 2:00 P.M. Sunday, June 22nd. In announcing the meeting, Dr. Donald Roberts, chairman of the local committee, stated that invitations are being extended to other organized citizens groups and interested individual citizens from all 37 parishes affected by the recent federal court decree which struck down "freedom of choice" in the public schools.

The regional meeting Sunday will provide an opportunity for delegates from other committees to exchange ideas and determine the best courses of action open to work for maintaining quality education in the public schools of the 37 parishes which have been ordered to have full integration by the fall school term.

Specific items on the agenda for Sunday's meeting include: formation of a state committee, with a representative from each parish, to work to maintain quality education and local control of school systems; functions of the various local Citizens Committees for Quality Education in working with their respective school boards for maintenance of high educational standards; the methods parents and others are willing to support to achieve these educational goals; the feasibility of forming a North Louisiana Private School Association.

The local citizens group, in approving the resolution establishing the 12-man committee, went on record favoring freedom of choice, with a private school system as a constructive alternative.

Concerned citizens from throughout the state, along with all interested parents, are invited to attend this meeting.

Non-commercial publicity release.

FOR IMMEDIATE RELEASE
June 10, 1969

CONSTRUCTION INDUSTRY
LEGISLATIVE COUNCIL FORMED

Formal organization of the Construction Industry Legislative Council for Louisiana is announced by P.D. Lambert, Jr., President. The Council is dedicated to promoting the views of the Construction Industry to all levels of government, and to the general public of Louisiana, Lambert explained.

Ten groups representative of the entire construction industry have affiliated within the Council. These are The Louisiana Architects Association (LAA); the Consulting Engineers Council of Louisiana (CEC); the State Council of Associated General Contractors Chapters (AGC); the Louisiana Council National Electrical Contractors Association Chapters (NECA); Mechanical, Plumbing, Heating and Cooling Contractors; Roofing and Sheet Metal Contractors Association; Louisiana Building Material Dealers Association; Shell, Gravel and Ready-Mix Concrete Dealers Associations; and the Building Specialties Contractors.

The Council will propose and support legislation which is good for business, industry and the public, and oppose that which is contrary to its best interest, Mr. Lambert commented.

Another typical publicity release.

NEWS

OFFICE OF PUBLIC RELATIONS
Contact: Jack Hess; Lee La Combe
(202) 783-6505

NATIONAL RIFLE ASSOCIATION OF AMERICA 1600 RHODE ISLAND AVE. N.W. WASHINGTON, D.C. 20036

For Immediate Release
(Tuesday, June 10, 1969)

COUNTDOWN NEARS CLIMAX
FOR U.S. SHOOTING TEAMS

Washington, D.C.----The countdown to the Final Tryouts for selection of the U.S. World Moving Target Team neared its climax this month as invitations were sent out from headquarters of the National Rifle Association to several hundred qualifiers.

The Final Tryouts are scheduled to be held at Lackland Air Force Base, Tex., and the International Gun Club of San Antonio, Tex., during the period July 11 through July 20.

Competitors will be vying for positions on one of three teams----Running Boar, International Skeet and Clay Pigeon. Four firers will be selected for each squad.

All entries will fire a full course on three successive days with total score used to determine the four team members.

Skeet will be the first event with 100 birds each day July 11 through July 13. This will be followed by Running Boar, July 16-18, with a 60-shot course scheduled each day. International Clay Pigeon July 18-20, with 100 birds daily will wind up the eliminations.

Lackland will be the site of the Running Boar and the shotgun events will be at the civilian gun club.

Publicity from the National Rifle Association sparked an idea for a commercial promotion.

special

PROGRAM
MATERIAL FOR
RADIO AND
TELEVISION

COTTON INSECT CONTROL

Here's an item that should be of interest to you. A premix formulation of Sevin carbaryl insecticide and molasses is now available for commercial use to control bollworms and other insects on cotton, according to Union Carbide Corporation, manufacturer of Sevin. The new specimen label for Sevin and molasses premix, designed as a guide for insecticide formulators to follow in preparing their own product brands of Sevin suspensions in molasses, states that the product contains 1.6 pounds of carbaryl per gallon. This molasses suspension of Sevin can be mixed with water and applied with regular ground or airplane equipment. The use of at least three gallons of mixed spray per acre is recommended, with an increase to higher dosages on larger plants. Molasses in the formulation is intended for improved bollworm control. A tank mix of Sevin and molasses also can be applied, with one gallon of blackstrap molasses (feed grade) per acre added to regular recommended dosages of the Sevin Sprayable formulation right out in the field. Tests by agricultural experiment stations have shown that molasses preserves the spray on plants longer to extend residual activity. This reduces the number of sprays needed per season. The combination of Sevin and molasses gives excellent control of major cotton insects, and a key advantage is that it controls bollworm moths before they lay their eggs. Molasses provides a food supply for moths. They congregate in molasses-treated areas, and while they are feeding, the insecticide does its work. By controlling bollworm moths, the grower can prevent sudden build-ups of worms, Union Carbide pointed out. The company cited statistics from recent tests. Dead moths in fields treated with insecticides without molasses totaled 144 per acre. Areas treated with Sevin plus molasses, in the same field, yielded 804 dead moths per acre. Figuring that 660 more moths in the molasses area were unable to lay their eggs, 33,000 worms per acre (about one per plant) were stopped before they got started. (SOURCE: Mr. Richard Gibbs, Albert Sidney Noble, 52 Vanderbilt Avenue, New York, N.Y.)

This commercial publicity release promotes a product of Union Carbide.

THE PACESETTERS

starring JOEY HEATHERTON

Last April, Joey Heatherton married Larry Rentzell. This marked her move into the "young-married" set, the generation that truly can be called Pacesetters.

But, like many young married women of today, she did not give up her career; fortunately for us, since she agreed to become the hostess-narrator of "THE PACESETTERS", a new, exciting radio series which will be available to you free-of-charge beginning September 1, 1969 just in time to help get your Fall off to a great start.

"THE PACESETTERS" will bring to your listeners five, 4-minute programs per week, each of which will emphasize the role the modern woman plays in her home, community, or career. The programs will also bring to your listeners inside news and views of personalities who are considered Pacesetters.

One program for example, will give listeners a close-up look at how Lee Remick's New York apartment is decorated, along with Pacesetting decorating advice the listener can use to her own advantage.

In addition to this kind of decorating information, Joey Heatherton will interview noted personalities about the decor of their homes, about their careers, their home life. She'll talk to well-known Pacesetters like Margaret Mead about the family of the future; Dr. Rose Franzblau about psychology; Joan Rivers about combining motherhood with a demanding career; Dr. Haim Ginott about solving the problems that arise between parent and child.

In other words, Joey, through these programs, will be setting an exciting pace that your young homemaker listeners will be only too eager to follow, and which will make them feel like Pacesetters themselves. Of course, Joey will impart her own zingy quality to the scripts - a quality born out of a career that embraces Bob Hope's Xmas shows in Viet Nam, regular guest star on programs such as the Dean Martin Show, Johnny Carson Show, Hollywood Palace, Jonathan Winters Show, along with smash tours in summer stock plays and her signing for the leading role in the musical stage version of "Bus Stop".

We'd be very happy to include your station, for exclusive broadcast in your city, among the many that will air "THE PACESETTERS",   Just fill out the enclosed postage paid, broadcast reservation card and return it to us. You will receive the first two weeks of programming well in advance of the starting date of September 1, 1969, and every two weeks thereafter.

"THE PACESETTERS" is being provided as a special service by Springs Mills, Inc. Retail outlets such as department stores, fabric shops, decorators, etc. would be likely prospects for local adjacency sales.

Hoping to hear from you soon.

ROBERT G. JENNINGS CORPORATION

A program series designed to promote Spring Mills, Inc.

date __18 June 1969__

We agree to air the new free-of-charge radio series "THE PACESETTERS", starring Joey Heatherton. The five, 4-minute programs per week will be aired as follows: **WE WILL BE HAPPY TO GIVE THIS ON OUR COMMERCIAL RATE CARD**

_____ at _____
(days)   (approximate air times)

Population coverage _____

Station Format _____

name __SI WILLING, GEN MGR.__   station __KMAR__

address __WINNSBORO__

city & state __LOUISIANA__   zip __71295__

Here's the best way to reply to an offering such as the "Pacesetters."

Sports......Immediate Release....Radio/TV

Union/Pure's Racing Panel of Experts had Cale Yarborough pegged to win the first annual Motor State 500 at Michigan International Speedway Sunday...and win he did...in one of the most thrilling victories of his career.

When Cale survived a last-lap brush with Lee Roy Yarbrough to take the first NASCAR super speedway race in the North, he handed first place honors in the Union/Pure Panel poll to motorsports writer Dwight Pelkin of the Sheboygan, Wisconsin Press.

Pelkin figured Cale would win the race at an average speed of 140.000 miles per hour...just seven-tenths of a second off Yarborough's actual race speed of 139.254 miles per hour.

Second place in the nationwide poll went to John Rogers of the Raleigh, North Carolins News and Observer, while Jimmy Smyth of the Johnson City, Tennessee Press Chronicle was third.

David Howell of the Greenville, South Carolina News was fourth.

The Union/Pure Panel forecasts major races throughout the year. Next race they'll predict is the Medal of Honor Firecracker 400 at Daytona International Speedway on July 4.

####

From: Daytona International Speedway Press Dept. 6/16/69

Some publicity releases have genuine value but mention a commercial name.

ADIRONDACK INDUSTRIES, INC.
Dolgeville, New York 13329

WILLIE MAYS 600TH HOME RUN

CONTACT: Ronald Endres
Conklin Labs & Bebee, Inc.
Box 375 GM Circle, Syracuse, N.Y. 13201
(315) 437-2591

CONTACT: Evan H. Baker
Rowan Industries, Inc
2 Crescent Place, Oceanport, N. J. 07757
(201) 229-5000

FOR RELEASE:

ADIRONDACK TO HONOR MAYS' 600TH HOME RUN

DOLGEVILLE, N. Y. -- Adirondack Industries, the company that makes Willie Mays' personal bats, today announced that they will honor Mays' record-breaking 600th home run by presenting him with a $12,000 de Tomaso Mangusta sports car.

In addition, Adirondack will present Mays with one share of stock in their parent company, Rowan Industries, Oceanport, for each foot his 600th travels.

Since joining Adirondack's advisory staff in 1951, Mays has had quite a record-breaking career. In 1954, he was voted the National League's most valuable player. After breaking the 500th home run mark in 1965, Mays was again given the most valuable player honors.

When Willie hit number 512, he broke the National League's home run record -- an achievement that retired his personal Adirondack bat to the Baseball Hall of Fame.

Mays' 600th (only 5 home runs away) will give him the distinction of being the only professional player besides Babe Ruth ever to hit 600 home runs. Willie is the only major league player to hit 20 or more home runs for sixteen consecutive years.

Another publicity release with a commercial name mention

P. I. Deals

P. I. means "Per Inquiry." Boiling this down to simple terms it means that a radio station will broadcast an unlimited amount of commercial messages for a sponsor who will reimburse the station for each inquiry they receive from those announcements.

We make no recommendation for or against this kind of advertising. It is mentioned herein simply because it is a form of radio advertising. Many stations have made a great deal of money; others haven't fared so well.

Per Inquiry arrangements have been and are being used for dozens of products. Certain record companies offer radio stations a percentage of the money they receive from the sale of their "package of the Greatest Hit Records for a Bargain Price." Baby chicks, tulip bulbs, garden seed and many other products are included in the "P. I. arrangement."

Advertising Agencies prepare the sales messages for their P. I. clients and also contact radio stations to persuade the stations to use these "P. I. Deals." Some examples of typical Per Inquiry deals are shown in the accompanying illustrations.

NEVER TAKE THINGS FOR GRANTED

A midwestern radio station had been enjoying prosperity for years. They were in a single-station market in a rather large town. The owners became rather smug and complacent. Business was good; rates were raised at frequent intervals. Service was poor; no competition. As long as there was a monopoly, no one seemed to care much whether service was given to sponsor or listener. Lose a customer? Who cares! There's another to take his place. But, while this station was wallowing in its complacency, other broadcasters were eying the market. They searched the spectrum and found a frequency. They filed with the FCC.

This finally twinged the nerves of the complacent owners. "Economic chaos!" they protested. "Two stations can never survive in this market!" "OK" was the answer, "We'll just file for your frequency and prove that we can do a better job of serving the needs of this community than you have done." "FOUL!" yelled the aroused owners. But they realized they were licked. Anybody could do a better job and they knew it. The decision was to allow the newcomers to file for a second station without protest. All of a sudden there was a general housecleaning. The manager was fired because, after all,

Box 12006, Alcott Station   Denver, Colorado 80212   303-455-9262

June 23, 1969

Dear GM:

My client, Ambassador Motels, is interested in advertising on your station and developing business in your coverage area. They train men, women and couples for careers in motel management. Motel management is a profitable, attractive career in over 75,000 motels throughout the country.

Ambassador needs good sales leads for their new national campaign. I am interested in placing them with you on a PI arrangement. I can offer you $4.00 per mail lead to get started. Our program calls for net pay to your station of $4.00 per inquiry for the first three months, $5.00 per inquiry for the second quarter, $6.00 per inquiry for the third quarter and $7.00 per inquiry for the fourth quarter. All inquiries received beyond the fourth quarter will be paid at the $7.00 rate. The only stipulation is that our spots do not lapse over 30 days in any quarter of activity. In small market areas where a station is unable to produce 25 inquiries in a quarter then pay schedule is based on groups of 25 inquiries. Most stations beat their normal spot rates at these prices as training is widely sought for this field. Of course this agency guarantees payment.

The client's motel training program is VA approved and with thousands of men and women leaving federal service every month for new careers, your mail pull should be excellent. During the past seven years I have placed motel training spots on hundreds of radio stations throughout the country. Some stations have run my spots steadily for over six years. The response on motel training is hot now and I know you can make good money as soon as you start this account on your station. All spots come produced on tape. When can we start?

Sincerely,

Jack Diamond
jd/gs

P. I. (per inquiry) commercial offer motel management training.

140

wasn't he to blame for such a shoddy operation? Although an honest effort was made to improve the service and sound of the station, it was too late. "Why didn't you do this in the first place?" was the general attitude of sponsor and listener alike. The new station flourished. The old station also ran. The moral of this story is that no matter which market you're in, you should always act as if there was a new station going to open tomorrow. Also, you have a right to choose your employer as well as he does to hire you. Avoid stations that care not about service. Avoid stations that think only about making money and seldom about serving the public. Select a station that has the right attitude and then give generously of yourself to help the station in its effort.

THE TRIPLE PLAY

We have considered the three essential parts of a sale separately. Now, let's put them together. Making a sale consists of three distinct parts. The approach, the presentation, and the close. Unless your approach is correct, you'll never get to part two, and if you cannot accomplish a presentable presentation, you'll never close the sale. It's as simple as all that. Something like the game of musical chairs. Many salesmen insist that introducing yourself first is the thing to do. I disagree. I believe that the idea comes first. The introduction of a good idea should be the first order of business. If the idea is appealing, the sponsor will be interested enough to ask who you are. Let me illustrate this with a little story.

The Case of the Jangled Jingle

I was seated at my desk one day when a salesman called. He introduced himself, told me the name of the company he represented and then said, "I hope you're not too busy because I have some station break jingles that are simply wonderful." The truth of the matter is that I was busy and had made up my mind in that brief 45-second introduction that I didn't have the time to spare. I was honest with the man and told him to leave his card and I would get in touch with him. He left.

Salesman number two visited me a few weeks later. His approach was better than the first salesman but he didn't make the sale. Here's why. He said "Mr. Willing, let me show you how you can turn your loss into a profit." Now, we weren't experiencing a loss and I resented the fact that salesman number two presumed that we were. "We don't need any

Box 12006, Alcott Station   Denver, Colorado 80212   303-455-9262

June 23, 1969

Dear GM:

I'm pleased to announce that my agency has been appointed exclusive advertising and marketing agent for Don's Hair Formula. Don's is headquartered in Oklahoma City with packaging and shipping out of Denver. This preparation has been used by thousands of men and women for the past six years. People who have been bald for years have actually been known to grow hair after using Don's. It will help an unhealthy scalp condition and prevent falling hair. The product carrys a money back guarantee and meets all FDA requirements.

Don's Hair Formula sells for $5.00 a bottle and is sold strictly by mail order. I would like to place Don's on your station for $2.00 per unit net to you. In my seven years of advertising and promoting mail order products I've never seen one quite as strong and proven as Don's orders for this product are really exceptional. Of course you have complete freedom in scheduling spots. Spots come produced on tape and you can either deduct your commission or bill this agency. We quarantee payment. Drop me a line or call and I'll be happy to forward spots and contracts. Don's is a producer---and is ready to go to work for you.

Sincerely,

Jack Diamond
jd/gs

Another P. I. offering a personal grooming product.

outside help," I said. Our station is doing quite well and we don't need any gimmicks." "But these aren't gimmicks," defended the salesman, "these are clever station break jingles." "We've got plenty of good sound effects," I told him. "Sorry, but I can't spare the time to hear your audition tape. Please let me have your card and I'll get in touch with you when we need some jingles."

Getting Better!

The third salesman used the right approach. He said, "Mr. Willing, I've been monitoring your station for about 30 miles and I like its sound." I thanked him for the compliment. He smiled and continued, "I have some clever station break jingles that will help you maintain the fine quality sound of your station." That interested me because I was aware of the fact that jingles, promos, etc., have a limited life and that it is necessary to keep a perpetual inventory of good sound effects in order to maintain continuity of listener insterest. It was then that I asked him whom he represented. He mentioned his company's name, then his own. I asked him to play his audition. I listened, but I didn't buy.

This Ernest Hemingway summation of the demise of salesman number three is related that way because I don't want to bore you with trivial facts. The answer in a nutshell is that his jingles were bad! The salesman was on the right track but he had the wrong train. His product was poor and didn't match his presentation which was good. He had succeeded in capturing my interest with his approach but had let me down with his presentation.

Best!

Here is how salesman number four made the sale. "Mr. Willing, competition in the radio business is keen. Please listen to my clever jingles and you be the judge as to whether they will be in keeping with the excellent quality of your station's sound." He then told me his name, the company he was with, and continued, "Our product should please your audience and perhaps attract more listeners." What he said made good sense. After all, how can you keep an audience without quality sound? I listened. I liked, and I bought. Salesman number four had succeeded. Here's why. He presented a good ideal first. He introduced himself second. He presented his good product third, and closed the sale last.

143

A popular theory among top-notch salesman is that you should start closing your sale from the very beginning. That is true because if you aren't in the business to close sales, then you should find other employment. Many salesmen are impressed with this philosophy but go about it the wrong way. What this actually means is that each card you play in the game of selling should score another winning point. It doesn't mean that you should ask a sponsor to buy a schedule right off! It means that you should sharpen the triple action sequence consisting of the approach, the presentation, and the close. The approach should be the introduction of an idea that will create more business for the sponsor or help him keep his present accounts happy. The salesman should subordinate himself to the profitable idea. That is why I recommend that whenever possible, you should introduce yourself after you have given the attention-getting suggestion.

IF AT FIRST YOU DON'T SUCCEED

Many busy men will not see anyone unless they know who he is and what he wants. Well trained secretaries are expert in the art of "getting rid of salesmen." The manager of a small, busy company can be short with a salesman by asking curtly, "Who are you and what do you want?" Now, here's where your salesmanship comes to the surface. The well trained "get-rid-of-the-salesman secretary" may be sufficiently impressed with your good idea to persuade her boss to at least give you a hearing. Particularly in the case of a small but busy company with the impatient manager, you can tell him your idea before you tell him who you are even though he doesn't ask the questions in that order. Let me illustrate what I mean. Here are some sales openers that I have used and that have worked. They must be concise, simple, and tell a story that captures the imagination:

"Mr. Sponsor, my job is to help you create more traffic in your store. May I show you how?"

"Mr. Merchant, your business is probably very good, but let me show you how we can improve it."

"Mr. Sponsor, we don't keep secrets and neither should you. Don't keep your sale a secret; let us tell thousands of people all about it."

"Mr. Sponsor, it won't cost you a penny to let me tell you how we can increase traffic in your store."

"Mr. Sponsor, we can tell more people about your sale in 60 seconds than you could in a year if you were to visit them one by one."

These openers are actual sales-starters that I have used time and time again and are carefully documented in my portfolio of sales experiences.

THE IMPORTANCE OF KEEPING RECORDS

While we're on the subject of sales experiences, I want to impress you with the importance of keeping records of your sales calls. This not only helps you separate the wheat from the chaff but it also builds a scenario in which you are the star player.

Some readers may take this to be a contradiction to what I have alread said. It's true, I've stated that a salesman should subordinate himself to his presentation of the attention-getting idea; now I'm recommending that you become a star player.

Actually, it is a contradiction, from the **negative** viewpoint. Here's what I mean. When you go to see your favorite football team play, you hope they will win. You hope there will be enough goals made to produce that win. A play is made. The ball is tossed. You're on your feet now. Your eye is on that ball. Will it be caught? Will it be a first down? A touchdown? A step toward winning the game? The play is successful! Your favorite team is closer to final victory. It is only after this dramatic action that you heap praise on the players involved. Jones passed, Smith caught. They **became** the stars of the play. They earned the distinction as a **result** of the **action**. This should be quite obvious. Other players were on the field, and, they may have assisted in the action but the attention of the audience was **first** on the ball, **second** on the passer and the receiver; therefore, those two men were credited with the action.

Perhaps this is not fair to the other nine men on the winning team but that's the way the game is played. History books tell about **winners**; statistics give facts about the "also-rans." Your diary should include all the facts. The reaction of your sales prospect to your opening lines. How long did it take you to make the call. What was the reason for failing to close the sale. What was the formula for making the sale.

I had my house painted once. The painter mixed his own paints to produce a very pleasant effect. The only trouble was that he didn't keep a record of his paint formula and couldn't for the life of him remember what went into that concoction. He was never able to duplicate his fine work for me. It is because you deal with such a diverse clientele that you must keep records. Not only keep them but **study** them!

REMINDER MEMO

In the Jangled Jingle episode we learned how a good approach and a poor product added up to no sale. A salesman for a broadcasting station has a most difficult product to sell. He must know it thoroughly, be able to demonstrate it to the sponsor's satisfaction. So, I suggest that before you hit the street as a salesman for a station, learn the component parts of a radio station. If possible, start as an announcer. This way, you'll become familiar with the makeup of copy, the programming, the importance of keeping kindred accounts away from each other. Most of all, you'll start to appreciate the sound. You'll learn about availabilities.

So you cannot announce; you don't have the voice. Then, listen to your station. Study the program log. Visit with your program director. The sound of the station is the product you are selling and you must know your product as well as your market to make sales. We learned that the approach must lead to the presentation. If you cannot make an acceptable presentation, part three, or the close, of the sale will not be made. Your entire sales pitch is like a chain; as strong as its weakest link.

Section 4

SALES Excel

WHY RADIO ADVERTISING IS NECESSARY

Radio advertising is the most economical method of informing masses of people. It creates new customers. Although I counsel against "knocking the competition" you should be able to counteract the propaganda that is constantly being put out against radio advertising by the other media.
For example: "Mr. Sponsor, when you advertise on radio, there is never a problem of setting type. It takes just a few short minutes to make changes in your commercial copy. Radio is everywhere, all the time. No need to wait for a convenient time to listen. People hear it in their cars, on the beach, in their bedrooms, bathrooms, kitchens. Radio keeps the housewife company while she works. It stimulates the imagination. It is the most flexible advertising medium known because it works for you all the time. Another thing, if we should make a mistake with your copy, we can make an instant correction. You don't have to wait for the next issue or anything like that. Radio advertising is immediate! It is now!"

Important Consideration

The product advertised is the thing! That's the most important part of the project. It must deliver as promised or else the advertising should not be accepted. Also, never accept products or services that are known to be deceptive or misleading in nature.
Reminds me of the fortune teller who came to see me about advertising her talent. I told her that I didn't accept that kind of advertising. She insisted that she was an accurate fortune teller. "You are?" I questioned. Then why couldn't you predict that I wouldn't accept your or any other fortune teller's advertising?" This put a "quietus" on her insistence. Believe me, the cash that she had to offer was tempting but I'd rather go out of business than depend upon that kind of business.

SPONSORS BUY IDEAS!

Fresh, creative ideas make sales. That is why the big Blue Chip companies always have plenty of ideas on their planning boards. The soap companies constantly do research. They add green crystals, blue crystals; they develop soaps that wash in cold water. They constantly change their packaging and design. The public is fickle! That is why ideas that motivate are always welcome. Big cars, little cars, two-tone colors.

Learn to think creatively. You do a great deal of your sales planning before you ever leave the studio. An old success story about Listerine illustrates the point very well. For 20 years, Listerine was a good mouthwash and enjoyed good sales. Competition was getting keen, so the Lambert people invented the word "halitosis" and claimed that Listerine was the cure for that social disease. What had appeared to be a saturation point during the first 20 years was only a leveling off plateau compared to the second phase when someone was called "Hal" even though his name was not Harold. Do some market research and I'll bet you can get at least one scintillating action-getting idea for every account on your list.

YOU MUST CHANGE WITH THE TIMES!

The town crier was replaced by the newspaper. The newspaper was soon in contention with magazines, Sunday supplements, etc. Radio came along and everybody thought that was the ultimate. Then, TV's appearance panicked the men in radio. Now satellites are being mentioned as the thing. Facsimile newspapers may be in vogue even before the print in this book dries. To keep up with the pace of change you must be malleable, mutable, pliable, and viable. FM radio is growing by leaps and bounds. Teenagers are growing into adults. Children are becoming teenagers. If you remain static, the world will pass you by.

In the beginning days of broadcasting there were only AM radio stations. FM radio didn't really get started until after World War Two. The National Association of Broadcasters (NAB) recently publsihed a pamphlet about the dramatic growth of FM radio.

In 1945 there were only 53 FM radio stations; at the time of this writing there are 2,170 FM stations! That's progress! The NAB publication describes the differencc between AM (amplitude modulation) and FM (frequency modulation) radio, as well as multiplex stereo. So, for the broadcast salesman opportunity grows bigger and bigger and bigger!

FOR EVERY ACTION, THERE IS A REACTION

With the tremendous opportunity growth in our time, we are naturally concerned primarily about advertising on radio both AM and FM. However, we must be aware of the fact that other people search for other methods of advertising also. Remember this, whenever a new kind of advertising develops, it becomes your competition. Your constant aim should be to make your case for radio advertising so strong that it will be difficult for other methods of advertising to encroach upon your sponsor's budgets. The following article from the front page of the WALL STREET JOURNAL describes several offbeat media.

OFF-BEAT MEDIA proliferate as ways to sell to consumers.

Portable billboards towed through downtown streets prove successful in Philadelphia and Dallas. A New Jersey concern does a brisk business selling ad space on vending machines in schools and factories. Some advertisers put their messages on high school bulletin boards. Newly formed Nite-Ray Advertising Co. in Dallas outfits a plane to transmit nocturnal ads on an airborn, 36-foot-long, computer-controlled electric sign.

Ted Bates & Co. includes ads painted on sidewalks and printed on milk cartons in its latest directory of specialized media. The ad agency also lists "Midnight Postings" as a media accepted by "politicians, gurus, and small retailers." But it warns that this tactic of furtively placing signs on buildings and fences late at night to avoid discovery "is a form of defacement, frowned upon by most local authorities."

One Dallas ad agency head sees a trend away from such media, however. "These gimmicks, like painted rocks and skywriting, are marginal media that succeed only in times when people have a lot of cash to spend," he says.

BE WISE, MERCHANDISE!

In this day and age, competing products vie for merchandising space. A product that is popular will get more of the space that usually goes for a premium. To get maximum mileage out of any advertising campaign, help your sponsor merchandise at the point of sale. This can be done easily and inexpensively by having attractive signs printed that read:

AS ADVERTISED ON RADIO XXXX

A clever printer can make a raft of variations on this theme. Such signs should be eye-catching and should always be displayed over clean, desirable merchandise. I say again, never accept or identify with any product or service that cannot meet your quality standards.

LEAD, DON'T FOLLOW

Things were tough. There was a crop failure. Advertisers started cutting their budgets. The station owners were getting fidgety. Instead of throwing up my hands in despair, I looked for ways and means to meet the crisis. It took a lot of doing but I convinced several sponsors to not only stop their budget cuts but to increase their budgets! It was a job getting them to hang on. Then, when we had a bumper crop the next year, those advertisers had a big headstart over the competition. Moral: Keep your morale.

INTRA-COMPETITION

I don't advocate back stabbing or tearing down your co-workers, but I do encourage clean competition within a sales organization. Somebody has to set the pace so why not let it be you? Go after bigger schedules that result from fresh ideas. Any salesman who has a competitive streak will have to increase his track record to keep up with you. This is healthy and lots of fun and it makes money for everybody. But again, I caution you, compete honorably and above-board; let service motivate you rather than monetary gain. This formula will automatically create monetary reward.

UNDERSTANDING AND BEING UNDERSTOOD

When a hotel reservation clerk received a long distance call about a reservation he asked, "do you want a room with a tub or a shower?" "What's the difference?" asked the caller. Replied the clerk, "With a tub, you sit down." A friction point developed because each person had his own interpretation of the word "difference." Throughout this book we shall see how a lack of uniform interpretation can create mountains out of molehills.

THE ADVANTAGES OF BEING A SALESMAN

For some inexplicable reason, many young people regard being a salesman as a lowly occupation. Just the opposite is true. A salesman is actually in business for himself. Compared to a man who is in the business, the salesman has many advantages. A salesman has no weekly payroll to meet. He has no financial investment. He doesn't have any capital risk. As a salesman for a radio station, you are the one whom management depends upon to get a return on his investment. All you have to do is use your enthusiasm, intellect, and other God-given attributes to create sales. You are in an enviable position indeed. You have the opportunity to give of yourself, which is the greatest satisfaction a man can have. And, you get paid for doing it.

THE MAN WHO COULDN'T GIVE AWAY A MILLION DOLLARS

Once upon a time there was a very wealthy man. He had millions of dollars in cash! He wanted to be generous, so he decided that he would give one million dollars as a gift to the first person who asked for it. But, he didn't make this idea known to anybody. He had an aberration in spite of his tremendous wealth. He thought that because he was so wealthy, somebody, someday would ask him for a million dollars as a gift, with no strings attached. He went to his grave still waiting for someone to ask him for the million.

Admittedly, this is a far fetched way to illustrate the power of advertising. If the greatest company in the world invented the greatest boon to mankind and they kept it a secret, they would never be able to market it and make a profit. As a salesman for a radio station, you must understand consumer motivation. This is a never-ending process. People change. Products change, and you must be in step with the change. In 1919 such companies as General Motors, RCA, and other Blue Chip companies of today were not even listed among the top 20 businesses. There were, however, some businesses then that were among the top 20 but are not even in business today. Unless you keep abreast of the times, you too can go out of style.

HEAD-ON COLLISION

The manager of a chain store was in a hurry. He wanted me to give him my best deal. "Mr. Manager," I said, "I have no best deals. I have one rate card and it applies to all accounts." He asked what the rates were. I told him. He bought a crash campaign schedule that called for saturation over a period of five days.

When I called back, the manager was smug. He scooted his company's inter-office paper over to me and pointed with pride to his sales increase amounting to 220 percent. He had won first place in his division. "Congratulations," I said. "I am glad that we helped you win first place." He answered, "My sales were the result of the telephone calls that my girls made to customers."

"How did you determine where your sales came from?" I asked him. "Dunno, but my girls did make a lot of telephone calls and told many of our customers about our big bargains." Instead of becoming indignant, I became inquisitive. "Do you know how many telephone calls your

153

girls made?" I asked. "Oh about six an hour," he drawled. "How many girls on the project?" was my next question. "About three," he admitted. "If three girls made six telephone calls an hour and there are about seven working hours in the day, that means there were about 630 calls made during the week, isn't that correct?" I asked. "Guess so," was the short reply. "I presume that your paying the minimum hourly wage of $1.60." "That's right," he said. "That means it costs you about 27 cents to make your message known to one person about two products. Whereas, we have 40,000 listeners in our trade area and, using our per message rate of $4.00, it costs $.001 (one thousandths of a cent) to get your message across to one listener. And, when your girls make calls, they generally contact your regular customers. Our radio station reaches potentially new customers. Besides, your company became tremendous because of mass production and mass advertising. Don't you agree that radio advertising has a great advantage over the laborious, tedious, expensive system of making telephone calls? You must also agree that the percentage of completed calls is small because mothers have housework to do, babies to feed, etc., and they sometimes resent an intrusion on the phone. But when they listen to radio, we are invited guests in their homes and they appreciate our sales messages." I rested my case.

His reaction came as a surprise because he agreed with me. I thought that I had blown the whole bit because I had deflated his ego. But a salesman should also have ego. He should give service without servitude; argue without being argumentative. Don't brag or boast but document your case for radio advertising with intelligent reasoning. If you are talking to a rasonable man, you will generally gain a good sponsor. If your man is unreasonable, pig-headed, stubborn, you will probably lose a sponsor, but you will keep your self respect. Before I end this little narrative, let me qualify it by saying be sure that your facts are right! Don't make false or misleading claims. If somebody denies the truth, he is not worth keeping as a sponsor!

PRODUCTS AND SERVICES

Radio stations advertise products and services. There are more products that are "advertisable" than there are services.

Many services are prohibited to advertise by law or ethics. Doctors, dentists, lawyers, certified public accountants, to name just a few of the services that cannot be advertised on radio. But, then again, there are scores of services that can be advertised: Dry cleaners, laundromats, repair shops, gardening, tailoring, and many more. In the prohibitive list of product advertising, there are: hard liquors, certain feminine and personal hygiene products, etc.

As a general rule, radio stations get more revenue from product advertising than they do from advertising services. Consequently, it behooves you to be very much aware of this situation. Your job is to sell as much advertising as you can, but you must take into account that the public to whom you are broacasting your sponsor's sales messages does spend quite a bit of its income on necessary services that are not advertised. Therefore, much of that spendable income is not available for buying the products that are being advertised.

Market research is very important in this situation. Search all sources of available information to find out just how much money was spent on unadvertised services. The balance that is left could well be spent to buy your sponsor's products. Be sure to take into account the interest paid to banks and lending companies that is being siphoned off. Going hand-in-hand with this kind of market research is trying to estimate the take-home pay after compulsory deductions are made (Federal and State Withholding taxes, OAB, mileage taxes, etc.). If you are pretty well able to determine how much money is waiting to be spent to buy your sponsor's products or services, you won't knock yourself out trying to sell a Cadillac in a Chevrolet market.

OF PIQUES AND BOOS

A salesman must build an inner fortification against disappointment, unfair criticism, and unexpected bad news. Easy to say, hard to do. This comes with practice and self-conditioning. If you're apt to be a piqued at the boos, slings and arrows that salesmen fall heir to, you'd better start doing something about it. My formula works for me and it's quite simple. I imagine that I have an invisible shield that causes slurs to bounce off but permits compliments and applause to enter.

Such conditioning is a continuing process because sometimes, the sudden shock of a sharp rebuke can be quite upsetting. The old, old tried-and-true method is a good antidote in this case; count to ten and then count to ten again. One of the most severe critics you'll always encounter is yourself: self-condemnation for missing a sale, self-reproval for any number of things. Here again, you should start a training course to analyze instead of criticize. Search for the cause instead of censuring the effect. Like we said, this sounds quite simple, but it is difficult; yet can be mastered if you stay with it.

One of the great golfers of our time became a professional golfer because he wanted an occupation that depended upon his talents and his alone. He had been a successful businessman and often found himself at the receiving end of criticism even though he was innocent. He chucked his successful business so that he could be in a position to blame himself for any and all errors. But, when he considered the situation carefully, he concluded that criticism from any source is wasted energy. Constructive suggestions for improvement replaced harping and carping. Consequently, he went on to win the big money in national tournaments. This therapy is an important part of any salesman's homework. As a radio sales representative, you are on your own when you call on sponsors. You can go far in your chosen profession if you have inner fortitude.

FRIENDS, FRIENDLY PEOPLE, AND PERSONAL ACQUAINTANCES

A wise man once said, "We go through life making lots of personal acquaintances, meeting many friendly people, and making very few friends." Good friends are rare indeed. Reminds me of an old joke:

1st man: "We're friends to the end!"
2nd man: "Great! Lend me a hundred dollars
1st man: This is the end!

Remember that many a true word has been said between false teeth. Start now to differentiate between friends and acquaintances; between "friendly" people and pleasant strangers. The main thing is to sell your product based on its quality and ability to produce as specified. Don't sell on the presumption of friendship.

SALESMEN APPRECIATE

Many salesmen neglect to put a value on their time. As you grow in stature, you become more valuable. This is the equivalent of taking an appreciation of valuables when you file your tax return. It's like the aging of good wine or the increasing value of a rare painting. We can make these comparisons to a certain point. You reach a peak of production.

Then, you start downhill; this is your depreciation period. Don't waste your time in idle pursuits. Yes, have fun, live it up when you have time for these purposes. Get all you can out of life, but don't squander your productive years.

Only you can assess the value of your time. Establish your own formula. For example, make a determination that you will earn so much money each year; say $50,000. There are only so many working hours in each day. Decide how many hours you will work in a year's time and divide those hours into your anticipated gross earnings. The answer that you get is your value per hour. Keep this firmly fixed in your mind. Every time you waste an hour of your precious productive time, you have to hurry up and double up to make your goal materialize.

BRAINPOWER

An old vaudeville joke goes like this: "I'm so smart that I've got some brains that I haven't even used yet." Robots should be programmed to follow explicit instructions and perform mechanically; people should use their brains and be creative. Challenge inherited knowledge. Develop intellectual curiosity. Get inquisitive without being an inquisitor. Study, observe, ask questions, and learn. Don't ever let it be said that the unused portion of your brainpower became atrophied.

KNOW YOUR Ws

Who? What? Why? When? Where? You should know these things about your market, in addition to knowing the important characteristics about people alone. Become familiar with who your potential customer is. Learn what they are doing. Determine why and when they are doing it, and last but not least where!

Populations shift. Some communities prosper, others dry up. Babies are being born at an astounding rate (so they are wetter). Longevity increases with the "golden years" group. Leisure time becomes more leisurely. Yes, there is constant change and you've got to know your Ws. Don't be afraid to discard old information. Personally, I'm more afraid that I won't have the freshest information than I am of weeding out the old statistics. Unless you keep pace, you'll lose the race!

ORGANIZE OR AGONIZE

It is most necessary to recognize and then organize priority matters. The method we suggest consists of the following:

1. Find a quiet place, away from any distractions.
2. Mentally review all of the things that must be done.
3. Write a list of these things.
4. Review your list.
5. Put a value on each project.
6. Revise your list, putting the most urgent projects on top of the list. For example: 1. Call Mr. Jones at 9 AM for purpose of finalizing year's schedule. 2. Be certain to remind secretary to call Mr. Smith at 9:30 to confirm price reductions for his sale. 3. Write letters to agencies advising contemplated rate raises. See Jones at 3:30 to discuss available football game sponsorship.

The success or failure of this routine depends on your talent to recognize top priority matters and discipline yourself to take care of them in their order of importance. If you cannot complete a priority matter for any reason at all, reschedule it on your next day's list and move on to the next order of business. Continuous effort will train you to tell the difference between essential and non-essential matters. After a while, you'll look back and wonder why you ever started and ended your day hedge-hopping from one inconsequential matter to another while the "big ticket" items died for lack of attention.

The Promissory Note

Let's put some teeth into the project of establishing priorities. The old cliche "that we are only human" is a truism and must be recognized. Being "only human" we become derailed by petty details and our resolution to stay with the priority list joins hands with the traditional New Year's resolutions that go down the drain on January 2nd. To make your priority list more meaningful, write it in the form of a promissory note. Like this:

I (your name) do hereby pledge that I will do thus and so. When I sign my name to this pledge it will be as binding as my name on any contract that I enter into. If I renege on my own pledge to myself, then I cannot ever expect anybody else to honor my word.

A word of caution: Before you sign that pledge, be certain that you will take it seriously and honor it the same as the note you signed to the bank. Simply because you have only yourself to account to in case of default doesn't make it any less binding than solemnizing a pledge by taking that one step forward or consummating your marriage with the words "I do."

THE BUDDY-BUDDY SYSTEM

Familiarize but don't fraternize! This simply means that you should know about your sponsor but that you should not get on a "buddy-buddy" basis with him. Your station should be accepted on its proof of performance and not as a result of your friendship with your sponsors. Mutual respect is of paramount importance, but familiarity breeds contempt.

A salesman once asked me to help him analyze why he didn't make the sale. He recited the events of "that evening out on the town with his sales prospect and wife." He said, "We got along famously. Went to the finest night club. Enjoyed the delicious food. Drank the finest liquor. After dancing with the prospect's wife, she told her husband that I was a great dancer and a wonderful guy. I thought I had the sale in the bag but learned that I didn't get the schedule after all; it was given to my competition." The salesman's presentation consisted mainly of romancing his prospect's wife and that's a sure way to kill a deal.

A sale should be consummated either in your sponsor's shop or at your studio. It should be based on your technique as a salesman to present the best reasons why your station is the best buy. Once the sale is closed, take leave of your sponsor after exchanging a few bread-and-butter bits of chatter. Provide entertainment for your sponsor if you think it is necessary, but don't participate in that program. Give him tickets to a theatre, ballgame, etc. Arrange for him and his wife to be your guests for an evening out, but have these items charged to your account while you stay out of them!

EXCHANGING ACCOUNTS

Some radio stations require salesmen to swap accounts with each other if those accounts haven't been sold within a specified time. To better explain, supposing you have been assigned to call on several accounts. If some of those accounts cannot be sold by you within a certain time, you give one of the other salesmen that list of unsold accounts and he gives you the ones that he couldn't sell. This is a good idea because not all salesmen can sell every account.

This procedure is most effective if the name of each unsold account is accompanied with all the important information about why the sale wasn't made, every known fact about the kind of man who refused to buy, the nature of the business, etc.

MAKING SALES REPORTS

Most radio stations require salesmen to make daily, weekly, or sometimes monthly sales reports. If you are required to file reports it is not because the sales manager or station manager is spying on you. He must know all about your activities in the field. Such reports help you as well as the station. The reports can be simple in form or detailed; depends entirely upon the station.

HOUSE ACCOUNTS

A "house account" is a sponsor that is not commissionable to a salesman because the sale was initially closed by the owner, manager, or sales manager. Many stations will relinquish a house account to a worthy salesman who earns it through his performance as a salesman. That makes good sense. In my own experience, whenever I turned over the house accounts to a salesman, he would produce little more than the accounts that he received from me. My policy now is to give some house accounts to those salesmen who first do a certain amount of selling on their own.

SALES TECHNIQUES

A good salesman anticipates his sponsor's thoughts. "But I'm not a mind reader," counters the skeptic salesman. "True," I reply. "You don't have to read his mind, just do some market research." This is a capsule summary that can be the beginning of something big. First, be assured that your prospective sponsors are bombarded with all types and kinds of salesmen; high pressure, low pressure, impatient, too patient. They are confronted with neat dressers, sloppy dressers, salesmen with sloppy habits. The reason you can take this for granted is because no two salesmen sell in the same manner. However, your sponsor remains almost constant in his attitudes. The big thing to remember is that you must calibrate your techniques to your sponsor's speed. You are an ever-changing catalyst. Here is how you can make it easier to anticipate your sponsor's characteristics. Mind you, I said easier, not easy.

Just as your radio station is judged by the kind of programs it gives, you can quickly size up the kind of shopkeeper your sponsor is by the store he trades from or the condition of his office. These are giveaways, just as the graphologist can detect personality defects and attributes, in spite of carefully guarded outward appearances. So can you get a key or index to your sponsor's true character. There are exceptions to everything. Critics will argue that you cannot always take for granted that a sloppy store indicates a sloppy sponsor. Granted! But you should certainly take this into account, at least until you have evidence to the contrary.

THE BIG DIFFERENCE

Some time ago in the French Chamber of Deputies a battle was raging about woman's suffrage. An indignant deputy stated: "Women should not be accorded the same privileges as men, after all there is a difference between a man and a woman!" Whereupon his opponent exclaimed, "Vive la difference!" Translated this means, "Long live the difference." In salesmanship, there is a difference between winners and losers. The intention of this book is to convert losers into winners.

Character plays a big part. What a man actually is and what he really thinks about himself is reflected by his action in the arena of life. Two men, confronted with the same situation, react differently. The actions of the loser usually are:

Fright and emotion.

Rebellion about a small loss causes reason to flee and the losses mount.

He scents a small profit and blinds himself to signifcant gains.

He is unyielding. Doesn't compromise. Instead, he indulges in internecine arguments.

Now look at the winner's methods:

He is confident. He controls situations; they do not control him. There is a will to win. He clings to his ideals but plays the game according to the existing ground rules. He parries, thrusts. All within the legally prescribed limits. Winning becomes a way of life. Satisfaction guaranteed because he can overcome roadblocks intelligently. He never keeps hitting his head against a stone wall; this can dull the senses and keep you in the losing column. Remember, the big difference between success and failure is **indifference**! And that's a big difference!

SHORT-RANGE & LONG-RANGE GOALS

The immediate business at hand is to earn a decent living for you and your family. That's your short-range goal. You can spend your entire lifetime "just earning a decent living" if you want it that way. In that case, your short- and long-range goals are one and the same. But suppose you set your sights on eventually owning a radio station. That's your long-range goal. You plan to reach this goal through successive steps up the ladder.

Each part of your long-range plan should have a completion date. Just making a goal for yourself and then forgetting about it will get you nowhere. Here is a plan of action that I prescribed for myself. I never lost sight of it. I had a copy of it on my mirror, my windshield, also in the bill section of my wallet. When I reached my first goal, I set up a new goal and have recently achieved that plateau. Never rest on your oars. Once you get to where you want to go, look for other interesting challenges. This was my first goal:

To illustrate, allow me to cite the timetable I followed. While in the service during World War II, I realized that it would be necessary to be useful in civilian life after the war. Accordingly, I chose the broadcasting industry as the field in which to work After completing a course in radio production and engineering I started as an announcer at a small station in California. My aim was to eventually own my own radio station. To do this, I planned to learn every phase of broadcasting. The timetable looked something like this:

         Announcer: 1947 - 1950
         Producer: 1950 - 1952
         Salesman: 1952 - 1956
         Manager: 1956 - 1958
         Owner: 1958 forward

Through hard work and study I got into sales much before the specified time. I arrived at the goal of ownership three years earlier than the timetable called for.

PUT FLESH ON THE SKELETON

A naked presentation needs some flesh. For example: "Mr. Sponsor, how about putting a saturation schedule of weekend specials on the air?" This is an obvious loser. Now let's dress it up. First, do some sleuthing and make a list of some real "door crashers." Then, prepare some good copy, like this:

Put your money to work for you! Let your money earn its keep. In other words, keep some of the money you earn. Shop and save for much needed items at great savings. Here are some excellent values for this weekend only at Smith's Department Store (mention about THREE GOOD MONEY SAVERS). And that's not all, SMITH'S also has (THREE MORE ITEMS). Remember, the money you save is the profit you make. It's profitable to shop at Smith's Department Store (address and city), most people do!

Now you've clothed the skeleton. It shows your sponsor that you care enough to be of service and that you are not an order taker looking for a handout.

MEMORABLE MESSAGES

Communication between and among people is absolutely necessary. All living creatures must convey messages to each other. There would be no progress at all if this were not so. From the beginning of time when primordial beings called to their mates on up to the contemporary sophisticated methods of contact, there is a constant stream of information.

A significant factor in this process is that discouragement, despair, doubts, fears, joys, happiness, and a myriad of other sensations and reactions result from these communications. You can go berserk if you try to imagine how the course of history would have changed if some of the more memorable messages were not sent. For example, cavemen used their clubs to clout other cavemen when theirs was a contest for food or cavewomen. God's message to Moses in the form of the burning bush. Christ's admonition to his disciples to go forth and spread the word. Sutter's announcement that he found gold. The message to Garcia. Lincoln's proclamation of emancipation. "What hath God wrought?" Edison's recording of "Mary Had a Little Lamb." "Remember the Main!" "We have nothing to fear but fear itself." "We shall never surrender." "I do not choose to run." "Ask not what your country can do for you, rather what can you do for your country."

How about the billions of letters that have been written through the centuries. The zillions of telephone calls and millions of radio and television programs. Yes, the message is the thing and without messages there would be no exchange of information and ideas and, consequently, no progress. Remember this the next time a stubborn merchant insists that "nobody pays any attention to advertising anymore!"

THE CUSTOMER IS ALWAYS RIGHT.

Do you believe that the customer is always right? You do? Well, you're wrong. Let him think he's right but don't you believe it! When we analyze a relationship with an advertiser we discover that he instinctively has a negative attitude. He simply doesn't want to advertise. Now, if you accept that customer's thinking you'll ring up a "no sale."

The reason the prospective sponsor is negative about advertising is because it requires him to make decisions. It means that he has to get out of his routine orbit. He thinks that he has to write the copy, plan the schedule, etc. Here, Mr. Sales Message Salesman, is where your skill comes in. You have two things to do. The first is to make your radio station acceptable to him as an advertising medium and the second is to relieve him of his fear that he will be responsible for creating the advertising.

ONE KIND OF SALESMAN WHO DIED

The slap 'em on the back, bowl 'em over kind of salesman died about fifty years ago. He has been replaced with the confident, respectful and respectable salesman. Don't whisper but keep your voice in a low, natural, confident key. Don't be raunchy or raucous. Be neat, informative and inquisitive. Be observant. Your sponsor may be hard of hearing. He could be vain enough not to wear a hearing aid. A tell-tale sign is evident if he asks you to repeat what you said. If he cocks one ear toward you, turn your volume up until you think he can hear without straining. The right voice key can unlock the door to many sales.

DON'T FLATTER, COMPLIMENT

Don't flatter; instead, compliment with comments well meant. A good sales counter display deserves a sincere compliment. An appointment kept on time earns a vote of thanks. Good service always rates a note of recognition. All human beings, lest they be made of granite, need recognition. A smile and a compliment will go far. But avoid false flattery. "Don't damn my soul with faint praise" was uttered by John Pope when his alleged friend gave him left-handed compliments. "I love your coat but didn't they have it in your size?".... Sprinkle your compliments generously to all people. A smile and a note of appreciation for a job well done often goes farther than a generous tip.

KEEP A MORGUE

The title sounds gruesome, doesn't it. The morgue we're talking about is a file of effective commercial copy. "Morgue" is the definition given to files that contain newspapers and I'm applying it to commercial copy. Often, a perfectly good commercial theme runs for a short duration and then is never heard from again. The rule-of-thumb is this: "If you should be fortunate enough to hit paydirt with an effective sales message, continue to use it as long as you get mileage from it. However, there is no reason why you can't come up with variations on that theme and elongate its usefulness.

Also, all of us run dry sometimes. We ponder, grope, search for ideas, but nothing comes. It happens to the very best creative people. That's when your morgue comes in handy. Like an oasis on a desert. Again too, if you switch jobs, go from a small station to a larger market, you'll be very much in the need of ideas. Here again, however, many of these sales messages have limited life because products and services change. So, get the maximum usage out of ideas and keep them bright and fresh. Don't bury them permanently in your morgue but refer to them.

DON'T BE A HIT-AND-RUN SALESMAN

Regardless of the size market you sell in, you've got to depend upon repeat business. If you are hungry for the fast buck, you can stretch the truth, Don't do it. Remember, you want this man back as a sponsor. If you've given your sponsor a fast shuffle and he finds himself on the short end of the stick, your reputation as a hot-shot salesman will precede you whenever you call in your market. True, you may make some big sales but they'll be one-time-only sales and you can't pay off a 20-year mortgage with one-time-only deals.

THE BIG SHOT SALESMAN

The big shot salesman is impressed with his own importance. He plies his sponsors with hot-shot deals. He's a name dropper; he knows everybody. He's the guy with social connections and let's his sponsor know about it. He tells his sponsor what a nice guy he is but rakes the sponsor's competition over the coals. Keep yourself out of this category. No, don't be a lilly white puritan but keep that label "hot shot salesman" off you. Be humble but not a doormat. Firm up to a situation but don't be overbearing. Be knowledgable but not offensive; the other guy knows a thing or two also.

HOLLOW SHELLS

The salesman who turns a discussion into an argument; the salesman who's not interested in anybody else's problems but his own is a hollow shell. He continues to talk when he should listen. He bullies customers who complain. "What do ya mean, you didn't order a saturation schedule. My boss says you'd better pay us or we'll sue, etc." Also, a hollow shell is the high-pressure man who likes to keep his sponsors in a pressure cooker. Don't you become a hollow shell. Smart sponsors are smart because they can smell a high-pressure salesman.

PATIENCE HATH ITS OWN REWARD

There is a period of gestation in all sales work. After you've dissolved the objections and the sponsor says, "let me think it over," he generally has already done so. If you let it go at that point, chances are that the sale will never jell. The way to handle this is to reply, "A good idea, but let's make an appointment to get your final decision. In the meantime, I'll search the program log for good availabilities and be ready to firm them up when we meet again." Now, suggest a date and time for your next meeting. Although not guaranteed, you'll have an infinitely better chance of closing the sale if you follow this procedure.

WEIGH IT BEFORE YOU SAY IT

A sponsor once told me that he thought he was wasting his advertising money because he never had time to listen to our radio station; therefore, he reasoned, no one else listened. An ostrich-like approach, eh what? I called the station, asked the announcer to invite all people driving cars down Main Street to honk their horns. I waited. Held my breath. The response was wonderful. The combined din of the horns should have caused the sponsor to be reborn. He said he had sufficient proof of listenership so I asked the announcer to stop the noise. That was even more sufficient proof that we had listeners.

"If all those people are listening to the station, how come that I don't get any response to my announcements?" was the next question. The sponsor was telling me one thing in the beginning but meant something else all along. He wanted to let me know that people were not hearing his messages. The reason he didn't tell me that in the first place was because he thought I couldn't prove my audience. I was flush with victory about the horn-honking response so I became a bit arrogant. "Now you know that we have listeners, so perhaps they are rejecting your product because you don't have what they need" said I. "Then why am I advertising," said he. "Don't know," said I almost inaudibly. "Cancel my schedule," said he.

If I had weighed my words wisely, I never would have given him the stupid answer that I did. I should have remembered that he accepted the idea that his was not an impulse buying commodity. He had agreed to an institutional type plan in an effort to build an image. But, we both forgot that original intention. Think before you speak. The spoken word, once said, cannot be recalled.

I. O. U.

Many of us have the bad habit of using the first person personal pronoun I too often. We can get on people's nerves if we talk about ourselves too much. This is especially true when trying to make a sale to a sponsor. To cure this habit, when you catch yourself using the word I, think of I. O. U. Drop the word I, delete it altogether but retain O. U. O. U. simply means OF YOU.

Lesson learned: By making the person to whom you are talking the most important person, you will be forced to delete the word I, then your end of the conversation must concern itself with him. This assignment is not easy but can be mastered if you understand why we have a tendency to talk about ourselves.

The tendency to talk about ourselves so much is due to the fact that our natural attention span to other people is very limited. Sooner, rather than later, we switch the conversation to ourselves. Once you become aware of this natural weakness, you will better be able to overcome this failing.

A man built a successful business. Many of his employees had been with him for years. They were loyal and devoted because the owner always thanked them for their good work. He complimented them by using the term: "We did a great job." "We are a great team, etc." The owner's son was taken into the business. Pretty soon, some of the men resented the son's attitude because he would boast about himself. He would say "I did a great job. I did this. I did that, etc." The son's father suggested that he get on better terms with his faithful employees by saying "We did a great job. We did this. We did that, etc." About six months later, the son walked into his father's office and said, "Dad, we are in trouble with your secretary."

ATTACKING PROBLEMS

The essential part of attacking any problem is to first recognize the problem. Many of us consider the effects of the problem to be the problem itself. A salesman for a radio station may say to himself "What a mess I'm in; those dern reports have delayed me so long that now I'm behind on my calls."

What he actually means to say is, "My work is so disorganized that I should take time to get them in order." That's the real problem, his being disorganized! Yet he blames having to make out reports to be the culprit. It's almost like blaming the thermometer for the heat.

If the salesman throws up his hands in despair and broods about his situation, he'll get nowhere fast. But, if he takes pen in hand and writes down the real problems first and then lists the options and alternatives, he'll start to move toward the sunlight.

The salesman's problem-solving format should look something like this:

Problems

Stayed out too late last night. Overslept this morning. Began compiling my report too late in the morning and consequently missed my first two appointments.

Solutions

Will call the sponsors I missed seeing this morning and apologize and ask for other appointments.

Will start my reports immediately after dinner tonight. No dilly-dallying.

After writing the report, I'll sct up my priority list of things to do tomorrow and I'll not deviate from it UNLESS ABSOLUTELY NECESSARY.

So, the project is first to recognize the problem and then start solving it. Think a minute; would it be possible for your doctor to heal you if he didn't know the nature of your illness? If he considered the results of your disease as the disease itself, you'd really be in trouble!

More on Problem Solving

Difficulties spawn, develop and grow to maturity in a hurry. They lay in wait; they trip you up when you least expect them. Here's a typical day of problems and how they were dealt with.

The priority agenda called for a visit with Jones at 9 AM. 10:30 AM appointment with Mr. Smith. 12-1 PM, lunch. 2 PM appointment with Mr. Taylor. 3 PM back to office to shape up commercial copy for accounts starting tomorrow. 4:30 PM, see if manager can accommodate hour-long teenage program at 3 PM in place of MOR program now on schedule. Now see what happened.

There's Many A Slip Twixt the Cup and the Lip

9 AM: Jones had an unexpected death in his family and couldn't keep the appointment.

9:10: Called Mr. Howard, asked if he could spare some time to hear a new idea for his program. Howard says, "Get here as soon as you can; I can spare about 15 minutes."

9:45: Mr. Howard sent word out that he'll be there in just a few minutes.

10:15: Closeted with Mr. Howard but uneasy about 10:30 appointment with Smith. Got permission to call Smith and tell him about unavoidable delay. Smith rescheduled appointment to 2 PM on Wednesday. Howard impressed with idea. Wants to have lunch and then call in his partners so they can review new program ideas.

1:45 PM: Howard's partners just arrived. Call made to Mr. Taylor, apologizing for not being able to keep 2 PM appointment with him. Rescheduled to 3 PM on Thursday. Howard's partners like program idea. Conference ends at 3 PM. Call made to station manager by phone to discuss conversion of MOR program to teen program. He says it can be done.

4 PM: Finally get to studio to shape up commercial copy.

Lesson learned: If scheduled appointments were ignored because of extenuating circumstances, chances are that two good accounts would have been lost forever.

Use Your Problem-Solving Scalpel

Don't panic when you are confronted with a problem; instead take it apart with your scalpel, just like surgeons do when they are probing for an offending member. Approach your dilemma with confidence, but also bear in mind that some problems cannot be solved. However, when you write down every part of your roadblock, you will be able to tell whether anything has been omitted. If you neglect to do this, it is certain that all important data will not be taken into consideration. Explore every avenue and opportunity. Select the most workable solution. Consult an expert if possible.

Once you have decided on the course to follow, devote every talent and energy you can muster. If you are on the wrong course, stop and reconsider. Perhaps all you have to do is make a detour to get to your objective. Most important is don't let the problem grab you; you grab it. Don't let the problem stifle you; you stifle it. Lay your ego and pride aside. If you think that you are infallible, you're adding to the burden you have to bear.

DON'T BORROW WORRY OR TROUBLE

All of us worry about things that will never happen. My mother told me the story about the actress who went to bed one night and suddenly thought that she was suffocating. Frantically, she picked up a shoe, threw it at the window and heard a smashing of glass. Then she slept soundly, breathing easily. When she woke in the morning, she was surprised to see that she had broken a mirror and not the window. That started another worry because thespians believe that breaking a mirror is hard luck.

To cope with worry, here's what to do. Weigh the odds about the potential consequences. Consider whether the inevitable can be avoided. If there is no escape, brace yourself and prepare to accept it. Chances are that things will not be as bad after all. Then, too, things may not go as well as you expected them to. Most important, you must innoculate yourself with antidotes against needless worry.

Bisect
Detect
Examine
Explore!

    Affect
    Effect
    Search
    Forevermore!

        Grope
        Hope
        Listen
        Ignore.

            He's right
            I'm right
            You're right
            We're right.

                              Ad infinitum.
                              Who's right,
                              From birth
                              to death's door!

   Take the above for what it's worth. It adds up to the
conflicts, differences, doubts, and fears that plague all men.
The man without a problem may be alive but he might just as
well not be. It has been wisely said that many people die at an
early age but are buried at an old age. These are the people
who play it safe. Never take a chance. Life is too risky for
them so they don't live their lives; they merely vegetate. Is
your life limited by a narrow horizon? Do you prefer to take
orders and not have people buy from you? Do you fret about a
lost sale? Do you follow-up and follow-through? When your
sales prospect says "no" do you accept it as his final decision?
Are you more aware of yourself than of your sponsor and his
needs? Do you consider your work "a day at the salt mines?"
   There are two things that will make you age faster than
most anything else. The first is to become bored with your job
and the second is to accept the aggravation that comes from
sponsors demanding servitude instead of service. Boredom
sets in when you get on a too familiar, buddy-buddy basis with
your sponsors, when your calls are social calls and not sales
calls. Hear me and hear me well. Remember, familiarity
breeds contempt. "But how can I avoid this ferment?" ask
thousands of broadcast salesmen who ply their trade in the
same markets year after year. The answer is simple but not
easy. Don't take your customer for granted. If possible, avoid a
first name relationship. No, you doubters, you don't have to
call a man by his first name, or vice versa, in order to "warm
up" to him. Build a bridge of respect and not a wall of
resentment. Be certain that he pronounces your name
correctly and that you reciprocate. When you first meet him,
pronounce his name; then spell it and pronounce it again.
Don't crush his bones when you shake hands but then again,
don't give a weak handshake. Make it a firm handclasp.

HERE'S AN ICE CREAM SCOOP!

   A giant food chain made a deal with an ice cream company. The deal was that in return for carrying that unknown
brand of ice cream, the ice cream company would use local
media for advertising. A representative from that ice cream
company visited me to get the best deal for the least money.
He had already succeeded in getting "package" deals from

other stations in the area. I side-stepped the question of price and deal and showed him our vast file of success stories. I qualified our rate card and explained that we had no special deals or rates.

The ice cream rep then proceeded to tell me about an experience he had with a station that operated similar to ours He said that his company ran a call-in contest that seemed to have terrific response. When he visited the newspaper in that city, the editor suggested that perhaps the contest wasn't so successful after all. "Because," he said, "there are just a few radio-contest buffs who participate in all guessing games on radio. They flood the switchboard and it seems like a big audience."

Ice Cream Company Rep Swallows Bait

To prove his point, the editor invited the rep to call several names out of the phone book at random and ask if they were listening to the radio. If so, to what station. The results were appalling. Out of 50 calls, just one person was listening to the radio and that was to a station other than the one that carried the contest. The rep cancelled his radio program and allocated his budget to the print medium.

I listened to the story. Then I said, "Mr. Rep, we don't have any listeners at all. But, somehow, our phantom audience has managed to respond to our sales messages and please our sponsors." I went on, "To satisfy yourself, just visit any merchant or business in town and ask them!" He took me up on this. He returned in about an hour and bought a schedule on the rate card. The schedule was for 13 weeks. That was four years ago and he is still on the air with us.

Don't Be A Vulture

Remember this: Don't do like the newspaper editor did. Don't knock the competition! You must compete on an honorable basis, not on your competition's lack of talent or inability. Demonstrate your phantom audience to the next sponsor who questions your audience. Before you do this, however, be certain that you do have a dependable, reliable phantom audience!

ILLUSTRATE, DON'T DEMONSTRATE

At the moment, riots are taking place on most college campuses. I hope that peace will be the order of the day when this book finally gets to you. The "Phantom Audience" episode clearly depicts how a sensible approach to difference of opinion can resolve a matter. Every person is different. Even identical twins have several individual characteristics. So, you must adjust to people. This happens only when you study people. What makes them tick? You are the catalyst that ferrets out the real objection from the stated objection. Learn how to differentiate between an excuse for not buying and a reason for rejecting. Be firm without being arrogant. Lose a battle but win the sale.

He's To Blame!

People are so complex! People are stubborn; unyielding; blind. They can never see your point of view. Is all of this true? You bet it is if you ask any dissident salesman. He'll swear that it's the unvarnished truth. He'll rattle off experience after experience that the stupidity of his sales prospects causes him to lose sales.

Consider now, that communications is a two-way deal. Some people argue this isn't so, because look at the captive radio and TV audiences. "You can't talk back to a radio receiver or a TV tube." That is correct, but listeners can and do react; they switch to other stations or channels. If programs are dull, if commercial messages lack candor and truth, they can be ignored.

NOTICE TO RATE-CUTTERS

Your merchandise (radio advertising) is perishable. It evaporates with every minute that passes. It's impossible to run a clearance sale, fire sale, rummage sale or any other kind of sale. True, you can sell special packages but avoid it if you can. The reason you can't afford to tamper with your product is because you have just one item to sell. Just one! If you take a markdown, you reduce the value of your entire inventory.

A cut in your rate card, a special deal, a one-time-only package or any other alteration in your rate card spreads like a prairie fire. No matter how secret or sacrosanct your deal appears to be, you are doomed to become disillusioned because you will be vulnerable to attack by faithful sponsors who accepted your rates without question. "Cut your rate card and you cut your throat," is what I preach to all broadcast salesmen.

If you happen to get a job with a station that "looks the other way" when you make special deals, be careful. This practice should not be indulged in by salesmen nor permitted by management. For whom does the bell toll? It tolls for thee and me. In other words, no matter where you happen to be, if you sell off the rate card, it hurts the industry generally and affects every one of us.

To prove the point, just compare established premium rates made by insurance companies with the rate-cutting policies of some radio stations. People never even ask for a premium reduction because they know it isn't possible. But talk to some radio advertisers and they'll tell you a different story; that they are paying less than some comparable sponsors in the same city on the same radio station.

DOES YOUR RATE RAISE RATE A RAISE?

A radio station that keeps plugging along with the same old everything including its rates, year after year, does not have much to offer. When the cost of most everything creeps up gradually, it is necessary for a radio station to also increase its charges for advertising. A radio station must keep pace with the times and that is not possible if it is still charging 1950 rates in 1969. There is a big BUT attached to this simple premise and that is: Charging more money for your advertising just for the sake of charging more money is a lesson in futility. It must be a qualified rate increase.

If the sound of your station is good; if it is acceptable to a big, loyal audience; of your station keeps things lively, informative, entertaining, and interesting; if your station gets response for its sponsors with today's ideas and today's methods, then and only then can you qualify a raise in rates. When the decision is reached to raise the station's rates because it is in order, then be proud to be on the staff of a radio station that is going places. Don't ever be timid about the rate increase if it is well qualified!

CHALLENGE INHERITED KNOWLEDGE

"It can't be done," is a very familiar phrase that is applied to most innovators. "You can't harness the energy of steam to a boat!"it was said. But a gentleman by the name of Robert Fulton did it in spite of the unkind tag, "Fulton's Folly!" Albert Einstein challenged Gallileo's theories and found the correct formula for atomic energy. Every day, people who are daring and courageous are investigating inherited dogma and finding their efforts quite rewarding. Try this on for size. Accept the premise that the greatest reward you can have as a sales representative is to have your sponsor buy from you, rather than you sell to him. You can achieve this more quickly when being of service is the motivation, rather than "what's in it for me?"

A Challenge to Reject

"I've got some junk that I haven't been able to move and I want your station to sell it for me." Do not accept such a schedule. Radio advertising is not intended to achieve the impossible. The purpose of advertising is to motivate people to action and direct them to the merchandise or service. Then, it's up to the salesman at the point of purchase to complete the sale. But, if the quality of the products advertised doesn't satisfy the customer, all is lost. You are blamed for poor results, the store itself loses customers. The best thing is to steer clear of these challenges.

Switch Bait Advertising and Lotteries

"Here is a piece of copy that I want to run for saturation til further notice," you are told. The copy says: Pick up the remaining payments of $9.95 a month and this merchandise is yours. See ZZZZ Machine Company (Name street and city). You check this out. There is just one machine for sale on those terms. The intention is to attract a lot of unsuspecting customers. This kind of advertising is not only unethical but it is illegal. Even if there was no law against it, your own conscience should persuade you not to accept it. Temptation becomes nascent when things are tough and you could cave in if you are hungry. The best advice is to leave the station or quit selling altogether if you have to make a living that way. Illustrated are several public notices and warnings from the FCC and FTC regarding illegal and "shady advertising." The FCC talks about lotteries and the FTC addresses itself to "switch bait" advertising.

THINGS TO REMEMBER

Does a car dealer sell automobiles? No! He's selling transportation, style, and comfort. Does a grocer sell groceries? No! He sells delicious taste, nutrition, etc. Elmer Wheeler said it best when he uttered these words: "Sell the sizzle, not the steak." Customers think they are buying an automobile, but the dealer must prove that his cars have

PUBLIC NOTICE

Federal Communications Commission ▪ 1919 M Street, NW. ▪ Washington, D.C. 20554

31229
FCC 69-611
June 3, 1969 -

APPLICABILITY OF LOTTERY STATUTE TO CERTAIN
CONTESTS AND MERCHANDISE SALES PROMOTIONS

    Contests and other promotional schemes which have recently come to the Commission's attention have made it advisable that we remind licensees of their responsibility to avoid the broadcast of matter regarding lotteries, and that we clarify the construction of Section 1304, Title 18, U.S. Code, which provides criminal penalties for such broadcasts. The principal purposes of this Notice are to set forth our interpretation of Section 1304 with respect to the availability of free chances in certain promotional schemes and to remind licensees of their responsibility to assure themselves of the accuracy of advertisements for such schemes.

    Although the statute does not undertake to define a lottery, it is well settled that the necessary elements of such a scheme are (1) the awarding of a prize, (2) upon a contingency determined by chance, (3) to a person who has paid or agreed to pay a valuable consideration for the chance to win the prize. Ordinarily there is less trouble in determining the presence of the elements of prize and chance than in determining whether a particular promotion involves the giving of consideration.

    Clearly, consideration is present when the contestant is required to pay money or give something else of value for the chance to win a prize. Therefore, the promotional scheme must not require a purchase or the risking of money or other things of value. The mere acts of appearing, registering and securing free paraphernalia, standing alone, do not constitute sufficient consideration to support a finding of a lottery. See Federal Communications Commission v. American Broadcasting Company, Inc. 347 U.S. 284 (1954); Caples Co. v. United States, 243 f. 2d 232 (1957), and Garden City Chamber of Commerce v. Wagner, 110 F. Supp. 769. However, the availability of free chances must be real and not illusory; i.e., free chances must be available on a basis which is reasonably equal to that on which contestants who purchase a product may obtain them.

    Thus, in a scheme in which bottle caps constitute the chances, free chances are not available on a reasonably equal basis if it is necessary to obtain them from a bottling plant or the local route salesman, since chances are available to purchasers at all places of business selling the bottled drink. In general, if free chances may be obtained from most or all customary outlets, such as grocery stores and supermarkets, the element of lottery consideration would be eliminated. Equal availability means at least this. However, efforts should be made to insure that the non-purchasing contestant is able to obtain free chances at all places where the product is sold.

Typical Public Notice from the Federal Communications Commission, warning broadcasters about illegal practices.

the mileage, comfort, style that the customer wants, because that is what the customer has come in to buy.

The grocer depends upon his suppliers to package food items so that they are taste-tempting, nourishing, weight-reducing or weight-increasing; his produce must be attractive; his meat items should be fresh and appealing to the eye. People do not knowlingly or willingly spend money unless they believe they'll get the desired satisfaction out of their purchases. So it is with radio advertising. Side-step discussions about cost by translating that item into an investment. Satisfy your sponsor that the purpose of his radio advertising is to attract new customers when he gives you the old ploy "everybody knows me." Your job is to sell the results of advertising rather than the schedule itself.

BUILD A PRISON; BECOME YOUR OWN JAILER

Don't paint yourself into a corner. Before you discard the idea, realize that this is an imperceptible process; it envelopes you before you know it. For example: You become so immersed in your job that you lose your capacity for fun and recreation. Even when you have time off, you cannot forget your business. That old cliche, "All work and no play makes Jack" holds true. But what good is "Jack" if you can't enjoy it. Your attitude affects not only yourself but also your family and friends. Sure, be the most conscientious salesman on your team but temper your work with time out for wholesome recreation.

BOREDOM, THE POISON OF MANKIND

You're doing well as a salesman for a radio station. Your calls result in sales. Commissions are healthy. Easy come, easy go. When challenges become scarce, look for them. Create them. If you don't, you'll drift from a "new idea man" to order taker and then get caught in the vortex of boredom.

This syndrome can make you old before your time, so avoid this trap. Make a conscientious effort to create at least one new challenge every day. "How can I increase Smith's schedule?" "Jones has been on a schedule of announcements long enough; time for a change. How about switching him to a meaningful program? Taylor's account has been off the air too long; time for him to join our family of happy sponsors." These are self-imposed assignments. Write yourself a promissory note: "I (your name) will make every effort to complete my project with Mr. Smith no later than (date). Sign

ADVERTISING ALERT

Federal Trade Commission
Washington, D.C. 20580

ORDERS ISSUED BY FTC IN LITIGATED CASES
(Such orders represent final action by the Commission. They become effective at the end of 60 days after issuance unless respondents appeal them to the courts. Violations of the orders are punishable by fines up to $5,000 per violation.)

Home Improvement Products   (D. 8738)

The Commission ordered five affiliated home improvement concerns to stop using bait advertisements and other unfair and deceptive practices. They are: All-State Industries of North Carolina, Inc., 1130 W. Lee St., Greensboro, N. C.; ABC Storm Window Co., Inc., 1128 W. Lee St., Greensboro; All-State Industries of Tennessee, Inc., 910 Eighth Ave., South, Nashville, Tenn.; All-State Industries, Inc., 660 Eleventh St., N. W., Atlanta, Ga.; and All-State Industries of Illinois, Inc., 2111 State St., East St. Louis, Ill.

In its opinion by Commissioner Philip Elman, the FTC upheld the finding in Hearing Examiner Andrew C. Goodhope's initial decision that respondents have engaged in a "bait and switch" operation.

The Commission said "Respondents' principal method of advertising is through mail-outs which include return mail cards. These mail-out advertisements promote an inexpensive product within respondents' product line which they refer to as an 'ADV' product. The ADV product is ostensibly offered at a substantial reduction from a fictitious 'regular' price

The Federal Trade Commission keeps an eye on advertising practices, too.

your name to it. Now it's a binding document. Now you've got to work at it or else lose your self respect. That's how to fight boredom. This is an important part of any salesman's homework. Unless, of course, he prefers to spend his productive hours watching a matinee movie and blaming the world for his own inaction.

BUILD ON YOUR EXPERIENCE

Who can say that every possible objection has been stated, who can say that every objection has successfully been dissolved. It's just the same as calling the patent bureau to ask them what hasn't already been invented because you want to invent something. No matter how many books you read you'll never get all of the subject. It's up to you to carefully document your experiences and use them to the best advantage. It's hardly possible to span the volumes that have been written on salesmanship. Author's suggestions about how to sell are valuable. But, nothing is more important than your own participation. Keep track of your day-to-day sales experience and then you too can write a book.

Take No For An Answer

Some authors insist that you should have a canned or memorized dynamic close, a close that answers all objections at the same time. Others suggest that you get the buyer into a "yes" frame of mind; get him to agree with everything you say, then it'll be easy for you to get him to say "yes" at the crucial moment. I say that a salesman has a responsibility. That responsibility is to be certain that the product offered for sale will function the way it should. Objections should be encouraged. Yes, take no for an answer but be prepared to turn that no into a yes by dissolving the objection with honesty and integrity. If you cannot give him the correct answer on the spot, be honest; tell him that you'll get the answer as soon as possible. Thank him for giving you the opportunity to share this knowledge with him. A reasonable man will appreciate the fact that you are not a "know-it-all"; a smart man knows that you are bluffing if you pretend to know it all.

SALESMANSHIP INGREDIENTS

Making a sale is like baking a cake. You have to have all the ingredients needed and learn how to use these ingredients to get the best mixture. Pure sugar, salt, flour, etc., is unpalatable. But, when you mix the correct amounts and bake for the proper time, the results are delightful. That's the way it is with your efforts as a broadcast salesman. Know your product; know your market, and know yourself in relation to both product and market. Learn how you fit into the picture.

NOTHING NEW UNDER THE SUN

Many people say that there is nothing new under the sun. Perhaps that is true. But, everything is new to the person who has not heard it before. Even stale jokes are uproariously funny to people who have never heard them; yet, they bore people who have already heard them. Each year a new generation is fascinated by Santa Claus; to you and me, Santa is old hat. How often have you heard someone say "that's news to me!"

So it is with your efforts to have your sponsors buy radio advertising. They may have already used the very same techniques that you are using. The thing that will set your efforts apart from theirs is the way you package your presentation. If you are a copy cat, it'll be noticed very soon. Be yourself; just being natural will give your presentation (no matter how shopworn the theme) a new look.

GREATEST POLITICAL COMEBACK IN HISTORY

Richard M. Nixon was elected to the Presidency of the United States in 1968 after losing the same race in 1960 and California's gubernatorial election in 1962. During his 1968 campaign, he had the most astute advertising men and public relations experts on his team. He avoided the errors of his ill-fated race against John F. Kennedy. The Republican Party poured a fortune into his battle for the Presidency.

Nixon had to create a new image; from that of a chronic loser to that of a winner. A decision was made to have Mr. Nixon participate in an old-fashioned whistle stop tour by train. Talk to the small people in the small towns; see 'em in person. And it was in a small town that Richard Nixon saw a little girl carrying a simple sign with three little words. Those words gave Nixon the theme for his new administration. The sign read: "Bring Us Together!" Remember now, millions of dollars had already been spent; the finest advertising talent worked day and night writing speeches, directing every activity for the would-be President. But it was a simple sign with three little words that precisely stated what the candidate wanted to present to the American people, something that had failed to surface from the thousands of words he had already said. Nixon rose to the stature of his office. He thanked his high-priced talent for their help but credited the little girl for synthesizing the intention of his campaign: "Bring Us Together!"

TURNING POINTS

The story about President Nixon and a little girl's simple sign is quite significant. It shows that you never know when you might say or do something that will be the turning point in your life or career. Your smile may please some, annoy others. You may be long-winded to some, too short to others. Some may understand you, others may be confused. Let's use President Nixon's successful campaign again for a yardstick. He, like other candidates, was a victim of the mobs who used the riot technique to make their voices heard. Suppose small groups, instead of rioting, had quietly presented their case in the form of petitions or some more orderly method. Would this have been a more effective approach? Who knows? Who can tell whether or not the soft-spoken method would have influenced the election. Many blame Hubert Humphrey's defeat on the riots in Chicago during the Democratic Convention. Would the course of history have been changed had there been no Chicago riots? Nobody can say with certainty.

CONSIDERATION

Many years ago I was groping for a future. The textile industry appealed to me. Accordingly, I went to Textile High School to register. While waiting in line, I was told by a much older man (he did speak with authority) that I was wasting my time; that the textile business was for older men. Stupidly, I listened to him and went home, never to return. The point of this true story is this: Would I have become the czar of the textile industry? After all, I was interested in the course. Tempting as it is sometimes, I never advise anybody that he is wasting his time in the pursuit of a career or occupation that he wants. If an applicant is not suitable to my radio operation, I tell him so and suggest that he seek employment elsewhere. One man who received this treatment from me is currently manager of a big radio station. From this I learned that a good salesman may not be able to rise to the full measure of his talent in one market but do very well in another market. A little encouragement goes a long way.

LISTEN AND HEAR

Most people, at some time or another, get fussed at because they appear to be listening but obviously are not hearing what the speaker has to say. Many people think that listening and hearing are one and the same. They are not. The difference between a good salesman and a mediocre sales rep is his ability to focus his attention on words being said and the meaning of those words. It does take practice. Show your sponsor that you are paying attention to what he is saying. Sprinkle your part of the conversation with enough acknowledgement signals to indicate that you are giving him your full attention. Examples: "It's good to know that you have just received a shipment of men's shoes." Or, "It's just like you said, Mr. Sponsor, the weatherman does predict cooler weather." Don't overdo it though. It takes good judgment on your part to let your sponsor know that you understand him and a great deal of tact and instinct to employ this technique in the right way.

OPINION MAKING

Have you ever analyzed the ingredients of an opinion? It usually consists of a small measure of information; about three teaspoonsful of imagination, a large portion of prejudice, flavored well with emotion. If a sponsor has an unfavorable opinion of your station, you've got to defuse this time bomb. Getting into an argument will only hasten the bomb's explosion. No sponsor will change his opinion of your station if he has been mistreated, ignored, cheated, etc. Best way to proceed in this matter is to acknowledge the mistakes made in the past. Don't apologize or blame. Simply acknowledge. "Yes, Mr. Sponsor, you are correct. We have inadvertently neglected to service your account. But I personally promise you this will never happen again. I have taken measures to correct this condition. Won't you give us the opportunity to be of service?"

KNOW IT OR ELSE YOU'LL BLOW IT!

Andre Maurois, the French writer, correctly said, "The most difficult part in an argument is not to defend one's positon but to know it." If an irate sponsor hits you hard with distorted facts, keep cool! Let him get it off his chest. Once he does that he will be easier to talk to. Then, don't argue or defend but dissolve. Yes, dissolve his allegations one by one with facts that he either didn't know nor cared to mention. Above all, don't make him out a liar.

A colleague of mine told me a story about a preacher who was scheduled to make a series of morning devotional talks.

The morning announcer was late in opening the station. The preacher complained to the manager. The manager cautioned the morning man. It happened again. The preacher became angry and expostulated that the announcer was obviously prejudiced against his church because the announcer was of a different faith. He said he would tell his congregation about the mistreatment and urge all sponsors in the congregation to cancel their contracts with the radio station and let the sponsors who belonged to the announcer's church support it.

The station manager wisely let the preacher blow off steam. When he had calmed down, the station manager said, "Mr. Preacher, what you say is correct. You have been mistreated but not intentionally. Won't you please consider what you are about to do this Sunday? Remember, even Christ asked The Father "to forgive them because they know not what they do." What you say on the pulpit is your affair, but I want to spare you the possibility of being criticized for asking vengeance on a radio station when the misery you suffered was not premeditated and where no discrimination exists." Suffice it to say, this did make sense to the preacherman and nothing more was said.

CHAIN REACTION

The manager of a chain store told me that his company was circular oriented. This was a decision made by the president of the organization. It seems that the president had bailed the company out of its financial difficulties with some of his own finances and now it was doing very well indeed and the president ruled supreme. One day, the printing press broke down. A fast directive came from the president: "It's OK to use radio, provided you get the most announcements for the least cost." When I quoted my rates to the store manager he said, "too high." "Higher than what?" I asked. "Higher than the station in the town where I came from," he said. Now, there I was, I had a distinct advantage and could have been a real wise guy by saying," OK use that station," or some other stupid answer. Instead, I asked him what his circular budget was. He told me. A quick paper and pencil routine revealed that he could buy a saturation schedule on my station for considerably less than the double-truck handbill and that was on our established rate. He was interested and then asked, "What guarantee do I have that the schedule will accomplish what the circular will do?" "What can the circular do?" was my counter question. "Don't know, it always seems to get good results." Then he added, "And besides, the president insists upon handbills." "Do you believe in them?" I asked. "I have no choice," he replied. "Since we have no radio experience for your store, why don't you take a calculated risk and use the schedule that I suggested." Again, I could have been sarcastic and said, "unless you want to check with your president first." It was an emergency all right. Time was short so he went along with it. The response was wonderful. He was delighted. But, that's where it ended. The chain's chain of command wasn't impressed one iota.

Reasoning to the Rescue

Follow-up calls resulted in the same negative response. "Can't do a thing about it," the manager said to me. You did help us out of a tough spot and I am personally grateful. "One day I made a suggestion to him. I told him that big men, really big men welcomed good suggestions. I recommended that he write a letter to his president respectfully asking that the entire advertising program be reviewed with a thought being given to including radio advertising in the diet. "Nobody tells the president what to do," was his reaction. "True," I said, "but all that we want to accomplish is to have your chief be aware that this market is different. He already knows about our success story and maybe all that he needs is a gentle nudge." I went on "I'll be happy to help you draft the letter." He agreed and we made plans to write the letter that evening.

The Letter That Did The Trick

Here is the text of the letter that we wrote:

Dear Mr. President:

It was through your personal efforts that our (store) became so successful. Thanks to you I enjoy having a job as manager. With your help we will continue to grow. I would feel remiss in my duties as a loyal member of this (name of chain) if I did not offer my respectful suggestions to help you in your never-ending quest for improvement. During the recent breakdown of the printing press, I did use the facilities of Radio.... The response was excellent. It would be a good idea to review our advertising program in this market with an eye toward using more radio advertising in addition to our circulars.

We waited. The answer came. It was good and said in part, "I agree that we should use a productive radio station. See what you can do about getting us a good frequency discount." The manager told me that the schedule was mine if I gave him a good frequency discount off the rate card. My answer was a firm no. After lengthy discussion, he ordered a regular weekly schedule on the rate card. His sales improved considerably. He was promoted to district manager, then regional manager, and now he's in the home office in charge of all advertising. He wrote to me and confessed that it was my prodding him to write to his president that started him on the way up the ladder.

If you have an honest conviction and you state it respectfully and accurately, you have more chances to succeed. Use this formula: Don't criticize but encourage. Nurture men who have ideas. President Nixon proved the point by accepting three little words from a little girl carrying a small sign in a small town. Abe Lincoln proved it when he gave a little speech entitled, "The Gettysburg Address," and the general in charge of the allied forces during the Battle Of The Bulge proved it when he wrote a one word answer to the Germans who asked for his unconditional surrender. He simply wrote: "Nuts!" In so doing he gave his men a boost in morale and his enemy the rebuke they didn't expect.

FOLLOW UP AND FOLLOW THROUGH!

Here is an excerpt from a letter that I received:

"By the way, it may interest you to know that you were the only station out of 100 that I contacted initially that took time out to send me a second correspondence. I worked in local radio for some 15 years and often wondered why local stations did not get more regional and national business. Could be that local station reps don't pursue this type of account. Anyway, thank you for the follow-up memo and be assured that you will have the schedule.
Sincerely,
(Name of company and man available on request)

The failure to follow up and follow through in sales is a kin to defeatism. Defeatism is a first cousin of boredom and boredom is the poison that turns you into a walking corpse. These are harsh words and intended to be. Follow up and follow through to me is more than just a routine. It is an action that has zest and meaning. The writer of the above letter was a buyer for a giant company. He had sent out what appeared to be a routine inquiry about our station's operation, market, and rates. It was a form letter. I answered it in detail. Put a notation on my calendar to send a second letter in two weeks if there was no response from the company. I sent a follow-up memo that read "It is two weeks since we answered your inquiry dated (date). Is there anything we can do at our end to encourage you to make a decision to take a schedule on our station? We go the second mile in service and invite you to call collect for additional information, availabilities, or to place the schedule.

Sincerely,

It was my memo that elicited the response and got the schedule. The interesting part of it is that ours was the only small market station that did get the schedule on our national rate card! This was told to me by the writer of the letter after I called him to thank him for the business.

I compared notes with other owners and managers at a subsequent state broadcaster's convention. "John, did you ever get the Account?" I casually inquired. "No, never did, that was a routine inquiry; those guys never buy."

Other answers I got went like this: "Si, can't you tell when a company is conning you into doing their market research. I never answer those letters; toss 'em away."

"Now Si, you know better than that. Those companies will waste your precious time if you let them." It was a unanimous opinion, "You waste your time when you 'fool' with those routine inquries." To me, the breaking of ground for a new building, a letter from an agency or an inquiry of any kind is like a tonic.

SEARCH FOR NEW BUSINESS

I love to sniff the air for a potential sponsor and make plans to get him on the log. No letter goes unanswered; every call is followed up. I never make a call simply to visit. I go prepared to present something new and interesting. This keeps me on my toes. Gives life meaning and purpose. Don't get the impression that I am Jolly Rover or a playful puppy dog or a Don Quixote charging windmills in search of the Impossible Dream. No, not at all. I do a lot of sifting and sorting.

Don't Waste Time

Eliminate the things that can waste time like calling on 'pat' accounts simply to pay them a social call during their busy day. I don't indulge myself in the luxury of spending precious time in idle pursuits. The Good Lord alloted us a very small package of time and our stay on this earth is like a watch in the night. If you kill time, you are a murderer. We have a very fine trade school in this area. Anybody can attend and get a thorough course in electronics absolutely free. This leads to a First Class FCC License. I have persuaded announcers to attend these free classes. So far, to this writing, not one man has had the gumption to take the complete course. Drop-outs occur after five or six weeks. Excuses like: "I'm too busy with other things." "What good is all that junk anyway." "Got too many friends who depend on me to work in the (name) Club." Excuses, excuses, excuses.

DON'T NEGLECT YOUR SPONSORS

"John," I asked, "when did you call on Jones' Tractor Company last?" "Oh about two months ago but he wasn't interested." "Do you plan to see him again?" "Yeah, whenever I have time." "What will you see him about?" "I don't really know, I'll think of something but I don't think he's a good prospect so I'm not going to waste time with him."

That typifies the thinking of many so-called salesmen in our wonderful profession. The challenge of making a second, third, fourth and even a fifth call to get the business is missing. The energy it takes to create and plan a fresh new presentation is missing.

Build A Firm Foundation

Taking lines of least resistance is the order of the day. I try to correct this attitude by requiring daily sales reports. They do it for awhile. I remind the salesmen. The flow of reports starts to trickle in, then quits. "George," I said, "do you make notes on your desk calendar far ahead to remind you of appointments?" "I sure do!" But when I flipped George's calendar I saw only blank pages. I made this notation on a page dated two weeks in the future: "George, when you read this, you are fired!"

A month passed. I asked George how his follow-up and follow-through system is working. "Just fine!" "It is?" "Sure thing, Si"

Let's review your work, George; I notice that your sales are slipping. You're getting the old standard renewals, but what about those potential accounts you were going to see?" "Haven't gotten around to them yet." "Did you see Smith's

Department Store on the 20th? You did make a note on your follow-up calendar about him, didn't you?"

"Oh, I put him off for a while, letting him think things over; I'll get around to him." "George, I bet you skipped right past the 20th on your calendar pad." "Si, betcha I didn't." "Ok, look at it."

BOING! Now George is a trembling fool. "Si, you don't really mean that, do you?" "George, I do mean it! You are fired as of now! But, if you want to rejoin this organization, if you want to think, act, feel like, and be a sales representative, you're hired on a two-week trial basis." "Thanks, Si, I'll do better." Grateful George dashed off, full of "whims and vinegar," but he settled down into his "I don't care routine" after about 30 days.

George Didn't Do It

George is no longer employed by me. He's probably subjecting his lovely wife and two young children to the rigors of moving around in our industry, looking for that easy job that is chockful of house accounts, sure-fire sponsors, and easy money. Y'know what? There ain't such a paradise in any sales job! Slap happy hippies and slipshod sloppies are not welcome in my organization. Honest! I am not a Simon Legree. I insist that there is a world of fun, pleasure, and satisfaction in selling radio advertising. It pays very well and provides the opportunity to get a bang out of life.

JOIN, BUT DON'T BE A "JOINER'

There is a difference between joining worthwhile organizations and becoming a "joiner." Many salesmen make the mistake of becoming members of each and every civic club, group, etc. The result of this multitude of memberships is that you can scarcely find time to attend all meetings nor can you function well on the many committees that you are appointed to.

"Joiners" fall into this classification. They are motivated by the mistaken idea that the more clubs you belong to, the more sales you make. As a sales representative for a radio station, you are inevitably drafted onto many committees. The law of diminishing returns sets in when you find yourself making excuses why you can't "be at all meetings and do the work that is expected of a committeeman."

So, carefully select the area of civic work that you want to participate in and join one or two of those clubs. Become an active worker in those clubs. That, plus your work in your church or synagogue and in your state and national trade organizations, will give you a full agenda. If your main object is to make more sales rather than be of service, don't let it show through. On the other hand, saccharine altruism can also become suspect. The best way to proceed is to be a good working member of these groups and hope that someway, somehow, your reward comes in the form of bigger and better sales for your radio station.

EFFECTIVE COMMUNICATIONS BY MAIL

If you have a sponsor who is a "forgetter," write him a letter; then another one and still another. Write inter-city and intra-city letters; the same for state and national. We previously mentioned that it is not possible to communicate with smoke signals these days; many times the phone becomes impossible because: 1. The sponsor is too busy to talk. 2. The sponsor's phone is too busy (buzz, buzz, buzz) 3. You just cant' catch the sponsor in when you call. So write!

May I digress for a moment and go back to smoke signals? Many moons ago, an Indian brave was sending smoke signals. He noticed that his young son was sending the same message via smoke. "How come you write what I write?" asked the big brave. "I make carbon copies of letter you send," answered the young lad.

Getting back to letters, they do have a definite place in your sales efforts. Stodgy, stilted letters are of little or no value. Letters like: "Dear Sir, I beg to inform you that we have a station that you should use, etc. Very truly yours," have no place in this modern world. Your letters should **tell** and **sell**; brevity, that's what I mean, yet with an element of humaness and warmth. Get to the point in a sentence or two. So I hear some of my readers say "Look who's preaching about getting to the point! Seriously though, how do you like this:

Dear Mr. Jones:
May we help you? Our happy family of (call letters) sponsors include most of the major oil companies. I use the word 'most' because you are not on that list. We can change 'most' to 'all' if you give me the pleasure of a 10-minute meeting. Just 10 minutes to show why our listeners should know what your wares are for. Please call me collect for instant service.
Sincerely,

Dear Mr. Smith:
Six months is simply too long to stay off the air. Our listeners miss your clever sales messages. We miss doing business with such a fine company. Please call me collect for instant service.
Sincerely,

Dear Mr. Jones:
This is my third letter to you. The others have gone unanswered. I flatter myself upon selecting such a busy man with whom to do business. A man who is obviously so busy and in demand that he cannot find time to write. A collect call to me will give us instant communications. Won't you please answer.
Sincerely,

Dear Mr. Taylor:
This note should take just one minute to read. It's an invitation to you to call me collect so that we can discuss a matter that should be profitable to us both. Then, two minutes on the phone will add up to three minutes well spent. Please call today.
Sincerely,

Dear Mr. Jones:
There is an ancient proverb that reads: "There can be no friendship without confidence; and no confidence without integrity." Please call me collect so that we can arrange a profitable meeting. I will prove the last part of that proverb to be true so that I can establish the first two parts.
Sincerely,

Dear Mr. Smith:
Honesty is the best policy. Yes we did make a mistake but we admit it and we are sorry. Reminds me of the doctor who was advised by the coroner not to sign his name in the space marked 'cause of death.' Said the doctor: "Mr. Coroner, I did not make a mistake; that is an honest admission." Please call me collect so that we may further discuss the error (singular) of our ways and how we hope to make amends.
Sincerely,

Dear Mr. Smith:
A great writer once said that it takes at least two people to make one transaction. Please call me collect so that we can arrange a convenient meeting. Then, either you will buy from me or I will sell to you. No matter which way it goes, you will be happy with the results.
Sincerely,

I had fun going through my files, selecting these letters that all worked for me; they should work for you, too! There's more:

Dear Mr. Jones:
You have not answered my three previous letters. Reminds me of the most recent insurance statistics that show for every man of 85 years of age there are 8 women. But it's **too late** then! Don't let this happen to you. Don't wait for radio to go out of style before you make a decision to buy (station) advertising.
Sincerely,

Dear Mr. Smith:
No answer from you yet. It's easy to write a letter. Step one: You dictate. Step two: Steno's translate. Step three: Mail. Step four: Sale. And a profitable sale for you, indeed. If all this is too much, just call me collect for the same guaranteed results.
Sincerely,

Dear Mr. Jones:
Do you still question the value of advertising on (station?) One minute of your precious time please. Read this:
The members of the Body decided that they were doing all the work and the Belly was getting all the food. So, they decided to strike until the Belly agreed to do its share of the work. The hands refused to take the food. Consequently, the mouth and teeth became idle. After a few days, the Members of the Body were in bad shape. They were weak; could hardly function. Thus they found that the Belly, in its own, quiet way, was doing necessary work for the Body and that all must work together or go to peices.
This bit of wisdom from Aesop should give you an idea how important it is to advertise. For if you have a product to sell and you don't let the public know about it, your machinery will soon become idle too. Please call me collect for instant service.
Sincerely,

Dear Mr. Smith:
We never guarantee it but we do work hard to help you make a profit. The difference between the driver of a new automobile and the owner of a new automobile is about 24 payments. Maybe, with our concentrated advertising efforts, we can at least make you the owner of that new car in twelve months. Let us help. Please call collect for instant service.
Sincerely,

Dear Mr. Jones:
The product advertised by your agency is advertised in flights. Since you are the flight engineer, please be sure that you don't take off before we have a chance to get on board. Please call me collect for availabilities.
Sincerely,

Dear Mr. Smith:
We do a great deal of research before we do your advertising. You can never be too careful. Reminds me of the salesman who was hungry. Needed a sale awfully bad, so he said, "Lady, you can save enough on your food bill to pay for this refrigerator." The housewife replied, "We are paying for a washing machine with the laundry money that we save; we are paying for our TV set with the money we don't spend at the movies, and our car is being paid for with the bus money we don't have to spend. It appears as if we cannot afford to save any more money at this time." Mr. Smith, we look for and find the flaws in our sales messages before they are aired. Won't you give us a chance! Please call me collect for instant service.
Sincerely,

Dear Mr. Jones:
Radio (call letters) is the advertising workhorse of this area. We invite you to ride the saddle. Get your letter in at post time or call me collect for instant service. Results never quaranteed but certainly worked for!
Sincerely,

Here are some letters that I have written to progressive sponsors in our area. Sponsors who may have touched up their storefront; renovated their store, etc.

Dear Mr. Jones:
"Brighten Up The Corner
Where You Are."
It is good to see that you have such wonderful civic pride. The front of your store is very attractive and we sincerely hope that many customers will enter your new, beautiful glass doors. Keep up the good work!
Sincerely,

Dear Mr. Lord:
"Pluck a weed,
plant a flower" L. Burbank
You have made this community a much better place in which to live. The interior decorations of your store are delightful

and I know your many customers will appreciate the good work you have done. We salute you for your Civic Pride!
Sincerely,

Dear Mr. Smith:
     "We Pass This Way Just Once,
     Make The World More Beautiful."
              Anon.
Just one word to describe your newly decorated store: Delightful! Keep up the good work.
Sincerely,

 Yes, communications by letter is most important. Your letterhead should be the finest, engraved, preferably. Remember, a letter is an extension of yourself and your station. Yes, I know, there are many salesmen who read this and say, "there goes Willing again, suggesting something over which we have no authority." That's true if you limit your horizon; if you think small; if you conform with little men who think little. But, you can have your own stationary printed and your own calling cards, too. I purposely get into these nitty-gritty situations to make practical suggestions from bottom to top. And, I must remind you again if you are going to be a sales representative in broadcasting, then get out of a station that will not let you take pride in your job; a station that really has no right being in business in the first place. There are plenty of these stations, and I say at the risk of offending plenty of readers. If you don't believe what I say, select stations at random. Write to them. Request replies. See what sloppy letterheads they have and how poorly the letters are written.
 Letters should have a touch of humor, wisdom, be concise, compelling, sincere and sarcastic too, if necessary, and once in a while it is necessary to be sarcastic. I'll show you what I mean.
 Not too long ago, a representative for my station indulged himself in commissions that were not due him. After writing letters of respect, showing him the error of his ways, I received a real nasty reply. Here's how I answered:

dear smith: (Mr. intentionally omitted)
The way that I have written your name indicates just how big I think you are. If the commission that you appropriated illegally means so much to you, then, by all means, keep it. I will gladly endorse your candidacy for the Poverty Program.
Have fun with your ill-kept gains.
After keeping this letter for a few days, I tore it up!

Letters Are Forever

"He who writes himself down a fool, remains a fool." Be careful what you write but be **certain** about what you mail. Writing a letter can get a lot of things off your chest. If you write in anger, don't mail the letter for a few days. Read it; re-read it, then by golly tear it up; unless, you are absolutely certain that what you wrote is warranted; that you will not regret what you've said once it is mailed.

Letters should be written also for the good and welfare of the reader. Put a proverb or familiar saying in the upper right hand corner to set the mood or the tone of your letter. Your letters should not be run-of-the-mill. If the recipient of your letter selects yours out of the heap that is on his desk because even the envelope is attractive, then you're really getting there. There's a lot of competition in the mail these days, so you start practicing how to write brief, informative, appealing letters. It should never be necessary to use more than one page if it's a business letter.

EFFECTIVE COMMUNICATIONS BY PHONE

The phone rang. My wife answered. She said "Oh, you don't say! (pause) **You** don't say! (pause) You **don't** say! (pause) You don't say! (pause **You don't say!** (long pause) Thank you and goodnight." "Who was that, dear" I asked. "She didn't say," was my wife's coy reply. This familiar, silly narration is to point up how even the most trivial recitation can capture attention.

Proper Use of The Phone

Use the phone wisely. Use it when you are detained by one sponsor and sponsor number two is waiting for you. Call sponsor number two and tell him that you are unavoidably detained. Tell him that you couldn't anticipate the delay and then reschedule your appointment.

You waste time when you make "cold turkey" calls to sponsors whom you already know and have on the air. Call him only if you have a real good reason for wanting to see him. Never telephone a sponsor just for the sake of making idle conversation. The only exception here could be if you have neglected him too long and you call to say that you are thinking of him and will see him soon. If you call him just to pass the time of day, it gives him the impression that you have nothing better to do; he is busy and you are wasting his time.

Be Brief When You Phone

Have consideration for your sponsor's time. A typical call should be pleasant, brief, and to the point. Avoid being brusque when you intend to be brief. Example of a brief, pleasant and informative call: "Hello, Mr. Jones, the audition tape we've been waiting for has just arrived. When will be the most opportune time for us to meet?" These few selected words state the nature of your business. You give him the opportunity to set the date and time for your appointment.

Use The Phone To Collect Past Due Accounts

It's amazing how much you can collect by calling delinquent accounts. Handle these calls this way: "Mr. Jones, my bookkeeper advises me that your check for the November schedule hasn't arrived. Could be that it got lost in the mail. We make these routine calls to all sponsors who have a pattern of prompt payment. If you have alread sent the check, it probably got lost in the mail. Simply put a 'stop' on the one you've mailed and issue another one."

This kind of approach gives the sponsor the chance to 'get off the hook' if he is delinguent, or thank you for advising him about non-receipt of the check that he did mail. He will appreciate the "escape hatch" that you provide because he could advise you about his financial problems and indicate a target date when he plans to make payment. At any rate he doesn't get the idea that you are "hounding him." Your well planned phone call pays off!

Telephone for Regional and National Business

Whenever possible, write to the out-of-town time buyer or representative before you call. This gives him a chance to study your pitch on paper. Indicate that you plan to call him long distance after he has had time to study your letter. He may reply by mail, saving you the cost of that long distance call. Supposing you have written him, offering a certain schedule. He doesn't answer. That's your cue to make the call by phone. Let's simulate the conversation:

"Mr. Taylor, this is my follow up call to the letter that I sent you recently." Such a statement gives your man a chance to gather his wits. If things are in order he'll assure you that he read your letter, was too busy to answer, and that your schedule will be on the way soon.

Should your station not be included in the campaign, he may side-step the issue to buy enough time to write you the bad news. His conversation in this case could go like this: "Yes, I remember your letter but we've been snowed under. No definite plans have been made yet; I'll let you know." Then, of course, his "Dear John" note will soon follow, giving you the sad news about how they had to trim the budget, etc.

If your rep or time buyer says: "I've been too busy to digest my mail," or "I can't remember what you wrote," or words to that effect, then you have a good reason to consider that he is stalling. In that case, ask him to get your letter out of the file so that you can review it together. If he says he is too busy, then you should remind him about the subject of your letter. "Mr. Taylor, I appreciate your being so busy, but I know that the flight for the (sponsor's) schedule is slated to start on (date) and that's just a week away. Is our station included in your plans?"

Now you're closing the gap. You're either in or out and he may just tell you. Since you already have him on long distance, you can make the effort to salvage the account or at least find out why you lost it in the first place. A question like this can do the trick. "Mr. Taylor, is there anything we can do to be reconsidered?" "Was our presentation sufficient or is the situation hopeless?" Mr. Taylor will advise you whether you can get the account by doing some repair work or he'll give you a final "no." Whatever the result, you will have saved a lot of time and apprehension by making your long distance call.

Local Calls

Cultivate small local accounts by phone. A good way to pursue a small account over the phone is like this: "Mr. Smith, I notice that you have a special on fresh river catfish. Since that's one of my favorite foods, I thought you'd like to listen to a sales message that I've prepared for your consideration." Then give him the sales message so that he'll be satisfied that you really mean it. Mind you I said give the sales message, don't just read it to him. Using the telephone is a great way to sell small accounts.

THE IMPORTANCE OF OUR TRADE ORGANIZATIONS

Your radio station limits its horizon if it belongs to no trade organization. The National Association of Broadcasters invites every radio and television station to belong. This great outfit concerns itself with the complex problems that plague broadcasters everywhere. They use newsletters very effectively. NAB is the eyes and ears of the broadcasting industry and has access to information that would cost individual stations a lot of money were they to do their own research. The same holds true for the many state broadcaster associations. Every radio and television station should join and support its own state broadcaster's association.

The accompanying illustration will give you an idea how both the NAB and the state associations disseminate news in a hurry to all of their members. When quick action is needed, out goes an urgent notice! You simply cannot afford to barricade yourselves within the confines of your own market and cut off communications with the outside world. Work for a station that already belongs to NAB and its state association. If this is not possible, respectfully suggest that your station join one or the other, or both if possible.

THE IMPORTANCE OF TRADE PAPERS

Salesmen in the broadcast field should be avid readers of the many fine trade papers (magazines). This is a must! It's as important as attending state conventions and NAB Conventions. You learn through reading. Broadcasting Magazine; BM-E (Broadcast Management-Engineering), Billboard, Broadcaster-South, Broadcasting-Engineering are just a few of the magazines you should read. Don't depend upon reading your boss's copy; subscribe to these yourself. The modest cost is well worth it.

THE IMPORTANCE OF ATTENDING CONVENTIONS

When you are being interviewed for a salesman's job, ask a few questions yourself. Ask your potential employer whether it is station policy for them to let salesmen attend any conventions at all. Let them know that you are interested in the entire industry and that you would like to attend at least one convention a year. Tell your employer that you will take the business sessions seriously and, of course, participate in the entertainment of the convention when it is scheduled.

A JOB WORTH DOING IS WORTH DOING WELL

Strive for perfection. Avoid sounding like a perfectionist but do put a ring of steel around your presentations. Check yourself for credibility gaps, omissions, distorted facts, etc. Don't be satisfied with your "rough drafts." A good analogy here is the repair work that is being done to Niagara Falls.

LOUISIANA ASSOCIATION OF BROADCASTERS

LOUISIANA STATE UNIVERSITY   P. O. BOX 16078   BATON ROUGE, LOUISIANA 70803

JOHN H. PENN-BAKER
EXECUTIVE SECRETARY

PUBLIC SERVICE AND THE COTTON COUNCIL

Si Willing has sent me a file of material relating to a problem that should be of interest to most of you. It concerns the National Cotton Council of America and its efforts on behalf of the cotton growers of America. As a part of these efforts, $10 million was budgeted in 1969 for "cotton research and promotion." In this period, however, the Council has continued to request public service time from radio, while apparently buying time from television and space in print media.

The issue was brought home forcefully to Si when, during his term as President of the Winnsboro Chamber of Commerce, he heard a talk about a contemplated advertising campaign for cotton given by a representative of the Cotton Council. Slides accompanied the talk and the virtues of print and television were extolled--while not one word was said about radio.

Soon thereafter Si wrote to the President of the Cotton Council and objected to such a presentation. He concluded the letter by saying, "We gave everything public service here while there were no advertising funds; we even helped promote the vote to have farmers have their cotton bales taxed. Unless we can get some commercial schedule from your Council . . ., we will not give any more public service announcements."

In his reply, the President said, in effect: What helps cotton, helps the economy of Winnsboro. What helps the economy of Winnsboro, helps KMAR and you, Mr Willing. Specifically, he said:

> The single purpose of the program of the Council and the Cotton Producers Institute is to increase the use of cotton so that farmers in Louisiana and other areas will have the opportunity to increase their markets, acreage, and profits. One guiding principle is followed in the funding of these programs . . . to place the industry's money into research and promotion projects which offer the greatest potentials for accomplishing the above objective in relationship to costs.

This seems to imply that radio just isn't as good a buy as print and television, and Si pointed this out by saying, "If radio was a good medium to use when there were no advertising funds available, it should be just as good when there is money to pay for those advertising schedules." He offered to match a paid schedule with a "non-commercial broadside" and repeated his refusal to carry anything from the Cotton Council without such a schedule.

The response was a beautifully brief brush-off. "Thank you for your response. . . . Please keep in touch. . . . If anything new develops . . . we will let you know." (Don't call us . . .)

State associations appraise broadcasters of legislation and other affairs which are pertinent to the industry.

FCC NOTES

Here Come De Fines

WACA, Camden, S. Carolina: $10,000 for willful and repeated failure to observe the terms of its station license by unauthorized pre-sunrise operation. It seems WACA would sign on at 6:00 AM at its daytime power of 1 kw. When the FCC insisted on a pre-sunrise power of 500 watts, the station replied that it did not have the equipment to convert to 500 watts and asserted that "on 1590 [it] cannot and does not interfere with any station . . ." and that there is no reason "why service at the perimeter of our signal should be denied our listeners." "Shut up.", the FCC explained, "And stop violating your pre-sunrise obligations." WACA refused to do so, stating that when faced with reduction of power at a time of day when its fringe areas needed "special announcements, encouragement and news," it could not decide on an alternative to using full power to "discharge what [it regarded] as [its] duty." As you can see, no licensee can talk to the Commission that way and expect to win its argument.

WJSW, Maplewood, Minn.: $5,000 for operating prior to authorized sign-on time, destroying station logs, and maintaining logs containing false information. Licensee argued that the violations were the result of actions by a general manager who had since been fired. The Commission said that was an interesting story, but read the Communications Act about the responsibilities of a licensee.

WWIN, Baltimore, Md.: $3,500 for broadcasting of lottery information and failure to have a properly licensed operator on duty. The lottery information concerned a Super Jet Money Man who was to visit homes at random [chance] to pass out $5.00 gift certificates [prize] to anyone with proof of purchase from the previous week from the Super Jet Super Market [consideration].

WFPM, Fort Valley, Ga.: $1,500 for double billing. Nothing more needs to be said.

KTFI, Twin Falls, Idaho: $1,000 for pre-sunrise violations.

KAPA, Raymond, Wash.: $1,000 because licensee, after being granted a construction permit authorizing change in antenna height and transmitter location, began regular programming with the new facilities without program test authority and continued operation for more than two months.

Association newsletters warn members of FCC actions, too.

IN STATE NOTES

Looking for Personnel?

Stephen Ruppe, 3055 Victoria Drive, Baton Rouge, (355-8215). 2 1/2 years experience including Program Director, News Director, news reporting, play-by-play, sales, production, traffic, and copy-writing. Interested in Program or News Director position with MOR or Top 40.

Charles T. (Chuck) Hudson, 47, 3032 Skyland Drive, N.E., Atlanta, Ga. 30341, (404-451-9076). Retired Air Force Officer seeking a "second career" in radio. Graduated from Elkins Institute of Radio, Atlanta, and Career Academy of Broadcasting, Atlanta. Has First Phone. Primarily interested in play-by-play sportscasting, but willing to work at any on-the-air position.

Roger Lee Beckmann, 28, 823-J Southwest Blvd., Jefferson City, Mo. 65101, (314-636-3460). Seven years experience as Program Director and announcer in Missouri. Wants to relocate in the New Orleans, Baton Rouge area and is willing to consider any phase of broadcasting. For reference, contact Stan G. Grieve, General Manager, KLIK radio, Jefferson City, Mo. Tape and extensive resume are available at LAB office.

Anyone looking for a job would do well to list his qualifications in an association newsletter.

199

HIGHLIGHTS
PUBLISHED EXCLUSIVELY FOR MEMBERS OF THE
NATIONAL ASSOCIATION OF BROADCASTERS

June 9, 1969

Dear NAB Member:

Broadcasting celebrates its Golden Anniversary next year and your Public Relations Committee welcomes suggestions to make it the best observance possible.

50th

At a planning session Wednesday, the committee approved for submission to the Board of Directors a comprehensive plan for national, state and local participation.

It wants to be sure industry participation is widespread and asks that any ideas you may have be sent to the NAB Public Relations Service.

The program recommended to the Board would include on-air radio-TV station presentations on the industry's past and future which emphasize its unmatched public service. Other highlights include cooperation by community and public service groups which long have been champions of broadcasting.

The committee also previewed a Careers in Broadcasting presentation that is half talk and half sound recordings in stereo. To be released soon, the presentation is designed for use by members in urging students to pursue a radio-TV career.

John M. Couric, NAB vice president for public relations, also briefed the committee on these NAB projects:

☆ A recording of radio's own march -- "Radio...The All-American Sound" -- which will be based on a martial air first use during 1968 National Radio Month.

☆ The May-long observance of "Radio...The What's Happening Sound" and the excellent support it received from NAB stations and networks.

☆ The new Build Television With Television campaign of spot announcements. (The second in the series will be released later this month).

☆ Cooperation with TIO in promoting TIO film spots which are designed to acquaint viewers with the many services offered on their behalf by TV broadcasters.

A National Association of Broadcasters' Communication.

URGENT . . . . . . URGENT . . . . . . URGENT . . . . . . URGENT . . . . . .
In the last issue of this Newsletter we discussed the Williams Amendment to the proposed new Copyright Law which would, in effect, force broadcasters to pay fees to performers on and manufacturers of phonograph records played on the air. These fees would be in addition to the fees already paid to ASCAP, BMI, and SESAC. It is estimated that the amendment, if passed, would cost radio broadcasters alone approximately $26 million a year.

We have been informed that Senator McClelland, Chairman of the Subcommittee on Patents, Trademarks, and Copyrights of the Senate Judiciary Committee, does not look with favor on this amendment and is very anxious to get the new copyright bill out of committee for passage. We would like to be able to show him that the bill will meet great opposition if the amendment is attached to it.

Excerpt from an NAB "Urgent."

NATIONAL ASSOCIATION OF BROADCASTERS

1771 N STREET, N.W. • WASHINGTON, D.C. 20036 • 293-3500

URGENT   URGENT   URGENT

TO ALL NAB MEMBERS

The cigarette labeling bill, H.R. 6543, is tentatively scheduled for consideration by the U. S. House of Representatives during the week of June 9. This bill would prohibit the FCC and FTC from banning or requiring warnings in cigarette advertising until 1975. The FCC proposes to ban all cigarette advertising after the present law expires on June 30, 1969.

    1. We challenge the validity of the Federal Communications Commission's effort to proscribe the advertising of a legal product without Congressional authority.

    2. Only the Congress has the power to prescribe what are permissible standards of advertising in the public interest.

    3. The FCC's assertion of authority to ban the advertising of a legal product is tantamount to a claim of power to promulgate advertising standards for all products. This is a principle for which we find no legal support. For similar reasons the Commission might seek to control advertising of products containing cholesterol; fluorides; beer and wine; proprietary drugs; insecticides, and many others.

    4. If the Congress does not act, the regulatory agencies will create a hodgepodge of conflicting and discriminatory rules.

Broadcasters are not insensitive to the issues involved. They recognize their obligation to the public in presentation of advertising and they will continue to meet their responsibilities.

We urge you to contact your Congressman immediately by phone, wire or in person to ask him to support H.R. 6543.

Paul B. Comstock
Paul B. Comstock
Vice President for Government Affairs

June 6, 1969

Another NAB "Urgent" alerting broadcasters to proposed legislation.

This great work of nature was found to be erroding. Engineers and geologists tackled the enormous job of diverting the water so that they could better study the rock formation of Niagara Falls. The plan is to reinforce the rock and granite to prevent the Falls from eventually disappearing altogether. That my friends is dedication and also work.

Sure, you're entitled to make mistakes but don't make 'em because of indifference. A sensible, positive attitude is what's needed. A pompous, know-it-all attitude is what is not needed.

MAKE IT COUNT

When King Richard The Lion Hearted decided to embark on his Great Crusade, he ordered his commanding general to forcibly explain the purpose of his mission to the soldiers. The General was eloquent. He used big words. He talked at great length. The result of his speech succeeded in drawing comments like these: "A wonderful speech." "How eloquent our commanding general is." "Beautiful rhetoric."

King Richard was very clever and he realized that the General's speech had gone over like a dud, so The King himself decided to talk to the men. The King inspired; he appealed to the soldier's emotions and patriotism. When Richard completed his hard-hitting speech, the majority of soldiers almost to a man exclaimed, "Let us march!"

Beautiful speech and lengthy talks do not often make sales. Count the words you say and make the words you say count!

DISTRACTIONS

Unless you are closeted in a sound-proof room with no telephones is it impossible to have a conversation with no distractions. Getting undivided attention these days is almost impossible. So, take distractions in your stride. You may be in the middle of making an important point such as emphasizing your low cost-per-capita rate; your station's coverage, etc., when all of a sudden, there is a phone call for your sponsor, or, one of his clerks barges in with a question. There can be a myriad of interruptions. Thing to do is wait patiently until your sponsor has disposed of the matter that caused the distraction, then go back a few words and continue your presentation. In other words, don't pick up your talk exactly where you left off because the train of thought might have been lost when the interruption began to develop.

RECOGNIZE PEOPLE

Generally, when you ask a favor of someone, you put yourself under obligation. But, there is a kind of favor that will make the sponsor from whom you asked that favor feel good. Ask him how he managed to catch "that big one" should he happen to be a fisherman. Or, if he is a hunter, ask him how he bags all of the buck. If he likes food, ask him where you can enjoy the finest food. Any one of these or other questions that will establish him as an expert and make him feel important. Mind you, I don't advocate a "snow job" but this is an excellent way to strengthen the bond of friendship. Part two of this action should be your telling him how helpful his information was. This will put the icing on the cake.

HEALTH! DON'T NEGLECT IT!

No matter who you are, what you are, or how much money you have, if you are sick, nothing matters very much. Don't make the mistake of neglecting your health. Get periodic checkups from your doctor and dentist. This sounds trite, corny, shopworn, but most of us don't get checked unless we start feeling bad. Preventive medicine and dentistry can make you a happier salesman. It's almost impossible to make many sales in broadcasting if you aren't feeling well.

THE MISSING LINK

Generally speaking, product advertising lauds the product but neglects to explain how to use that product. Years ago, I was taken in with the compelling reasons why a new additive to a certain brand of toothpaste would prevent cavities. My family and I used that brand exclusively. Then, we made our periodic visit to the dentist. You guessed it, we all had cavities. I told the dentist that we had switched to the new toothpaste and felt confident that the incidence of tooth decay would be greatly reduced. He agreed that it would if we brushed our teeth properly. He pointed out that we were relying on the toothpaste to prevent cavities but had been neglecting to brush our teeth correctly. Because we had been giving our teeth a lick and a promise with a soft toothbrush, the toothpaste had actually collected a film that developed into a tartar that hastened tooth decay. The business of brushing teeth is a universal ritual, yet few people know how to brush teeth properly.

I have given you this account of toothbrushing gymnastics for a very good reason. You will make permanent sponsors out of skeptic advertisers if you make them aware of the total function of radio advertising. If you give them the impression that all radio advertising is effective, you've overstated the ability of radio advertising just like the toothpaste people did. If you accept a thin schedule to promote a big sale; or, if you allow flat copy to announce that sale, chances are that the results expected by your sponsor will not materialize. Therefore, you yourself must first know what can be expected from an advertising schedule and you must transmit this knowledge to your advertiser. Don't let him expect one action when you know there will be an opposite reaction.

THE VEGETABLE PEOPLE

People who occupy space and serve no wothwhile purpose are generally referred to as "vegetables." An unfortunate person who is congenitally infirm; someone who is very old and worn out falls into this classification. But, a person who has all of his faculties, who is able to perform for the good and welfare and doesn't use his talents, is taking up much needed space without making any contribution. There are many salesmen who "dry up" because they don't use their minds to create new ideas; new approaches. They avoid challenges; play it safe. You miss the joy of salesmanship if you allow yourself to drift into a state of non-performance. Don't **YOU** become a "vegetable."

PARASITES, THE THIEVES OF TIME

Next to your good health, the most valuable possession you have is time. "Dost thou love life, then do not squander time," warned Benjamin Franklin. Planning your time will avoid wasting it. We have touched on the subject before, now here are some pointers how you can manage your time so that it won't become waste:

1. Get your important papers into finger-tip availability. Looking for misplaced papers and documents is not only frustrating but also time-consuming. Don't be a saver of

unimportant papers, periodicals, and things that clutter up your desk and files. You've got to develop a talent to distinguish between expendable things and important items. You've got to learn to discipline yourself to throw out the things that errode your time.

2. Keep your attention focused on the business at hand; do not let a "talker" get you off the track toward a point of no return. Some people like to meander into small talk. Unless it contributes to making the sale, steer the conversation back into its proper dimension. This kind of maneuvering takes tact and diplomacy. It takes plenty of practice but it can be done and must be done if you plan to get anywhere with a sales prospect. One little example: Supposing your prospective sponsor "just happens to have an album of his grandchildren." Admire the kids and say, "just think how much more you can do for these fine lads if you increase your business through the medium of advertising with us on Radio----." Use his weakness as your strength. Practice, practice, and more practice will help you achieve this most important gymnastic in avoiding small, needless talk.

3. A sponsor broke three scheduled appointments with me in succession. He always had a good excuse, for himself, that is, but he never did consider that he was not only wasting my time but also showing extreme inconsideration. I computed my time according to the value I had put on each hour. I visited him without any appointment scheduled and presented him with a bill for the time that I wasted. At first he thought I was kidding, but I told him I was dead serious. When he was satisfied that I meant business, he paid me. I promptly returned the money and told him that I wanted to bring into clear focus just how much importance I put on keeping appointments as scheduled. Now, there is never a waiting period when we plan to meet, and he is a very good radio advertising account.

4. Be prepared! Know your subject. Get to the point in simple, understandable language. I don't mean that you should be brusque or sharp. But be lucid and pleasant. Don't get to your point of the subject by way of three or four chapters. The measuring rod of progress is to ask yourself whether you are wasting your sponsor's time and your own all at once. Learn the art of the "silent sell." You accomplish this by

practice. The first step is to write your presentation. Second step is to go over it with a magnifying glass. Third step is to strike out all unimportant sequences. In other words, boil it down so that it is a lean, informative, and compelling discourse. Extraneous words and ideas can sidetrack a presentation. This is important homework so start to practice it now!

5. Categorize your prospects. Drug stores, dry goods stores, groceries, tractor dealers, car dealers; and so on. Your homework consists of creating new ideas for each account within each category. This can be frustrating if you let it, but it can be a rewarding experience if you let it exercise your mind. It is obvious that you will strike out if you give the same talk to each kindred account. Supposing you have five tractor dealers and you offer each one the same idea. Sooner or later you'll get cancellations when each dealer hears his idea on his competitor's commercial. It's the same reaction you hear from a woman when she sees another woman wearing a dress just like one of her own. This is where the order takers are separated from the salesmen. Use your imagination, it's one of the few things that is for free in this day and age.

6. Satisfied sponsors can be a source of new business. You compliment a sponsor when you ask him to refer to a prospective new sponsor. You can work this another way. Ask your satisfied sponsor if he will endorse your station should you be calling on a dubious prospect. Ask if he will give your dubious sponsor-prospect a favorable report if you have the doubter give him a call. This works wonders. Don't be afraid or ashamed to ask for references. This technique is a real time saver and a sales-maker.

7. Get out of a rut. Make it a conscious effort to see at least one new prospective sponsor a day. Remember what we said about the law of attrition erroding old customers. Again, we urge you to present new, sparkling ideas to your sponsors, both old and new.

THE EXTRA EFFORT MAKES THE DIFFERENCE

It may cost you a bit more but the payoff is great. Here's what I mean. When you write a presentation to an account or an agency, enclose a self-addressed envelope in which your prospect can return his reply. It is astounding how many

	POWER APPEALS						SECONDARY OR AUXILLIARY APPEALS								
	Happiness	Sex	Health	Wealth	Esteem	Security	Employment	Safety	Appetite	Comfort	Fear	Family	Snobbery	Acquisitiveness	Widely Variable
Air Conditioning	✓					✓	✓			✓		✓			
Automobiles (general)	✓	✓			✓		✓		✓			✓	✓		
Auto Accessories	✓	✓			✓					✓		✓	✓		
Banks	✓			✓	✓										✓
Bargains, general	✓			✓										✓	
Bargain Dept. Stores	✓			✓										✓	
Boats	✓				✓		✓	✓		✓		✓	✓	✓	
Book Stores	✓				✓							✓	✓		
Bread bakeries	✓		✓				✓	✓		✓					
Children's Clothing				✓	✓			✓		✓	✓				
Department Stores															
Promotion stores				✓	✓									✓	
Prestige stores	✓	✓		✓									✓		
Discount Houses	✓			✓										✓	
Drug Stores	✓		✓											✓	
Dry Cleaners					✓		✓								
Employment Agencies	✓			✓			✓								
Farm Implements				✓				✓	✓			✓			
Fashions	✓	✓			✓		✓		✓			✓	✓		
Furniture	✓			✓	✓	✓	✓		✓	✓	✓	✓			
Floor Coverings	✓			✓	✓		✓		✓	✓	✓	✓			
Hardware Stores			✓				✓							✓	
Home Builders	✓			✓	✓	✓	✓		✓	✓	✓				
Jewelry	✓	✓			✓		✓						✓	✓	
Men's Clothing	✓	✓			✓				✓			✓			
Night Clubs	✓						✓					✓	✓		
Pianos & Instruments	✓						✓					✓	✓		
Real Estate Brokers	✓			✓	✓	✓	✓		✓	✓	✓	✓			
Restaurants	✓						✓	✓							✓
Savings and Loan	✓			✓		✓	✓		✓						
Service Stations	✓					✓	✓							✓	
Sporting Goods	✓	✓					✓						✓	✓	
Supermarkets	✓			✓			✓			✓					
Theatres	✓						✓								
Tire Dealers			✓			✓					✓	✓			
Toys	✓				✓							✓	✓		
TV Service	✓		✓				✓								
Variety Stores	✓						✓					✓			✓

I. Neil Terrell's Motivation Finder Chart. It is useful in determining which aspects of a store or product to emphasize in copy.

accounts are lost because this added convenience has been omitted. When you make it simple and easy for a sponsor to answer your inquiry, you overcome at least several causes of inertia, which usually consists of 'being out of stamps,' 'not having time to answer,' or some other reason for putting your letter aside and then letting it get lost in the shuffle. I have kept a meticulous record of the results that I received from enclosing self-addressed (stamped!) envelopes. Nine out of ten letters were answered promptly. Make this a habit-forming practice.

THINGS GET OLD FAST

Just thumb through some 'how to' books written only five years ago. See how quickly those ideas have grown old, even obsolete. It can be so with this book or any book of this vintage. Automation is rapidly taking over. It is predicted that within the next 10 years, households will be run by computers. Meals will be programmed and the computer will not only prepare these dinners but also cook them. Yes, pushbutton living is rapidly approaching.

At this writing, there is nothing on the horizon that indicates radio advertising salesmen will be replaced by computers. It's that personal confrontation that makes the difference. Radio stations are now automated. You can buy insurance policies through vending machines. Satellites can well replace TV stations and possibly radio stations. The advance of "technocracy" is rapid. "You can be replaced by a button," is already an old cliche. The reason I brought up the subject is to make you aware of your expendability. You are not only in contention with expert sales representatives and dissident sponsors but also heartless equipment that can flatten you should you not become a human expert.

BE A DO-IT YOURSELF THINKER

When you are confronted with a problem, stop and think. Don't stand helplessly and wait for somebody to do your thinking for you. This is part of being a salesman. You are the person involved in the problem so figure your way out of the maze. George Bernard Shaw once said: "Few people stop to think more than once or twice a year. I've been able to earn an international reputation by thinking only once or twice a week."

EXAMPLE OF HOW NOT TO SELL

I was seated in the cafe enjoying a hot cup of coffee when a stranger tapped me on the shoulder and asked if he could join me. "Of course," I said. He introduced himself. He was a space salesman for a new agricultural newspaper that had been in business for about a year. Without much ado, he smiled and said that he would take most of my agricultural accounts away from me. "How do you plan to do this?" I asked. "Simple," he said. "We've mushroomed in the past year. Sales have zoomed and I'm hungry for more business." I admired his being so candid.

"How long have you been selling space in your paper?" I asked. "I don't have to sell it; it sells itself," was his smug answer. "Come again," I said. "Let me know the secret of your success." "Simple," he replied. "I never prepare a pitch. Just show the sponsor my newpaper; he sees the good company he'll be in and then he signs on the dotted line." "Tell you what," said I, "let's simulate a sales call. Perhaps I can learn a thing or two. Are you game?" "Sure," was his confident reply. "OK, let's go. I'm seated at my desk and you open the pitch," I suggested. Here's how it went:

Salesman: "Mr. Willing, my name is John Jones and I am the sales representative for Agricultural News. This is a new publication just about a year old. I'd like to have your account."

Me: "Mr. Jones, what is your Starch Report?"
Salesman: "My what?"
Me: "Starch Report"
Salesman: "Don't know what you're talking about."
Me: "OK, how about your Sindlinger Report?"
Salesman: "You've got me, don't know what you mean."

The rest of the interview is easy to quess. Very predictable. He was hanging on the ropes when I plied him with pertinent questions regarding his circulation, readership, etc. To make a long story short, the man confessed that he had a lot to learn, especially that without preparation you simply cannot sell any kind of advertising. This proved to be very true because recently I met this man. He was no longer representing the newspaper but he was selling vacuum cleaners, door-to-door. This is a true story, carefully filed in my portfolio of sales adventures. So if you want to be worthy of your profession, learn everything there is to know about radio broadcasting. Half-baked facts produce no sales.

REASONS WHY SPONSORS QUIT ADVERTISING

Neglect is perhaps the most common reason why a sponsor quits advertising. In the beginning, the sponsor is wooed and romanced. Promises are made. Promises are broken. Fresh copy becomes stale. The salesman neglects to call on him. He hears sparkling commercials from his competition while he is still on with the same old copy that he had several weeks ago. That's one reason why a sponsor quits and goes to another medium.

Your station's programming goes downhill. The same old sound; nothing new. Listeners are bored and they flip their tops and then their dials. Fewer listeners result in less response, consequently advertisers become fewer until eventually panic, despair, and all of a sudden the station is on the block for sale.

An unrealistic raise in rates is another reason for sponsor desertion. If the station is producing results; if there is a strong demand for space on the log, then a reasonable raise in rates is justified. But if a smug, complacent attitude prevails, programming gets shoddy, announcers are careless, and the manager plays too much golf or catches too many fish, look out! The ride downhill is swift and the impact is great. The climb to the top is difficult. Increased rates for neglected programming and service is a radio station's fatal mixture.

You work hard to get sponsors to advertise on your station. Why let all of this work go down the drain. Be alert. Service your accounts. Suggest new programming ideas. Again we say that new, bright, fresh, attention-getting sounds will hold a station intact and make regular sponsors out of your accounts. If you are a party to the demise of your station, your record follows you whereever you go. If you see that the station is disintegrating in spite of your efforst to save it, quit while the quitting is good and move on to greener and better pastures.

HOW TO SELL A NEWSCAST

The purpose of sponsoring a program is to "capture" a complete audience. Newscasts have universal appeal and are very salable. Here are the reasons why a good sponsor should be given the opportunity to identify his company or product with a newscast:
1. Exclusive sponsorship of a newscast guarantees that the sponsor is the only advertiser in that program.
2. Compared to advertising in a newspaper, this is an advantage because it is impossible for one advertiser to be the only advertiser in every newspaper issue.

Now remember, we are never going to knock the competition. We let the sponsor make his own decisions through inference. We do this with an exciting presentation something like this: ...."Mr. sponsor, our listeners don't have to thumb through countless pages to find your ad. They know you are the advertiser who is bringing the news because that's what they hear in the very beginning. You not only are guaranteed sufficient advertising within the news but you are also providing a service by bringing the latest news. Listeners don't have to wait overnight to hear what happened this afternoon; they know they'll catch the very latest news on your newscast.

Isn't that an exciting presentation? Just think, the freshest news in understandable fashion with only one advertiser. Your sponsor will quickly see that he has a terrific vehicle going for him. Without your telling him, he'll know that he couldn't buy an entire newspaper issue exclusively. Even if it were for sale, he couldn't afford to pay for it! That's why you should sell newscasts! A word of caution! Be sure that your newscasts have the latest news! Be certain that the announcer doesn't give a stale newscast and omit the latest breaking stories!

HORIZONTAL & VERTICAL PLACEMENT

You can sell a horizontal schedule or a vertical schedule. Here's the difference: Let us presume that 60 announcements per week is the schedule. You can schedule 10 announcements each day for six consecutive days; that's horizontal. Or, you can schedule a saturation of 20 announcements for three consecutive days; that's vertical selling. Each has an advantage. Horizontal scheduling gives fewer announcements each day over a greater period of time. It reaches less audience each day. Vertical selling is saturation. It concentrates more announcements in each day but for fewer days during the week. Vertical selling is suggested for a "crash campaign;" horizontal schedules are effective when there isn't the urgency of a big sale or closeout of merchandise. It is up to you to know the difference between these two methods and then recommend the kind of schedule that will create the best results for your sponsor.

Vertical schedules can also be used when a sponsor tells you that all he can afford is 60 announcements a month. He tells you that an average of two announcements a day is hardly worthwhile. He's right about that so you suggest that he use 15 announcements every Thursday in the month. That's vertical placement and a good way to get maximum mileage out of a limited budget. A saturation campaign one day out of each week in the month, but be sure that he has something important to say; otherwise the account won't be with you too long.

DIAGONAL PLACEMENT

A good way to guarantee that your sponsor will have his sales messages exposed to every segment of your audience is to place his messages diagonally:

MONDAY, JUNE 6th: 7 AM

TUESDAY, JUNE 7th: 8 AM

WEDNESDAY, JUNE 8th: 9 AM

THURSDAY, JUNE 9th: 10 AM

FRIDAY, JUNE 10th: 11 AM

SATURDAY, JUNE 11th: 12 PM

SUNDAY, JUNE 12th: 1 PM

MONDAY, JUNE 13th: 2 PM

TUESDAY, JUNE 14th: 3 PM

WEDNESDAY, JUNE 15th: 4 PM

And so on. Diagonal spotting is also called "round the clock" placement. Since these times are guaranteed, they are worth more and a premium rate should be charged for this arrangement.

PRIME TIME

A good number of stations classify their time into "prime" and "regular." Prime time is determined by the amount of listeners the station has at certain periods of the day. The more listeners, the more prime the time becomes. This information is gained through professional surveys.

Some markets may consider "drive time" as their prime time because that's when most people are driving to work in the morning and returning in the evening. This audience is sometimes called "listeners on wheels." Other stations may have an exceptionally good morning man who caters to families during breakfast. Almost any segment of the day may be classified as prime time provided it is authenticated by a reliable, up-to-date survey.

Many stations charge a premium rate for prime time, while many stations don't make a case of prime time. Therefore, become familiar with your station's policy. It is difficult for a salesman who has never sold in a market that has established a prime time rate card to negotiate in that kind of a market. Salesmen who move up to larger stations from small town stations also find it difficult to ask more per announcement than they did in the previous station. Consider yourself to be a prime salesman and it'll make the job of selling much easier for you.

COPYWRITING TECHNIQUES

Although this book is basically concerned with selling radio advertising, it is important that you know about copywriting, too. After all, the commercial copy is part of the merchandise that you sell. Neil Terrell has developed a fine course in copywriting and has given me permission to use some salient facts for the purpose of illustration. Here are some of the more important do's and don'ts that you should become familiar with.

VITAL STATISTICS

Many salesman rationalize their failure to keep records by saying that "Records can keep you." That is true if you let yourself become a slave to the records you keep. The best way for you to become master of your record file is to keep only the important information. Illustrated is a sample of a case history form that earns its keep as soon as you complete it. Daily entries in your record book build mounds of information that becomes invaluable. Don't confuse important homework with needless chores. Let the second-rate salesmen take comfort in the fact that a little extra work "is for the birds."

Do:

1. Always write from the **you** attitude.
2. Paint a beautiful picture of the **benefits** of using or owning.
3. Remember that buying is based mostly on **emotional** needs.
4. Remember that the six **Power** appeals are:

   1. Happiness
   2. Sex
   3. Health
   4. Wealth
   5. Esteem
   6. Security

5. Offer your prospect **more** than physical merchandise or service.
6. Relate your offering to human needs and wants.
7. Realize that self-love is the basis for buying.

8. Always start with an attention compeller, then:
9. Lay a foundation of aroused interest and desire for the offering, and:
10. Close with an urge to action.

Don't

1. Write from the advertisers viewpoint like "Special Selling" or "We've got to sell 100 cars this week" or "We're out to set a new sales record."
2. Assume that customers buy for purely logical reasons.
3. Take for granted that listeners will figure out benefits for themselves.
4. Sell on the basis of physical need only.

Do

1. Look for hidden **emotional** motivations.
2. Base your copy on **emotional** appeals.
3. Look for all **secondary** benefits or motivations.
4. Check your copy basics for hidden motivations.
5. Check national advertising when appropriate.
6. Review your own knowledge of the product or store.
7. See the merchandise. Know what you're selling.
8. Determine your prospects before writing copy.
9. Write more than one **type** of copy when identical merchandise is aimed at more than one type of listener.
10. Select the **type** of copy that will produce the **best** results.
11. **Emotionalize** then **rationalize**.
12. Avoid humor unless you have a real ability in that field.
13. Justify a bargain price in a logical manner.
14. Sell the idea that now is the time to buy.

Don't

1. Use minor appeal as a basis for copy.
2. Overlook the possibility of **hidden** motivation.
3. Discount national advertising as a source for valuable pointers on motivations and overall approach.
4. Write without seeing the merchandise unless it's absolutely necessary.
5. Start writing before determining who the prospects are.
6. Try to sell two widely different types of prospects with the same copy. (Some exceptions, of course, but be wary.)
7. Use wrong type of copy.
8. Rationalize without first emotionalizing.

9. Try to write humor copy unless you have a real ability for it.
10. Present a bargain price without justifying low price in a logical manner. (With price-list type of copy, one justification can cover it all.)
11. Assume that prospects will **buy now** unless you give them a reason.

Do

1. Use your lead to grab the attention of **prospects**!
2. Let the prospect's **imagination** work for you.
3. Use **emotional** motivation in addition to price.
4. Avoid price-list copy at every opportunity.
5. Reinforce desire by using the same motivation throughout a campaign or saturation schedule.
6. Always sell **cure** rather than **prevention**.
7. Be sure your lead has these three factors:

   A. Appeal to the self-interest of **prospects**.
   B. The right word, phrase, or sound stimulus.
   C. Arouse curiosity.

8. Consider using these appeals in your lead, also:

   A. Give news to the point.
   B. Make it believable.
   C. Offer quick results or fast benefits.
   D. Make it easy to understand.
   E. Contrast.
   F. Promise benefits.
   G. Mention product or business favorably.

9. Use standard words and terms.
10. Use "Do Something Verbs" to paint word pictures.
11. Use the four-step plan for writing **Power copy**.

   1. Attention
   2. Interest
   3. Desire
   4. Action

Don't

1. Use a lead without a direct connection to your subject.
2. Overlook the help the prospect's imagination can give you.
3. Use price-only motivation. It is not enough to produce maximum results.

4. Use price-list copy unless absolutely demanded by client.
5. Use different basic motivations in the same campaign or saturation schedule.
6. Sell prevention. Sell cure instead.
7. Use relatively new slang, jazz or hippie words and phrases.

WE LEARN FROM EACH OTHER

A free exchange of ideas is the best way to make progress. As a broadcaster, I always welcome ideas and suggestions. Conversely, I have always made an effort to share my experience and knowledge with my broadcasting colleagues.

Only you can profit from the experience that you, yourself, participate in! Reminds me of the man who said, "Boy, getting up at dawn and jogging for 30 minutes is great. Especially when you take a cold shower immediately afterwards and then follow up with a hearty breakfast. It's a wonderful way to start the day."

"How long have you been following this routine?" I asked him.

"Oh, I plan to start it tomorrow," he said.

Up to this point you've been reading about suggestions; ways, means, and methods. The final part, SURPASS, tells how the professionals handle themselves under fire. We hope that some of their success will rub off on you.

WCTR, Inc.
Chestertown, Md.

George F. Thoma   General Manager

BUSINESS ANALYSIS

FOR _____
ADDRESS _____
PHONE _____
SLOGAN _____

MARKETING NOTES

CONTACT_____

AD AGENCY_____

ACCOUNT EXEC._____

CURRENT LOCAL ADVERTISING

RADIO STATIONS_____ PGMS_____ SPOTS_____

TV STATIONS_____ PGMS_____ SPOTS_____

NEWSPAPERS_____ OTHER_____

+ + + + + + +
THE COMPANY AND ITS SALES OBJECTIVES

1. GOODS, ITEMS OR SERVICES
   a.
   b.
   c.

2. DISTRIBUTION AREA FOR GOODS OR SERVICES

3. PRINCIPAL OUTLETS

   a.   c.
   b.   d.

4. NORMAL BUSINESS HOURS

5. NUMBER OF SALES EMPLOYEES

6. UNIONS AT COMPANY

7. NEW PRODUCTS OR SERVICES ANTICIPATED

8. MARKET RESEARCH AVAILABLE

   a.   b.

Account analysis form recommended by Neil Terrell as part of his Power Technique approach. This is page 1 upon which you enter basic indentifying information.

219

THE COMPANY IN RELATION TO COMPETITION

1. MAJOR COMPETITION

    a.
    b.
    c.

2. LOCATION CONSIDERATIONS

3. MASS PURCHASING POWER

4. VARIETY OF SELECTION

5. ADDED FACILITIES (delivery, parking, custom work, consultation etc.)

    a.   c.
    b.   d.

6. PRICE COMPARISONS

7. SELLING HOURS

8. AFTER-SALE SERVICES

    a.   b.

9. STRONGEST COMPETITIVE ADVANTAGES

    a.   c.
    b.   d.

10. STRONGEST COMPETITIVE <u>DISADVANTAGE</u>

    a.   c.
    b.   d.

On this page (2) you enter information regarding the prospect's competition.

THE COMPANY PRODUCTS OR SERVICES

a. description

b. major uses

c. reasons for use

d. major consumer benefits
1)
2)
3)

e. secondary or auxilliary benefits

1)   3)
2)   4)

f. price or price range

g. customer guarantees

h. high-profit line, item, or service

1)
2)
3)

i. leader item or services

1)
2)
3)

j. life expectancy of products

____Days ____Weeks ____Months ____Years

k. other product information

Information about the prospect's products or services is assembled here.

221

THE COMPANY'S PROSPECTIVE CUSTOMERS

1. AGE ANALYSIS   <u>MEN</u>   <u>WOMEN</u>   <u>TEENS</u>

   PRINCIPAL USERS   %   %   %
   PRINCIPAL BUYERS   %   %   %

2. PEAK SALES MONTHS   (ranked according to importance)

   January ___   July   ___
   February ___   August   ___
   March   ___   September ___
   April   ___   October   ___
   May   ___   November   ___
   June   ___   December   ___

   PEAK DAYS

   Mon ___   Wed ___   Fri ___
   Tue ___   Thur ___   Sat ___

   PEAK SELLING HOURS

   6 - 10 AM ___%   10 - 1 PM ___%

   1 - 3 PM ___%   7 - Mid ___%

   Mid - 6 AM ___%

On the final page of the analysis form the firm's prospective customers are categorized. Armed with the information contained in this simple, 4-page form, a salesman can prepare an effective campaign for his client.

MANAGEMENT ROUNDTABLE

Order Takers Don't Sell

Needs and Wants — Radio's Advertising Strength

By Si Willing

"GRASS ROOTS" RADIO

By Si Willing

This letter reveals station involvement in community and area affairs.

Is Radio Becoming A Welfare Estate?

By Si Willing

Several articles by the author on sales have been published in BM/E Broadcast Management Engineering.

223

PARKES BROADCASTING CO. PTY. LTD.
307 Clarinda Street, Parkes, N.S.W. 2870
P.O. Box 295, 2870. Phone 62-1122 AUSTRALIA.
Telegraphic Address: "TWOPEKAY"

2PK

VOICE OF THE GOLDEN WEST

14th May, 1969.

MAY 19 1969

The Editor,
BM/E.,
Mactier Publishing Corporation,
820 Second Avenue,
<u>NEW YORK. N.Y. 10017.</u>
United States of America,

Dear Sir,

I have read with interest Si Willing's Answers to Questions, in the January and February, 1969, Issues of BM/E.

In the issue of August, 1967, Si Willing wrote an article under the title of "Order Takers Don't Sell", and I still have this issue in my possession.

As this Station is located in a very small market, I desire tp secure any other material issued by Si Willing.

Would you be so good as to advise if any other material by Si Willing is available and at what cost.

Yours faithfully,

PARKES BROADCASTING CO. PTY. LTD.

N. T. SPICER.
Manager.

A MEMBER STATION MBS   MACQUARIE BROADCASTING SERVICE

Letter in response to published material show the need for information exchange.

Section 5

SALE
Surpass

HERE'S HOW ITS DONE

To begin this part, we quote from letters received from other salesmen telling how they handled some sales problems. These letters came in response to a series of ads that I ran in leading trade magazines asking for real-life sales experiences. They are being published exactly as they were written. Salesmen, remember this! You may be alone with your problems when you call on a sponsor but other radio advertising salesmen have not only been confronted with these problems but they have solved them. Never let a problem defeat you! You defeat it!

Mike Rooney, KVOZ, Laredo, Texas, 78040

Bob Batson, 1210 Douglas, Odessa, Texas, 79760

Tom Longfellow, Arkansas Radio Network, 1001 Spring Street Little Rock, Arkansas, 72203

Steve Coco, KTRN, Wichita Falls, Texas

Randy Griffin, KBRZ, Freeport, Texas

Neil Terrell, Nashville, Tennessee

Roger S. Davison, WNBO AM-FM, Baton Rouge, La.

Mike Rooney writes:

After my return from the forum in San Antonio, I briefed our station owner, Mr. Bill Harrell, and sales staff. We all agree with you that we're selling "sales messages" and not "spot announcements." Many good ideas came out of the forum and I can't begin to thank you and Mr. Terrell enough.

I used your idea about playing a free demonstration commercial on the air for one customer. He signed up for a $1600 year contract. Up to that time he had been thinking in terms of $1200. The demonstration could have made the difference.

From Bob Batson:

Si, as for my most successful sales story, I think perhaps it was a sale I made, which I consider as the turning point in my career; in fact, the one that kept me in the sales game.

I entered the profession of Life Insurance in 1962 full of enthusiasm and with high hopes of success, but after the first six weeks I took home $95 total income. Naturally, you know my condition of mind was very low, but nevertheless I was making the calls and the presentations. I made a presentation to a doctor and had shown him a $120,000 policy with an annual premium of $1,800. Due to an emergency the doctor had to leave and I didn't finish the sale. I did, however, set a time and place for a callback. You know what a callback is, so naturally I thought I had lost it. He had said that he was interested in "some," perhaps like $50,000. That weekend we had a meeting of the Company, so I went to all the pros and told them the story and asked them what to do. From these men I came up with one statement and course of action. I wish I could remember the man's name to give him credit for it.

My callback amounted to this: I went in to the man's office, opened my briefcase started filling out the application (after all he said he was interested in "some"). I completed the application, except for the amount of insurance, and turned it to him. I took out a blank check and filled it out for the $1,800 premium and handed it to him. He looked at it and said, "I don't know if I want all of that or not." (Now the answer the pro gave me.) I said, "Doctor, it depends; do you want 100 percent protection or 50 percent, and I shut up. Believe me my heart was pounding. I was glad he was a Doctor—I could have had a heart attack right there. He said, "Well I would rather use my own check." Believe me, I flew home on wings; my commission on that sale was over $900 and this was the beginning that took me to earnings in excess of $50,000 per year.

I have had many sales more dramatic and with perhaps more of a message in sales ability, but, in the example I just mentioned I think you will find a different kind of message, a message for the man who is failing. At such a time a man needs hope; he needs confidence, and believe me every salesman finds himself on the ledge of failure. If he quits at this point he will surely fail. The other part of the message is seek help: The big men will always understand and help you with your problems if you ask.

Here's **Tom Longfellow's story**:

"I don't buy anything but personalities. You got any personalities?" These words kept ringing in my ears after my first meeting with Stuart Flanders, owner and operator of

Stuart's Muffler & Brake Shop in downtown Little Rock. My answer, "We don't sell personalities; we sell ideas and creative commercials..." so what to do?

Two weeks later I dropped in again with a tape recorder and a written presentation pointing out why Stuart's Muffler Shop should sponsor the 5:45 PM News. He liked the idea of sponsoring the drive-time newscast to reach motorists when they are most conscious of needing brakes, mufflers, or a tuneup; but, he said, "Who's going to be the personality?" I said, "You!" After he got over the shock, I turned on the recorder and just had a quiet conversation with him as to just what services he had to offer, without giving thought to timing or composition. A good editing job back at the station turned out some excellent commercials featuring the manager, speaking in a natural conversational manner. He knew his products and services well, and his voice was sincere.

Our "personality" really pulled in new customers. After a couple of months he said, "The results have been so good from this one program, why don't I run more and get more results?" So I set up a morning drive-time schedule of two spots per day on an alternating schedule: 7:00 and 8:00 AM one day, and 7:30 and 8:30 AM the next. After the first few commercials, editing was no longer necessary. Now Stu and I make 60-second ad lib conversational commercials on the spot in the shop with all the noise going on in the background. They really get your attention and they really sell mufflers and brake jobs. After a few months he quit using newspaper ads entirely, and in the fall, when business used to slack off, customers kept lining up for service. Now he has consistent year-round business, regardless of the weather. The second annual contract will expire in March, but he'll sign another at our increased rates without batting an eye.

Does radio sell? Just ask "Stu" at Stuart's Muffler and Brake Shop in downtown Little Rock.

From Steve Coco's letter:

I hate to admit it, and I hope the boss never finds out, but in retrospect I can see that many of my "greatest sales" were accidents. When you make a sale by accident, though, it's still a sale. The trick is to realize what you did by accident and learn to do it on purpose from then on.

One of my "accidental" sales involved a big order for broadcast advertising from the manager of the local outlet of a chain operation. That's all the description I can give, because I wouldn't want the name of the manager or the company disclosed.

I had worked up a pretty voluminous presentation. By the time I got through that presentation, no intelligent man could come to any conclusion but to "buy" my station. But the manager of the "X" Company either missed part of the presentation or wasn't too bright, because he was not going to buy.

We had been talking about using advertising material that was available from the "X" Company home office in the schedule of advertising that I had proposed. It was about the middle of the week and the proposed schedule was to start on the next Monday. I had just about given up on making the sale when an accident happened. I said to the manager, "Well, it's so late in the week now that you probably couldn't get the material in from your home office in time to get the schedule started Monday."

That did it. Within just a few minutes the manager was on long distance telephone to his home office showing me that he could get the material to us in time to start Monday. The point is pretty obvious. Instead of trying to impress your customer, let him impress you. It won't work every time, but it will work often enough to make you a lot of money in selling.

A Success Story From Randy Griffin:

For months I had been trying to get a supermarket in Lake Jackson on the air with a weekly spot schedult. The owner kept turning me down with the statement, "my newspaper ads and weekly circulars are all the advertising I need and can afford."

One day over coffee, we checked his full page newspaper ad and discovered about 20 percent was blank space. We checked the cost per thousand of his circulars delivered to only a fraction of his potential customers, then I asked him to try radio on a 13-week daily spot schedule, giving me the cost of the 20 percent wasted newspaper space and the cost of his circulars. He thought about it for a moment and agreed to try it. He would use approximately 32 spots (30 seconds) a week for 13 weeks.

The first week there was a small increase in sales but it wasn't enough proof. The second week I deliberately misquoted the price of a sugar special. It should have been 29 cents for a 5-pound bag, but I advertised it over the air at 19 cents, knowing that I would compensate him for any financial loss and also give him extra spots at no charge for every spot I broadcast using the altered price.

Less than an hour after he opened the following morning the owner was on the phone checking the price of sugar. It seemed there was an impatient line waiting for the doors to open to buy sugar at 19 cents for a 5-pound bag. Each customer told him they heard the price over the radio. The man was furious, to say the least!

I listened to his verbal blast quietly, then softly said: "Mr. Sponsor, doesn't this prove that radio should be the major medium for your advertising?" The phone was quiet for 30 seconds or more, then he answered: "Randy, you've made your point...you've sold me. Drop by and let's work out a weekly schedule on a 52-week basis. Wouldn't the rate be cheaper?" I assured him it would!

That was six years ago and the supermarket is still on the air as one of my best customers. Two years ago he sold out but sold the new owner on the merits of radio advertising who, I may add, leaned heavily toward newspaper for all their advertising. By the way, the owner wouldn't accept payment for the loss he suffered in selling the sugar at a reduced price. His answer was: "I noticed some brand new customers in that waiting line and it was worth it to me! Come on...let's go get a cup of coffee...and you can pay for it."

Neil Terrell is on the nose with his suggestions how to close!

Here are some rebuttals visualized mostly for larger markets where sales resistance is a practiced art and where many times a knife-sharp attack against untrue statements is necessary for the sale. Learn the basic ideas of each and adapt them to your own language in any size market. They'll make money for you. As Don Gilbert, general manager of KGLC, Miami, Oklahoma, said at the Dallas **Power Technique** broadcast sales seminar, Jan. 6, 1969, "If you can keep a prospect from lying to you, you can sell him."

I've Tried Your Station and Didn't Get Any Results

In larger markets, and especially in major markets, this is the most frequent objection you're likely to hear. It is used by the prospect to discourage you and send you on your way, as psychologically he holds a tight grip on his pocketbook. It is disconcerting to many weak salesmen. You can command a large measure of respect when you stand flat-footed and slug him with these ungarbled words. He'll never mention the subject to you again. This is **Power Technique.**

Mr. Prospect, that happens every day on the best stations. If you've used our station at all, I don't doubt that you've placed spots that didn't get results. All our advertisers have. Furthermore, you know very well that you don't get results from every spot on the station you now use. If you did, you'd advertise everything you've got instead of the two in the present schedule you have. If a man got results from every spot, or every second spot or third spot he uses, there would not be enough time available to carry all the advertising.

Mr. Prospect, the station is not responsible for advertising failures nor is it entitled to undue credit for the successes. The station has absolutely no control over results. Take our station, for instance. Almost a hundred advertisers will use our station tomorrow just as they do every day. Many of them will get the results they desire, while others will get mediocre response.

Let's understand this clearly, Mr. Prospect. The question of whether a spot will or will not produce depends on several factors beyond our control. First, is there a reasonable demand for the thing advertised? Second, does the quality compare favorably with others of its kind? Third, is the price mentioned and is it sufficiently attractive to interest careful buyers? Fourth, is the copy written in such a fashion that it would arouse a genuine desire for ownership in the mind of a listener? Last, and least important, perhaps, did the sales message appear on a station whose listening clientele is sufficiently large and diversified to include a reasonable number of prospects for this particular thing? You see, Mr. Prospect, the responsibility for results falls squarely on your shoulders.

I often think of a story that illustrates the point perfectly. Suppose you sent a message to Nelson Rockefeller by Western Union asking him for $100 to be sent by return wire. After you get no answer, would you go to Western Union and tell them their service was no good, or they didn't deliver the message? Of course not. You'd realize that the message you sent was so ridiculous, so asinine and so silly that it went right in the waste can where it belonged. Today, Mr. Prospect, thousands of dollars of advertisers' messages are going into mental waste cans all over town for the same reason. Mr. Prospect, our service parallels that of a telegraph company exactly, except that instead of directing the message to a particular person, we broadcast it to several hundred thousand. Whether or not any of them answer the message depends on the contents.

Adapt these ideas to your own language and viewpoint and be ready for the hard-nosed sales resisters and salesman-baiters. As long as you maintain a smile and a cheerful attitude, you have absolutely nothing to lose. You have a sale to gain. These ideas will make money for you. Use them.

When I Get Ready I'll Call You!

What you really mean, Mr. Prospect, is that you still don't believe you'd make money by using our station. If you thought you would, we couldn't keep you off the air. Now, here are the facts that show conclusively why you can use our station to make money.

Wrong Time Of The Year To Advertise

Mr. Prospect, the fur dealers once thought they couldn't do any business during the hot summer months. They decided to advertise during these months, and now any of them will tell you that August is now one of the biggest months of the year. In a city the size of this there are enough people and enough money to enable anyone to get business at any time of the year if he goes after it. I know a firm that makes a practice of increasing their advertising expenditure when their competitors lay off and get greatly increased results by doing so. I'm not saying that would be advisable in your case, but as your rent, your overhead and other necessary expenses go on just the same, it seems foolish not to make an effort to get the business.

I Don't Need To Advertise

By the same token, Mr. Prospect, the Coca Cola Company might say they don't need to advertise. Everyone knows them, and they are the undisputed leaders in their field, yet they are among the largest advertisers. No firm is ever so large or small that it doesn't need advertising. True, a firm might stay in business a great many years without advertising, but as long as advertising is the biggest business-building force in American business, and earns its way every day, it seems foolish not to take advantage of it. I'm sure you want new business and new customers, and the surest and quickest way to get them is to advertise for them.

One Station Is All We Can Afford To Use

Mr. Prospect, I wonder if you're not thinking of advertising in terms of an expense rather than an investment. That was a popular conception of advertising a few years ago. Advertising is either a useless expense or a profitable investment. If it is a profitable investment, you ought to use as many mediums as are necessary to reach the greatest number of people at the lowest possible cost. If it is an expense, you ought not to use any. I'm sure, however, that the station you're now using has proven profitable or you wouldn't continue to use it. Certainly that station isn't the only one that earns a profit for its advertisers. Let me show you that we can earn a profit for you, too.

Well, I'll Give It A Try (or similar doubtful committments)

Mr. Prospect, I'll be happy to have your business, but I want you to realize that the station is **not on trial**. It's a large and successful institution of the economic community and has been for a long time. Our product is highly esteemed, as evidenced by the fact that many businesses buy it every day and pay for it. Hundreds of advertisers use the station successfully and profitably every year. The only trial involved will be a trial of your ability to meet their competition. If you offer things that meet the demand and are priced as compared with competition, you'll get a favorable response. If you don't, the replies will probably be few and far between.

The "trial" bit is the most ridiculous situation you're likely to face. Herschell Smith, salesman at KEYS, Corpus Christi, advocates replying, "Ford is putting six million into radio alone this year (1969), and you want to test radio with $85?" Sears radio-only budget for 1969 was 695 percent greater than it was two years ago. This fact helps your specialty shop, hardware, drug, tire, and department store managers see a $100 "trial" in perspective.

I Don't Like Your Music!

I'm not suggesting that you listen, just advertise what you want to sell to the people who are listening. You, personally, may prefer a T-bone steak. But when you go fishing you may bait your hook with a worm because that's what the fish like. A lot of people do like the music we play. If you don't respect their musical taste, you certainly should respect their buying power.

Here bring out your own station data. Show the prospect success stories, listenership figures, promotional material on station personalities. Get across your point that your station has a tremendous audience composed of people who are prospects for what your prospect is selling, and that your personalities and music are popular with those people.

Why Should I Use Your Station When I Can Buy Another For Half Your Rate?

Mr. Prospect, every station is worth exactly what it can command. If, tomorrow, our good competitors could command the price which we ask, they certainly would do so. The fact that we ask and receive the price that we do indicates that we are able to produce accordingly and, therefore, the investment you make with us should be most profitable. There is no economy in buying "price." What you should buy is quality because it can produce. It's better to spend a dollar and make a dime than it is to spend a dime and lose it. Look at some of the businesses currently using our station. They, rather than we, are the judge of the rate. It is inconceivable that Mr. ___, who has built his business from the ground up, would be guilty of stupidity by buying us if it wasn't profitable for him. But the fact that he and many others renew their schedules with us time and again must stand as justification for our price.

Mr. Prospect, the advertising market is like the money market; you pay for what you get. If you "buy" $10,000 you know you're going to pay the going rate. If you want only $1,000 you'll still pay the going rate. It's just a matter of how much money and how much audience for your sales messages you want. If you want to get your story across to the big audience, the buying audience, the profitable audience, this is the way to go.

With Newspapers I Always Get Results!

If that's true and you always strike paydirt on every newspaper ad you run, then you've discovered a billion-dollar advertising system that has been baffling ad men ever since the cave man scratched the first advertisement on his wall with a spear. No medium's perfect and we both know it. If newspapers are really that infallible, why aren't you in tonight with five double-truck ads? You know newspapers can get results, but they can also lay an egg. With broadcast advertising in general, and my station in particular, you'll reach a large and interested audience that the newspapers in this town don't even touch. To prove that one point why not add a broadcast schedule right now to add impact to a couple of items you're running in tomorrow's paper. Your shrewd selection of specials is the key to success here. (You might want to suggest that the retailer check over his past print performance more carefully. Chances are, he'll find a number of times when the newspaper results were less spectacular than he thought.)

235

And Roger Davison clinched 'em this way:

As far as the success story goes, we had a recent success story of eight calls and eight sales for the FM station, totaling better than $1900. Using the Pepper Sales Stereo Library, we made up "spec" spots for eight prospects. We then sent our salesman out with the FM manager and bought a Craig Stereo playback, a tuner, and two speakers for $115. The two of them then made eight calls with the spec spots, setting the machine up on the client's desk. This is the most phenomenal happening around here in some time, and very effective.

HOW TO SIDE-STEP OBJECTIONS

Convert sponsor's objections into questions; that's how you not only acknowledge them but also side-step them and use them to your advantage. Here are some examples:

Sponsor: But Mr. Salesman, I can buy a package of 30- and 60-second announcements at a special rate if I take 5 newscasts a week on Station ———.

Salesman: Mr. Sponsor, if I interpret your objection correctly, you mean why doesn't my station have "package rates." The reason for this is that we maintain quality control for our sponsors and listeners when they buy on our rate card. The FCC allows us to give only 18 commercial minutes of time in each hour. If we gave generous package deals, we would destroy the quality of our programming, lose a lot of our audience, much to the detriment of the sponsors and the station.

Sponsor: "But I have so many items on sale that I can't see how you can list them all. Guess the newspaper is the best place for me to advertise.
Salesman: If I understand you properly, you are trying to tell me that you want my station to list all of your specials. Mr. Sponsor, radio is not primarily a listing medium. Radio creates impressions and builds a favorable image of your store. Our experience has been that if we mention just a few of your best specials and devote the rest of the copy to the service you give and the pleasant atmosphere of your store, you get the best results. A quick call to (mention a good sponsor) will confirm this.

Sponsor: "I never listen to radio anymore and I don't know who does."

Salesman: "Mr. Sponsor, what you're trying to tell me is that you're too busy to listen to radio. Here is our most recent survey. It shows that (number) of sets are turned on every day and that we have (percentage) of the listeners every day in the week.

Demolish Objections By Mentioning Them First

You: "Mr. Sponsor, it is generally believed that the attention span of the average radio audience is about 20 or 30 minutes at the most. Although there is no precise way to gauge the time with complete accuracy, let us presume that it is correct. That means we have a different group of listeners tuning in every 20 or 30 minutes. Again, let us suppose that each new audience consists of 2000 people; that means we can expect a bare minimum of at least 40,000 people who listen to us attentively over a 10-hour period. Mind you, we are taking minimum estimates into consideration. This in itself reinforces the reason why a sponsor should use a daily saturation schedule. Only one announcement each half hour will reach 40,000 attentive listeners over a 10-hour period. I daresay that you couldn't tell your sales message in person to all of these people in a Month of Sundays.

Lesson Learned: By anticipating this question that lurks in the minds of most sponsors and bringing it up before the sponsor mentions it, you satisfy him that you are thinking the way that he thinks and it helps to put him at ease; it clears his mind to be more receptive to the rest of your presentation.

You: "Mr. Sponsor, the print medium is excellent. I read the newspapers every day. I calculate my reading time to be about five minutes. First the headlines, then to the sports section. A look at the theatrical portion, and then over to the financial pages. I wind up reading some of the feature writers and portions of the editorial section. I estimate that it would take me several hours to read each and every word in the entire newspaper. I daresay that I would retain only about 5 percent of what I read. How many people do you think read every edition from cover to cover, and if they did, how long would it take and how much would they retain?"

Lesson Learned: Here you let the sponsor make his own conclusions. Chances are that he is a "skipper and a scanner," too, and will use his own habits as a yardstick for the other subscribers. Without berating the print medium, you have mentioned another subject that is usually brought up first by the sponsor to substantiate his advertising schedule in the print medium and raise an objection against advertising on your radio station. The thing to remember is for you to bring up the subject before the sponsor does. You must anticipate the more prominent objections; mention them first and then demolish them without knocking the competition!

You: "Mr. Sponsor, it's good to see that you believe in advertising. I think your double-truck ad in the newspaper (or circular) is very good. However, I have taken the liberty to suggest how you can save money on these ads. I've re-arranged the layout and, in so doing, have saved about 40 percent of the space that you now use. See how much easier it is to read the ad now that the eye can follow from one item to the other with little or no effort. There is no obligation for this suggestion. But, with the saving that you can make in the print medium, you can use just a portion of that money on our radio station and reach a vast audience that the newspaper (or circular) doesn't reach.

Lesson Learned: It shows the sponsor that you care enough to take a personal interest in his advertising program. Again, you do this without knocking the competition! This process of reducing space in the newspaper (or circular) by making the ad more effective can be done, should be done and is being done every day by radio advertising account executives who take time and trouble to go the extra mile to make worthwhile sales. It also serves to destroy his objection by using the standard "can't use radio this week because I've got a big ad in the newspaper or circular."

There are many more objections that you can anticipate and mention before your prospect does. As a matter of fact, you should itemize as many as you can and memorize the list. You must be subtle! Never walk over the backs of your competition when you employ the **anticipate first; demolish next,** technique. Always let your prospect draw his own conclusions by the facts that you offer first in evidence!

YOU MUST SELL YOUR STATION AS WELL AS THE ADVERTISING IDEA

A friend of mine related a sad but true story. He became obsessed with a fine new idea for one of his sponsors. He prepared an elaborate presentation for the sponsor. The sponsor was impressed and said, "Chances are that I'll use that idea because it sounds great!" The salesman was elated and left.

A salesman for the other radio station in town called on this sponsor. He showed the latest demographics, how good the station was. It was a real fine pitch. The sponsor was taken in with the ability of the station to produce so he took salesman number one's idea and used it on salesman number two's radio station! Therefore, you must always sell your station at the same time that you present a good advertising format.

THE NUMBERS RACKET

It's sad but true! Agency time buyers select stations that have the most listeners. These statistics are complied by professional survey companies. If your station should have a lesser rating than the others in your market, it doesn't mean that you have no case at all.

Suppose you are number five in a market of five stations. That means you have the least amount of listeners but the difference between your station and station number one may amount to only a few thousand people! It's time to get your microscope out and your thinking cap on. It's time to start preparing success stories of your present advertisers to prove that you have a quality audience, an audience that is loyal. It may be smaller in number but better in advertiser response.

Don't quit simply because you are a victim of the "numbers racket." Your station serves a worthwhile purpose. It may cater to fewer listeners but can possibly produce better results. If this were not so, you'd soon be out of business. However, never quit making the effort to gain more listeners so that you will become the number one station in your market!

DETERMINE THE TRUE OBJECTION

"Business is very bad; I can't afford to advertise."

"Nobody listens to radio anymore."

"I've never advertised before; don't have to because everybody knows me."

"If I increased my business, I'd have to hire more help and I can't afford that!"

"I've been using the other station for the past 10 years; there's no point in making a change now!"

"Don't have time to fool with advertising."

"I'll advertise as soon as I am ready."

"Can't get any coop from my suppliers."

And there are many more. It's like I've already said, there isn't any writer, no matter how brilliant he may be who can prove that each and every objection has been already stated and completely dissolved. An important thing to remember is that often the **stated** objection is not the **real** objection. Your skill as a salesman is to ferret out the real reason for the prospect's refusal.

Quite often it is a matter of instinct. How often have you heard a salesman say "He told me that he couldn't afford to advertise but I know for a fact that he's got lots of money and can afford it." Now comes the soul-searching; and the analyzing. It could well be that the prospect didn't like you personally. Please don't be offended. It happens to all of us. I "worked" on a potential advertiser for three years and finally threw in the sponge. He was very nice, cordial, and he treated me with respect. For some elusive reason I could never close the sale. I had (I thought) answered all of his objections to his satisfaction. It bugged me. It was almost like the story of Moby Dick; I was determined to get him on the air. Somewhere there was a solution and I was intent on finding it. Oh no, I didn't spend three years of my precious life making that the only project. Not at all, I continued the pursuit as just one of MANY endeavors.

One day I asked the owner of the station to call upon this man to act as a "spy for Si." The call was made and the sale was made! "Si," said my boss, "it was as easy as shooting fish in a barrel." "It was!" I exclaimed with astonishment,. "Tell me all about it!" "I don't want to hurt your feelings but I'll level with you," said my boss. Then he spoke slowly; "Putting it as gently as I know how, you don't belong to the right church. You were trying to sell a man who is prejudiced and you never could have done it in a million years." "In a million years, it would never matter," I mumbled. But there you go. It happens to all of us, even to thee and me."

Wait for the Opportune Moment

In some instances, after you've tried every kind of sales ammunition in your sales kit, you somehow cannot "get through to your prospect." I had a man like that and I knew the reason why I couldn't reach him with my presentation. This guy liked to imbibe during the day. He had a private bar in his office and after a few healthy slugs, he was inebriated but he didn't show it. There are many people like that. They conceal being drunk very well. This man was one of them.

One day I caught him sober. Don't ask me how this happened. I guess it was because he had run out of his supply of whiskey or maybe he made a vow to quit drinking, I really don't know. But the important thing was that he was sober. I took full advantage of the situation. Gave him a beautiful presentation and he bought a schedule. When the owner of the station complimented me for finally making the sale, I said that I had learned a real good lesson. "What do you mean," asked my boss. "Simply this," I said, "I learned never to call on that man during any month that had a fifth in it!"

HELPFUL SUGGESTIONS

Here is a good idea, provided you don't overdo it! When one of your accounts is having a big sale and has taken a saturation schedule, put your beeper phone to work. Call the station from his store and do a short broadcast. We call it "The on the spot, spot report." The call is a brief play-by-play account of the activity in the store. Sometimes we get the sponsor himself to say a few words to our listeners.

Remote Broadcasts

When something real big is being advertised, like a grand opening, a carnival, automobile show, etc., set up a live remote broadcast. Such a program can run in any length. There is excellent equipment available that enables you to announce and play music directly from the scene, get interviews and make it an action packed live program that'll attract plenty of customers.

A Substitute for A Live Remote Broadcast

If you think there won't be enough continuous action for a remote broadcast, suggest a delayed tape-recorded remote. You can stop your tape when the action slows down and then continue it when the tempo increases. You have complete control here because you are able to erase any inadvertent "slips of the tongue." Also, people interviewed on the tape have a chance to hear themselves when the tape is played on your station. They'll tell their friends to listen too.

A slip of the tongue, if you can call it that, once nearly wrecked my career. I was doing a live remote. I interviewed one of the customers at an automobile showing. The customer said (on a live mike), "If I had seen this car before buying the one I have now, I would not have bought the one I now own because it stinks." Then he mentioned the brand of car and dealer involved!

CHANGE OF PACE

The tempo of our times is to hurry, hurry, hurry. We eat breakfasts that contain the total amount of proteins for the day. We read abridged stories to get the "meat" out of them. Most of this book has been written in short form for fast reading and action. But many readers may wonder what happened before, during, or after an important suggestion. For example, I recently read about a man who was lucky enough to buy 150,000 shares of stock in a new company; the cost per share was 50 cents. The stock rose to $50 a share. It all sounded so simple. Make a $75,000 investment and become a millionaire. How easy, how pat.

After a lot of digging and probing, I got the play-by-play account of this man's good fortune; how he mortgaged everything he owned; how he borrowed money from personal friends and scratched and scrounged in order to make this investment; his moments of despair when the stock went from 50 cents down to 12½ cents a share. It made a fascinating story only after I searched for the facts.

In the several stories that follow we alter the previous just-the-bare-facts story format so that you will have a better appreciation of the facts.

How About Me?

This is a true story about two jewelers in the same town and one sales representative from a single-station market. The sales representative put a feather in his cap because he sold a terrific idea to jeweler number one. As a matter of fact, it is one of the few cases where a jeweler advertised 12 months a year instead of only during the traditional June Bride Month, Valentine's Day and Christmas seasons. The jeweler sponsored hourly time signals like this: "The time is .... o'clock, given to you with a great deal of pleasure by ..... Jewelry who reminds you to bring your watch to him for repair." Then, there would be other reminders after the time signal such as, "Time to buy your wife her birthday present from ..... Jewelry; "Time to buy a birthday gift from ..... Jewelry," and so on.

Meanwhile, jeweler number two was doing a slow burn because he considered himself a kind of "also-ran" in the sense that our sales representative didn't give him any ideas for a continuous advertising schedule. One day, jeweler number two said, "John, don't waste your time calling on me anymore. You've given my competition your best schedule and you haven't even given me any more attention than the usual sales promotions." This jolted our salesman but he recovered quickly. He said, "I'm glad that you brought that up, jeweler number two, because I've been giving that matter a lot of thought but hadn't worked out all the details. I do have a plan that will give you as much, if not more impact than the plan you mentioned being used by the other jeweler." This caught the interest of jeweler number two.

"What is that?" he eagerly asked. "Simply this," said the sales rep. "Every month has a birthstone, so every month for 12 consecutive months, we will advertise and encourage people to buy the birthstones they should have." "Haw!" exploded jeweler number two. "Who buys birthstones these days anyway?" Our sales rep was very clever and he said, "Very few people do, but when we remind them every day of every month, people will be buying birthstones!" Then he told jeweler number two about the man on Times Square in New York City swinging a broom around in a 360-degree circle. A policemen walked up to the man and asked him why he was swinging the broom around. Said the man, "To keep the elephants away." The cop said, "Man, there aren't any elephants around here!" Answered the man, "Of course not; I'm keeping them away!"

That was a good analogy, and it worked because it made the jeweler realize that because few people were buying birthstones, that was reason enough to start creating the desire for a birthstone. If jeweler number two had been selling a lot of birthstones, the sale would have been more difficult to make because the objection would have been "Why, everybody buys a birthstone every month."

There you have a success story that happened quite accidentally to a salesman who was treating one sponsor like royalty and taking the other for granted. He was jolted out of his lethargy by a valid complaint. And he was able to think on his feet, not recoil and lose an account. The moral here is to anticipate the needs of your sponsors. Don't show partiality, especially if you have kindred accounts. Be original. Be clever. Give 'em all a fair shake!

It Is Better To Give Than Receive

The day was cold and rainy. I was behind with my desk work. Things were slow downtown, so it was a good day to catch up. Suddenly, the door opened and in stepped a man who looked like he was down on his luck. He asked, "How much to advertise a used car for sale?" I answered, "Is it your car that you want to sell?" He said "yes." I quoted him the rate card. "Too much" he replied. He started to leave.

"Wait a minute," I said, "who are you and where are you from?" He answered in measured tones "My name is .... and I'm from .... My wife and family and I own two cars. We have to sell one of the cars to get enough money to go where we're goin'," he said. "Where are you headin' for?" I asked. "Nowhere in particular," he answered. "Don't you have a destination?" His answer was, "Wherever I can get a job to feed my family."

An idea struck me. "Supposing we can help you sell your second car on our station, would you consider selling your other car also. Then you'll have enough money to live here for a while, use the major portion of your combined sales to buy some cars at the Car Auction. Who knows, you can get into the used car business that way!" I fairly shouted, so overjoyed was I at the thought of being of assistance. "Can't afford your rates to advertise," he said quietly. "Never mind, pay me when you can afford it. Let me put on a saturation schedule and sell both cars at one lick!" I exclaimed. "Would you do that for me, a total stranger?" he asked with some excitement in his voice. "Not so much for you but for your family. How many children do you have?" "Seven," was his reply. "That's why we're a two-jalopy family," he said with half a smile.

"Let me go all the way for you, let me try to help you; how about it?" I asked. "OK," he said with some hope in his voice. "Go to it and let's see what happens. I've got $30 with me and that should keep us in groceries for a few days." "**Sold!**" I shouted.

Then I went to work, saturated the air with copy about his two cars for sale. First, let me assure you that I inspected the cars thoroughly and they were no bargains. I didn't advertise them as bargains either. I said they'd make good "fishing" cars or "second" cars or even would be attractive as antiques. The plan worked. We sold them the very first day. That put a reasonable amount of cash in the man's pocket, enough for him to stay at our local motel.

Then I drove him to the Car Auction Barn. He bought a fairly good car and another cheap jalopy. We hooked the cheaper car to the better one and he drove them back to town. We hit the air again. Good results; more profit. We repeated the same procedure; the trip to the Auction; bought two fairly good cars, and sold them. After a few weeks the man was trading two and three cars a week, then four and five. He rented an empty lot.

In six months he had made enough money to pay his entire advertising bill. This man lives and breathes. He has taken root. His life has meaning and purpose, and he is the most kindly disposed sponsor toward radio that I know of. You couldn't buy his schedule for all the world. I dare anybody to say a nasty word to him about my station or me.

The Bible gave me the idea. Radio made it work. It is better to give than receive! Try it, it works! You never know when you will have the opportunity to be a good samaritan.

Salvage!

The disappointment was keen! The sponsor had cancelled without any warning. What went wrong? Where did we fail? No sense in holding a post-mortem meeting without an autopsy. We discussed. We analyzed. No reasonable answer for the cancellation. Then we probed. The sponsor assured us, "you are a good station; have always benefited me; will be back soon."

That was good enough for about a week when all of a sudden, there it was, a double truck ad in the local newspaper! A switch from our station to the competing print medium! Why? Same smile; same reassurance; "Don't worry Si, we'll be back." But the double truck appeared with regularity, every week. Months went by and still the sponsor hadn't come back to radio.

Autopsy not complete because we couldn't find the cause of the sponsor's demise on our radio station. So, explore some more. Idea! Get some facts from that very pleasant clerk in the sponsor's store. We asked; we heard, and we were astonished.

"Remember, if you quote me, I'll deny saying it," prefaced the clerk. "I give you my solemn word that you shall be kept out of it completely, but tell me why did Mr. Sponsor cancel?" Then, in soft, whispered, almost inaudible words came the truth: "He cancelled because he was unhappy with the way your announcements were given. They were just so-so, no effort to sell. You seemed to take him for granted; gave his competition a full measure of service and selling ability." So, that was it! Indifference; the "He's a Good Joe attitude."

Obviously some repair work was needed. Summon your wits, Willing. Go to it! Do something! And, we did do something indeed!

"Mr. Sponsor, we've been giving a lot of thought to your account these past few months. Here is some fine action-getting copy. We honestly believe that you can put the full meaning into this message. Here is a microphone; please look the copy over and then let me tape your message when you are ready." The sponsor looked the copy over. He taped it. It sounded good to me, but he didn't like it! "Tell you what," I said, "let's have Jones make a stab at it." Jones was one of the clerks. Jones tried but failed miserably. "How about you making another effort, Mr. Sponsor?" He did and this time it was good!

Said I, "Mr. Sponsor, I apologize for not getting your signal during your last schedule." "What signal?" he asked. Said I, "You were trying to tell me that we were slipping and I didn't take the hint. Now I know! We failed to give you continuous good service." I blurted out the unvarnished truth; an honest admission. "We pledge good continuous service from now on!" said I with a note of optimism.

I continued, "One thing that I left out of the copy you just recorded was the fact that you have a double truck ad in the newspaper. Let's put that into the copy and refer our listeners to pages six and seven of this week's newspaper. Let's tell 'em that they'll find more information on those pages." The sponsor thought a minute. "OK," he said. We revised the copy on the spot. "See how flexible radio is, Mr. Sponsor" I said. He agreed. He renewed the schedule. Eventually he reduced his ads to one page, then a half page and that's the way it stood for a long, long time. Complete radio schedule restored, along with a cross reference between the radio and newspaper. "See our ad on page 6," said the radio sales message. "Hear all about it frequently on Radio ......," printed the newspaper in the sponsor's half-page ad on page 6.

Oh what a valuable lesson we learned from that experience. Never, never take a good thing for granted. Be honest; 'fess up when you are wrong. Right that wrong and use the objection as a tool to right that wrong. Many of us try to cover up our mistakes, blame everybody and everything but ourselves. I learned a long time ago that you can't kid anybody but yourself when you indict everybody and exonerate yourself. You are culpable. Admit it. There is no shame in being wrong. There is only shame in denying that you were wrong. One of the penalties that we pay in making a difficult problem become easy is that everybody says "Oh that's easy to do." Remember when you have a difficult problem do this:

Explore,
Explore some more.
Sooner or later
You will find
That you were blind.
Don't blame him,
Blame me!
Then you will see
the light; he was right.
Then enjoy peace of mind.

Si Willing

How Blue Monday Was Turned Into The Black

    Market research revealed that The Dixie Store was doing little or no business on Mondays. For some unexplained reason, shoppers just didn't frequent the store. This called for a remedy. First, let's examine the situation carefully. Aha! A clue!
    His weekend specials were so good that people took it for granted that was the best time to shop. But those weekend specials were "loss leaders." Hardly any profit when you are practically giving your merchandise away on the weekend on a storewide basis. Sure, business was brisk on Thursdays, Fridays and Saturdays. Why not? Prices so low, you could hardly see them. Clerks over worked. Big gross, little net. Then, Monday came along, prices were restored to normal. A bad situation.
    Make an abrupt change in policy? No! This problem had to be altered within the framework of "loss leaders," but with a different approach. Staff meetings; discussions. We brainstormed. It took about two weeks but we came up with a solution. Instead of giving most of his merchandise away during a few days, why not select just five items to attract customers on one day of the week. Let's go to work, and go to work we did! We prepared a jingle, like this:

(To the tune of Dixie): Shop your Dixie Store on Monday, all day, all day.

Then the copy followed:

Billy: Si, have you heard about the friendly Dixie Store Monday-only Five-Star Specials?

Si: No Billy, tell me about 'em!

Billy: OK, two pairs of nylons for 79 cents

Si: Tell me more.

Billy: Wash'n wear work pants, two pairs for $4.98.

Si: Where?

Billy: At your friendly Dixie Store, all day tomorrow!

Si: Say on, Billy!

Billy: Fifteen men's handkerchiefs for $1.25.

Si: Nothing to be sneezed at!

Billy: OK, so I won't say "Gesundheit."

Si: Easy, Billy, tell me more about the friendly Dixie Store.

Billy: All day tomorrow, ladies' briefs, two for a dollar.

Si: Don't be so short (haw)...

Billy: Don't be so snappy! (Haw, Haw) and (pause) and...

Si: (eagerly) Yes, yes...

Billy: Bonded-knit fabrics, $1.50 a yard.

Si: It clicks!

Si and Billy sing closing: Shop your Dixie Store on Monday, all day, all day. Tomorrow, that is..........

    A Sunday saturation schedule. Twenty-five sales messages. Then I checked the store from a distance, bright and early on Monday. People were waiting in line. Great response! The "loss leaders" did the job; business went way up! But now, how about the repair work that had to be done on weekends? Let's try the same idea. Use just five items instead of a general, storewide markdown. The manager agreed. We tried it. Worked very well.
    We generated traffic on Mondays, with the "Monday-only Dixie Store Five-Star special" format. On Tuesdays we used the "Two for Tuesday Specials"; on Wednesdays, we

proclaimed "A surprise for everyone who buys at your friendly Dixie Store from now through Saturday." This gave the manager control of the items he wanted to reduce. We didn't promise anything specific, only a surprise. Because Mondays were so well handled with five good items marked down, customers had faith and trust in the Dixie Store. We increased the schedule from a normal 30-sales-message schedule up to 75 a week. Here is an example of how market research paid off; how careful analysis paid off; how we increased our revenue through the process of being helpful to the sponsor. My first consideration was to go the second mile in service. Our station's revenue increase was the result of this endeavor and not the cause.

"Do noble things, not dream them all day
long; and so make life, death, and the
Vast forever, one grand sweet song.
Charles Kingsley

Combination Salad

Here's a real-life experience that combines most of the elements already suggested in this book. There's the use of a personal call; writing letters; using the phone, taped audition, and on-the-air-audition. The reason I am including this is because it shows to what effort I go to get a worthwhile sponsor on the air. It concerns a bank, a bank president and an executive vice president of that bank.

Many years ago, I was a sales representative in a city that had two banks. For some reason, the owner of my station couldn't get along with the president of one of the banks. The showdown came when that bank refused to give him a loan and the other bank granted the loan with very little trouble. Accordingly, he transferred his account from the one that had turned him down to his existing account in the other bank. He always kept active accounts in both banks, up to that time, that is. If I had known all this before the sales manager assigned me the job of getting the bank on the air, I would have had an easier job. But, as most usual, there was no information available about why we had one bank on the air and not the other. I did make some attempt to get the background and market information necessary before making my first call. A veil of secrecy always seemed to be evident; nobody knew 'nuthin.'

Here goes! Let's prepare some real good sales messages, have good avails ready should the presentation "take." The president 'shunted' me off to the exec VP. That alone was a danger signal. The veep listened to me, to my announcements, etc. He was pleasant; he seemed to be pleased. I tried to get him to talk to me but he kept saying, "You tell me what you have for me." These could have been interpreted as buying signals because they indicated an interest; but, actually, he was hastening the process to get rid of me. Optimist that I am, I refused to see it his way. I went through the meeting very well. He didn't offer one objection (which didn't suit me one bit) in spite of the fact that I tried to bait him into making an objection. For example, I said "Mr. Exec VP, isn't there something about our station, these announcements, or availabilities that doesn't please you?"

"No sir," he replied, "it all sounds good to me but (then he looked around, dramatically leaned over the desk as I cocked my good ear) I have to talk to the 'old man' about it." I leaped at the "open door" and said, "let's see him now, together, while I have my tape machine, announcements, etc."

"Oh no," he said emphatically, "that will never do." He continued (slowly, thoughtfully), "I'll see him alone, in good time. I can work with him where very few people can. You **do** understand, **don't** you?" He smiled when he said that. I supposed that I was to understand what he meant and I pretended that I did, but I didn't know what he was talking about. But, in order not to look stupid, I gave him a knowing wink and said, "Will you call me as soon as you have discussed it with Mr. President?" "You bet," was his reply. Two weeks passed. No news from the bank so I wrote a short note, like this:

Dear Mr. Exec VP:

You are always so busy when I pop in to see you that I am sending this short note to follow up my pleasant visit with you. Have you had an opportunity to discuss the matter with Mr. President? Do you need more information to help encourage you to make a favorable decision. I am as near as your phone. Please call when you can."

Ten days later, I wrote:

Dear Mr. Exec VP:

Please look at the enclosed sales messages. Our production staff has been giving a great deal of thought to your bank since I suggested that we could look forward to a regular schedule. Please let me know what you think of them and also what Mr. President thinks when you have the chance to talk to him.

One day, I decided to probe deeper. I actually didn't need additional money but I decided to make a small personal loan, so I walked into the bank, strode up to the VP who was busy, shuffling papers, etc. "Mr. VP," I said. He looked up "Oh, good to see you, but I'm busy. Can you see me some other time?" It was a pleasant rejoinder (if rejoinders could be pleasant).

"Sorry you're so busy," I said, "just wanted to borrow some money. Should I see Mr. Jones at the other bank?"

"Oh no! That transaction will just take a minute and I'm not that busy!" He quickly added, "have a seat." I sat down. He took pen in hand and said, "How much do you need?"

"Not much," said I, "about $300; I'll repay you $100 a month for three consecutive months. Do you need collateral?"

"For that small amount, you can borrow it on an open note," he assured me. The entire process of making the loan took two minutes. I asked him to deposit the money to my account. Then I left.

I made a few more visits to the bank. Everytime the VP saw me, he waved, shrugged his shoulders, pointed at his desk and that was the sign that he was too busy to see me. Then I wrote him a third note:

Dear Mr. Exec VP:

It took me exactly two minutes to negotiate a loan and five months to ring up a "no sale," so obviously I must have much better credit than salesmanship. Please let me know when I can see you to develop our plans to be of service to your fine bank.

The situation was getting to be a real challenge because my letters were never answered. What to do next? I know! A new approach! New ammunition! It was about two months away from Christmas so I created a Christmas spectacular. Choice Christmas music, itsy bitsy sales message. It was a program created specifically to present 30 minutes of pure Christmas music for ten consecutive days prior to that great Holiday. Then, on Christmas Day, just Christmas Carols with no commercial interruption except opening and closing credits. A good format because it gave the audience a chance to listen for long stretches of uninterrupted time to their favorite Christmas music.

What do you know! It worked! The Exec. VP liked it and bought it. For a "door opener" it was pretty good, but "pretty good" just ain't good enough for me. The only good accounts I know are the ones that are on a steady basis, with a sufficient amount of revenue and whose checks are mailed on time but never bounce.

The bank had all the qualifications of a good account so I set my sails again. This time I prepared a program of "popular" music that has withstood the test of time, the old standard classics written by Irving Berlin, Cole Porter, Rodgers and Hammerstein, etc. We compared the enduring service of the bank with the never-ending pleasure that this kind of music has provided, is now providing, and will always provide. Good symbolism. Then came the effort to see the exec VP. He was always too busy or just about to become too busy. I sent another note:

Dear Mr. Exec VP:

The minute you have a breathing spell, please call me because I have some real good news to tell you. Seems as if I can't ever catch you with a free moment at the bank. Please call soon.

One day, I made a decision. The bank would buy from me or I'd simply have to write them off for a long, long time because I was afraid that I was wearing out my welcome. After all, several personal calls, phone calls, letters. So, I had a conference with the sales manager and decided to use the method of playing the program over the radio as an audition when I gave the signal to the radio station to play it. Then I went to the bank. The exec VP gave me his customary long-distance wave from his desk. I made a small bank deposit, then I walked up to the VP's desk and before he could say that he was too busy, I asked him to enjoy his work even more while I was doing some other business in town.

"What do you mean by that?" he asked. "Mr. Exec VP, sir, please let me use your phone," I blurted. Then, I dialed the station and simply said, "Now!" My attention was focused on the VP. "Here's what I mean, sir, just enjoy this music on my small portable radio. Then give me an honest opinion of what you hear, OK?" I smiled when I said (or asked OK!) Click! The radio was on and there it was:

"Ladies and gentlemen, we bring you this program of music that has become standard enjoyment through the ages. The services of the .... Bank is also standard for (area), having been in existence these (amount) years. Listen and enjoy as the .... Bank presents the Best of Irving Berlin," music up full.

I turned the volume down for my next short talk: "Mr. Exec VP, enjoy it. I'll see you later." I turned up the radio so that he could hear it, and departed.

It was agony for the next two days. I didn't go near the bank. I knew that sooner or later he'd want to return the portable, no matter what else he decided. On the morning of the third day, he called me: "Willing, don't you want your radio (pause) and don't you want to take our order for a schedule?" Wow! I had all I could do not to shout, "Yes!" But I played it cool, visited him, got the schedule and the radio, too.

Twinkle, Twinkle, Little Star

Our sales manager sounded the clarion call. He issued his command: "Get Star Furniture on the air!" Dutifully, I commenced to research the account. The owner was tough. I believe that he would have gigged the astronauts for not having shaved before splashing down from their trip to the moon. How this man managed to stay in business was a mystery. But, our station needed more business and now we were going over the non-advertisers and I drew this account.

First order of business: Visit this man; get his chemical reaction. Who knows, he might like me. Let's try.

I entered his store. He greeted me with a smile. "May I help you?" was his weak greeting. "Thank you no, but I believe that I can be of service to you, Mr. Sponsor," said I gleefully.

"Don't need any help," and all of a sudden he changed from a sunny day to stormy weather. He walked away. I stood there. Never follow a prospect. Always let him come to you. So, I just stood there. He busied himself with this and that in back of the store. He walked back. He saw me standing there. Looked at me. Turned his back. Walked halfway to the rear. Turned around. Approached me. "I told you that I didn't need any help!" Now it was raining; I could sense lightning also. "How do you know what help I propose to give you?" I asked with a silly smile on my face.

"Whatever it is, I'm not interested!" He underlined those last three words. "Mr. Sponsor, I have some used equipment that I would like you to sell for me. We'll split fifty-fifty; would you go for a deal like that?" I asked casually. "What kind of equipment?"

"For openers, how about selling a very good but used tape machine; you do sell used furniture and equipment, don't you?" He stopped raining. "Yes I do, but how do I know the quality of the machine?"

That's where Mr. Sponsor walked into my little "Sponsor-Trap." "A good question; supposing I bring it to you and let you be the judge." "OK," he said suspiciously. "Let's see," I mused, "How about tomorrow afternoon at, let's say 2 PM?" and my voice rose as I posed the question. "Don't waste my

253

time if the machine stinks." he said. "Check it out real good before you bring it or don't bother at all," was his short answer. "See you at 2 tomorrow, Mr. Sponsor," I said as I took leave.

Devilish little old me. I made sure that the machine would not only work but that this 'hard-to-get-sponsor' would take a schedule. Yes, I would bet anybody a hundred dollars that he would. Events proved that I would win the bet. Here's what happened.

I prepared a 10-minute taped program entitled "Star furniture store presents Kay Starr singing her star songs exclusively for Star Furniture Store that always has star values. "It's Startime! So let's go. Kay sings a song. Then the sales message:

Mr. Sponsor of Star Furniture Store is happy to present the Star Songs of Kay Starr. Star Furniture has setting sun prices. For example, you save $100 when you buy this 3-piece bedroom suite. Formerly priced at $290, but on sale now at Star Furniture for $190, plus easy terms. Exactly the bedroom suite to suit you. See Star today. Remember Star quality at setting sun prices, always yours at Star Furniture.

It was a fast moving program, 10 minutes of delightful music plus hard-hitting Star sales messages.

The next day, promptly at 2 PM, I made my appearance. I was carrying the tape machine. "Are you ready for a demonstration?" I asked the prospect. "Yes, but I don't have too much time." I busied myself and got the machine ready for the demonstration. The tape opened this way:

"Mr. Sponsor, it is said that you are a real rough man. I don't believe that. I was happy with the way you greeted me yesterday. I like to do business with a man who says what he has on his mind. I don't blame you for not wasting time with salesmen, for after all, they do intrude on your precious time. All salesmen should be banished because they take up so much of your time. That's why I am using this method to state my case. If this wastes your time, I'll be happy to pay you by the hour, whatever value you place on your time. Now don't move, but listen for the next 10 minutes and prove that you are the gentleman that I think you are.

Yes, that's what prefaced my "Startime 10-minute program." It worked! He bought the program! And he complimented me for being so ingenious. He became a steady sponsor, not because he liked me; no sir! Because the program helped him get business!

Converting A No Into A Yes

"Don't call on this man unless it is raining and you're caught taking shelter in his drug store." "Impossible!" "Whew!" These were the notations made on the fact sheet about a druggist in town.

I had inherited some impossible accounts when I started to work for a medium-sized midwest station. There were three salesmen on the staff; I was hired to mop up the difficult accounts. To make a long story short, it was raining. I had taken shelter in the drug store. While I was drinking a cup of steaming hot coffee I glanced at an almanac that was hanging on the wall behind the counter. I noticed that it called for a clear day. I kiddingly told the druggist that you can't depend on the weather. It'll purposely go out of its way to refute the weather bureau and even an almanac. The druggist told me that his almanac was about 80-percent accurate. He was satisified that the rain outside was just a fluke.

"Mr. Druggist," I asked, "is your almanac the only method of advertising you have?" "Yes sir!" he replied proudly. "Been giving then away for years. My customers depend upon them for reliable information."

I didn't want to get into an internecine argument about the fluke rain outside so I asked, "Sir, if you had your 'druthers' which advertising medium would you 'druther' have, radio or television?" "Why television, of course!" he said. "Hardly anybody listens to radio nowadays." Again, rather than get into a Mexican standoff trying to prove that there was plenty of radio listeners, I used another approach.

"When do you think most people refer to your almanac, morning, noon, night, or just when?" was my question. "Hmm, I would say mostly in the morning," was his answer. "How many almanacs have you distributed and what proportion of these people refer to the almanac?" I asked. "I have 2000 of them out and I would say that at least 600 people use them every morning." "Would you say they referred to them while having breakfast?" I queried. "I would say so," was his casual reply.

Now I firmed up and, like a lawyer, shot this out to him. "Mr. Druggist, I'll concede that to you; now will you make a concession to me?" I asked in a Clarence Darrow tone of voice. "Depends on what it is," he replied. In measured tones I said, "Will you concede that at least 600 people listen to my radio station at that time of the morning?" "Your radio station? What station is that?" he asked. I told him the call letters and then continued, "Now will you make that concession?" "OK," he said meekly. "That's only fair, tit for tat, you know."

This time I took real aim and fired, "Mr. Druggist, do you believe in achieving the impossible?" He was taken aback, "Depends upon what you mean."

"Here's what I mean. You said that if you had your 'druthers' you'd advertise on television, right?" "That I did," he said. "What would you say if I could prove to you that you can buy a radio schedule on my station and achieve the same results of television advertising?" "Go on, I'm listening," he said with a note of doubt in his voice.

I continued, "First, tell me why you don't use the TV station?" "It costs too much for what I want," he answered. "Exactly what do you want out of TV?" I pursued. "I would like to have motion, animation in the form of live announcers acting out their parts, like the big advertisers have." Then he continued, "This costs money, paying talent, the use of the equipment, film, and so on; it's too much for me to pay." I kept quiet. He started to talk again. "Guess I could afford a few of those announcements where they just show a picture of my store, or something like that, and give an announcement along with the picture," he concluded.

"Great!" I said. "Now let's examine what we have. You said that you have at least 600 people who refer to your almanac daily, every morning, and at the same time you conceded that 600 people listened to my station each morning, agreed?" "Agreed!" he responded. "OK, we also agreed that in the absence of an animated TV announcement featuring moving, living announcers, the less expensive way to go was to have a stationary billboard with a picture of your drug store, or something like that, along with an announcement in back of the picture. That is also a little too rich for your budget, right?" "Correct again," he said. "Now, if you had guaranteed sales messages on my station in the same time your cutomers were looking at your almanac, wouldn't that be the same as having a stationary billboard on the TV screen with an announcement in back of it; wouldn't we be achieving the same result, **sight** and **sound**?" I asked with a degree of triumph.

The druggist turned around, prepared a Coke for himself. "Want one?" he offered. "No thank you," I said. He sipped his Coke and I sipped my coffee. He smiled, looked up, and said, "You know, you've got a good point there; sight and sound is what we're after on TV, and you've given me a **sound** explanation with your keen **insight**." He laughed and said, "Hope you don't mind my puns?" "At the risk of using the oldest cliche in the world, I'll say that I enjoy your puns and this coffee; they go together just like my sales messages for your drug store and the sight of your almanacs," was my trite but sales-getting answer. The man bought a schedule from me, after I did a lot of research to determine when most of his "almanacers" would be "almanacing." I made certain that somewhere in his advertising copy we suggested that listeners refer to his almanac, and if they didn't have one to be sure to get one free at his store. It worked. The man was happy with the whole idea. That's how I succeeded in having an "impossible" sponsor buy from me!

ONE-LINE DISPOSALS

Sponsor: "Business is very good so I don't have to advertise."

Disposal: "My health is excellent but I wouldn't be caught dead without insurance."

Sponsor: "Business is very bad, I can't afford to advertise."

Disposal: "Advertising may be the only solution to your going out of business altogether."

Sponsor: "Nobody listens to radio anymore."

Disposal: "Nobody but the listeners who are shopping the big sale at your competitor's store."

Sponsor: "I've never advertised. Don't have to because everybody knows me."

Disposal: "Quite true, but do these people know what you are doing?"

Sponsor: "If I increased my business, I'd have to hire more help and I can't afford that!"

Disposal: "More help would relieve your workload, give you more time to attend to the things you do best, taking care of the big, important ticket items!"

Sponsor: I've been using the other station for 10 years; no point in making a change now."

Disposal: "Don't make a change; just sample my station. Then you be the judge about whether you shouldn't have total coverage."

SPEED READING

We have stressed the fact that there are some things to do; more items to read, more of everything, but the time in which to do these things remains constant. So, if you want to stay abreast of the news, develop the art of speed-reading. Many people think it is impossible to read at a faster clip but it can be done. There are many courses that you can take in this subject; however, the big secret of successful speed reading is practice!

LEAVE YOUR NAME

Doesn't it burn you up when you get a message that "somebody called long distance but he didn't want to leave his name!" If you have a legitimate message, leave your name and number when your man is out. This may sound like a small matter but I know lots of people who consider it very important. Don't you?

GOODWILL BUILDER

If your prospect is out when you visit for a service call, leave a note. This is a goodwill builder. It takes a minute to write something like this: "Mr. Jones, stopped in to see if I could be of service. Please call when you get a minute and let me know if I can be of service."

BE CONSIDERATE

If somebody calls you on the phone, don't keep him waiting too long. Again, doesn't it irritate you when you make a call and the secretary puts you on 'hold' and then doesn't get back to you for five minutes. If you are not able to talk with your caller, ask your secretary to tell him that you are busy, get his name, and number and return the call as promptly as you can. Remember, little things mean a lot.

MISS OR MRS.

Girls, when you sign a letter, please put Miss or Mrs. before your name. It makes it difficult for somebody to answer your letter if you don't indicate Miss or Mrs. Make a mole hill out of a mountain. Make a hit. Sign your letters with: (Miss) Susie Jones or (Mrs.) Susie Smith.

SERVICE WITHOUT SERVITUDE

Learn the difference between service and servitude. Once upon a time I called on a new account, a dry goods store. The owner was in a dither. Some of his help didn't show up. He was surrounded with unopened cartons and crates waiting to be opened and checked in, then be put on the shelves. Things were in a mess. Instead of bothering him with the necessity of having a good Grand Opening Campaign schedule on our radio station, I took off my jacket, rolled up my sleeves, and pitched in.

It took several hours but we managed to make order out of chaos. The man was grateful and offered to pay me but I refused. I also qualified my helping him by emphasizing that he was under no obligation. My purpose was to help him out of a rough spot. The station would have to stand in its own two feet and he would buy a schedule based on the ability of the station to produce results for him. To make a long story short, he did take a schedule and it worked. We enjoyed a long and pleasant business association. There is an example of giving service, without servitude.

SERVITUDE WITHOUT SERVICE

A salesman told me this story. He had an automobile dealer who liked to imbibe during the day. The dealer had two salesmen on the floor while he took "medicinal refreshments" in his private office. One day, my friend the radio advertising account executive, called on the dealer.

The only person on the showroom floor was a customer looking over the latest model car. The customer thought that my friend was a car salesman. My friend said that he would get the owner of the dealership to personally make the sale. He scurried up to the owner's private office. The owner was 'half-gone' by this time and mumbled "I don't know a damn thing about selling cars; get one of my salesmen."

Down the steps hastened my friend; he asked the customer to wait a few minutes and then he went looking for either of the two salesmen. They were nowhere in sight. The customer left.

The owner staggered down the stairs and said, "Where'sh the Shalesmen? Did they make the damned shale?" My friend said that he couldn't locate any of the salesmen, whereupon the inebriated owner said, "Get the hell out of here; if you can't shell my cars on the floor, how can you shell 'em on the damned radio.

If my friend had let it stand at that point, he would have been accepting servitude instead of giving service. He didn't do that, however; he did say, "Get yourself a doormat and be sure that UNWELCOME is printed on it." Then he left while the owner held onto a car for support.

SEE THE TOP MAN FOR BEST RESULTS

I was delighted when a contract came through for a 26-week schedule for a famous soft drink from a leading agency. The time buyer bought my station at the lowest frequency discount. Two 13-week flights with a one-month hiatus between those flights. We billed the first 13 weeks at out lowest discount rate and then the agency cancelled. I wrote the agency and told them we would be obliged to 'short rate' unless the second flight was used.

There was no answer. I wrote again. No answer. So I called and was shunted from pillar to post. I could get no satisfaction. I was being given the brush-off. One man laughed at me. "You small town operators are all alike," he said. "Be happy that you got a taste of a schedule and don't bother us with your short-rate threat. Who knows, we may give you some more business some day."

I wrote the president of this mighty agency. I stated the case and included copies of the letters that were exchanged between our station and his agency. I appealed to his sense of fairness. He responded by directing that the contract be honored the way it was written. Apologies came cascading through the mail from his junior executives. One man wrote and said, "I am sorry that I didn't write the script myself instead of having our president write it."

I had gone the second mile in service, extended our lowest frequency discount based on a firm contract. The agency had reneged. I took positive action and got positive results. A big man was president. A big man made an honest decision. The small men squirmed, apologized. I hope they learned a lesson. I hope that you learn a lesson. Walk tall; don't crawl, give service without servitude. Be humble. Be grateful. Be a man! (or a woman!)

"Nothing in life is to be feared,
It is only to be understood."
Marie Curie

VARIATIONS ON THEMES

Boy meets girl, then things begin to happen. Thousands of books have been written using variations on this theme. A song becomes popular, and eventually there are several different versions of the same song that also become popular. Books are written on salesmanship; sooner or later other writers take the basic principles of selling and also write successful books on how to sell. There is a never-ending variety of treatments on the same subject.

Also, people read books in different ways. Some just refer to the section or sections that offer the greatest interest. Others read the book from cover to cover. Still others start at the end, skip to the middle and then jump around from chapter to chapter. Very seldom do two people do things exactly alike. The same is true when it comes to applying the techniques of salesmanship. Let's consider some variations on the themes we've already established.

Give The Complete Sales Story

Take nothing for granted. Never imagine that your prospective sponsor knows all the facts about your coverage, ratings, rates, etc. A friend of mine told me how he lost a big sale. He thought that he had given the total sales story but he was keenly disappointed when he learned that the radio advertising budget went to the competitor's station. He asked the sponsor why he lost the sale. "Because," said the prospect, "Station K---- reaches the teenagers and those are the people who buy my product." "But," said the radio advertising salesman, "we have a terrific teenage audience!" "You may have but you never mentioned it to me," was the candid reply. So, give all the facts; omit nothing, especially the information that makes sales!

Sell The Use Of Your Product

A sponsor couldn't care less about the sound of your station unless it appeals to his prospective customers. Market research pays off in this instance. "Case" your prospective sponsor's customers. Try to determine what kind of radio appeals to them. If it's a country and western kind of clientele, then impress the sponsor with your C & W listenership. Obviously, every sponsor wants to know that potential customers will pay more attention to his sales messages while they listen to their favorite kinds of programs. It takes market research so go to it!

Nick A Nickname In The Nick Of Time!

"Hey Shortie!" "Hey, Leftie!" "Hey Tiny!" and other nicknames can be disastrous. Don't get nicked by a nickname. They only tend to demean you. If only parents and friends would realize how a nickname can ruin a personality. Generally, these point up a physical disability. Like calling a baldheaded man "Curley," a thin man "Skinny,' and so on. It may sound appropriate but would you ever vote for "Tiny " Johnson or "Curly" Nixon or "Lefty" Hunphrey for President of the United States? What's that you say, you're not running for Presidency? True, but you are aspiring to become one of the finest salesmen in broadcasting so why hand a loadstone around your neck on your way up the ladder?

Don't Forget To Remember

A good sponsor of mine once said, "Si, I'll service your TV set if I remember it." I tactfully suggested that he make a note of it and he was glad for the suggestion. If you have a tendency to forget things, write them down and them remember to refer to your notes. All this should be entered in a memo book or calendar. It's true, we do get busy and make promises and then forget them. I never buy from a salesman who stands me up due to forgetfulness. Does this sound silly? Well, try it on for size. Deliberately forget several of your promises and see how your sales take a skid. Remember, jot it down, then go to town.

Encourage Your Sponsor To Say "Yes!"

Radio advertising is difficult to sell because many merchants are afraid to make decisions. They are plagued with many unstated questions such as, "How many announcements should I use?" "Must I prepare the copy?" "How do I know whether this will work?" etc. The usual answer from these doubting Thomases is, "I'll let you know later." This is your opportunity to make him decide to advertise now! Here's how you do it.

"Mr. Sponsor, I've covered the entire story of our radio station. You've got what the listeners want and need. Why wait? Competition is keen; make your bid for a share of the business. The longer you wait, the further ahead your competition gets. Mr. Sponsor, we do all of the work; we write the copy, subject to your approval. We place your announcements in the most strategic places on the program log. We worry for you. Don't let your merchandise be subject to a clearance sale after the season passes. Let us help you encourage customers to trade with you now!"

Notice, please, that I didn't ever say that you should guarantee that he would sell all of his merchandise. All you can do is assure him that every effort will be put forth to make his messages most palatable so that listeners would be encouraged to shop at his store. Let me remind you that you should have reasonable assurance that the merchandise he is selling is of quality and that it is what people want and need. All the advertising in the world will not sell inferior merchandise to people who don't want or need it! Let's remember the big point of this sequence; that is, to dissolve your sponsor's doubts and fears so that he'll say, "Yes, I'll advertise!"

One Detail Can Make The Sale

"We never put an announcement on the air until it is approved by the sponsor." "We can make a copy change in just a few minutes; all you have to do is call and tell us what to change. If necessary, call me at home in the evening and I'll guarantee the change will be made for the morning." Little things like that prompt sponsors to select your station over other stations that may not be as conscientious. Small details mean a lot, especially to sponsors who need these assurances. This technique also enables a prospect to make comparisons between your station and your competition without your mentioning him by name or by knocking your competitors.

Turn "Just Some" Into "Total Sum."

A difficult part of selling radio advertising is going back for renewal orders every week. This uncalled for, time-consuming method of selling is enervating and can be remedied; here's how:

Supposing you have a sponsor who believes in schedules only for his weekend business. Supposing he doesn't advertise every weekend; he leap frogs. Explain that consistent advertising is cumulative. It not only motivates his regular customers but also gains new customers. Explain that if his advertising is spotty, listeners will certainly patronize the other shops they hear advertised. On-again off-again advertising gets on-again off-again customers. Clinch the deal by explaining that he can earn your best frequency discount if he contracts for the required amount of announcements. All of these reasons, plus suggesting new ideas, will make a regular account out of a "skipper." That's how you turn "just some advertising" into "the total sum of advertising."

See More Sponsors

Plan your calls for the following day and then add two more accounts to that list. The more calls you make, the more sales you'll make. The trick of this assignment is to be so well versed in your subject that you can cut the time it takes to make a sale down to bite size. Mind you, I don't mean that you should give a half-baked presentation or give a "rush" job. I mean that if you can prune the time you waste in unnecessary talk, you'll have enough time left over to make those extra calls, and that's where you'll start making more money.

Confirm Every Order

Leave nothing to chance or imagination. Confirm every schedule. Check out all copy. Be sure that the facts are right. It's this extra effort that keeps customers happy. Happy customers are much better to have than unhappy sponsors.

Take Personal Inventory

Is the growth of your station leaving you behind? "Billings were never higher" proclaims the owner of the station; and yet, you're still earning about the same commissions that you earned six years ago. Time out for self-analysis. Maybe the owner feels sorry for you and doesn't want to replace you. Maybe you're satisfied with your little slice of the action. You'll die of boredom unless you get into high gear. Take personal inventory of yourself. Be a self-motivator. Get into the race. Become a real salesman!

Automotivate Or You'll Be Automated

Motivate yourself or you may become automated. "Automotivate" means to motivate one's self. Check yourself for the following deficiencies. If you are weak in any of these, you must recharge your battery: 1. You resist change; 2. you're getting flabby and lazy; 3. you play it safe; 4. you fly off the handle; 5. you blame the other guy; 6. your imagination is slipping; 7. you're on the defensive; 8. you're too stubborn; 9. No enthusiasm; 10. you're getting to be a "loner" and losing the "team spirit." Repair these trouble spots so that you can stay in the ballgame.

Be A Pseudo-Detective

Keep a complete file of every sponsor. Itemize every important fact. His likes and dislikes; his hobbies, his habits. Remember that you are the person who has to adjust to your sponsor's speed. The more you know about your sponsor, the easier it will be for you to adjust to this tempo. Here's an idea that reaps dividends. If ever you see a social or business article about one of your sponsors in a trade paper, newspaper, etc., clip it and send it to him. Suggest that he may need an extra copy for his scrap book. Be sure, however, that you keep a copy of that story in your own office file of sponsors' vital statistics.

Dont' Be A Whirlwind

Fast conversation doesn't make sales. Be knowledgable; have important information at your fingertips. Many salesmen in radio advertising haven't even taken time out to learn the difference between AM and FM radio. They don't know the difference between KiloHertz and MegaHertz. These alleged salesmen depend on fast patter to make a sale and then wonder why they can't earn enough to pay their rent. You've got to read the trade papers. You've got to go to conventions and listen to qualified speakers. If you depend on being a "whirlwind" to make sales, you'll never become a good salesman.

Not Everybody Buys For The Same Reason

Some sponsors use radio advertising because they want a tax write-off. Some advertise because they have to improve their business. Others advertise because they want to keep their names in front of the public." You must realize that one 'canned' presentation will not close deals with all sponsors. You must not only satisfy the need of your sponsor but you must also be versatile enough to reinforce this need with newer and better ideas.

Dont' Waste Your Time

Many salesmen consider studying as a waste of time. The opposite is true. If you don't improve your mind with worthwhile reading and market research, you are wasting your time. Sure, get your share of fun and pleasure, but don't do it to the complete neglect of that all-important market research and study.

Responsibility Of A Single Station Market

Where a radio station is fortunate enough to be the only station in a market, it is commonly called "a single-station market." That means the station has been licensed by the FCC to serve the primary needs of that market. This is a big responsibility. A single-station market is usually fragmented into audiences that have favorite kinds of programs. One group may prefer to listen to country and western music all the time. Another group insists upon having Gospel music as the main bill of fare. Still another may care for middle-of-the-road music.

Block programming is the best way to satisfy the majority of tastes in a single-station market. That means having a time segment that plays only C & W, another block of time that caters to the middle-of-the-road fans and still another portion of time that features Gospel music, and so on. If a single station market plays just one kind of music all day long, every day in the week, it is automatically shutting out other listeners who have their preferences. This makes the station vulnerable to a challenge for the FCC license.

The FCC encourages any interested party to file for an existing frequency and show how he can offer better entertainment, news, and information than the current licensee. It's easy for a challenger to emphasize that the present licensee is catering to a portion of the market and how he plans to remedy that situation by arranging his programming to meet the needs of the total market. If, you are working in a single-station market that features just one kind of programming, be sure to remind the owner or manager about the danger of that format. He could well be influenced by a militant minority that insists upon hearing what they like to hear. He should test the whole market and then arrange his programming accordingly. The important thing to remember is that you must cater to the majority of the people to the best of your ability.

Guaranteed Times Are Worth More

R. O. S. means Run Of Schedule. An R. O. S. schedule permits the station to place sales messages on the program log according to the times that are available. A Guaranteed Time means that a sales message will be logged at a specified time all the time. It could be adjacent to an important local newscast on just before the sports program, etc. Many stations charge a premium rate for a guaranteed announcement time. When you make a contract with a sponsor for a guaranteed time, be sure that is is scheduled for a sufficiently long time to make it meaningful.

Be A Showman

The attention span of most people is just a few seconds. Unless you have a presentation that commands attention, you could well be putting your sponsor to sleep. That is why we have mentioned, frequently, the importance of creating new, fresh, attention-getting ideas. Presentations that drag on ad infinitum can be disastrous. Presentations that are dull, ordinary, and routine fall flat. If you are calling on a new prospect, keep his attention focused on the fact that you can encourage new customers to shop his store or try his service. If you are calling on an established sponsor, point up the fact that he can have another successful sale because of the new approach you planned for him. Make sure your taped demonstration is full of life and vitality. Remember this, few people are duller than long-winded salesmen who have nothing to say.

Gain Your Sponsor's Confidence

Everything you do and say in your presentation should inspire confidence. Many moons ago, I wanted to buy a tape recorder. I had clipped a picture of the recorder that I wanted to buy from the store's catalogue. I asked the clerk where I could make my down payment on the instrument before taking it with me. My mind was made up. I knew exactly what I wanted to buy and how much I wanted to spend.

This did not satisfy the eager-beaver salesman. "Oh no," he protested. "You must let me demonstrate it for you," he insisted. "Not necessary," said I. "My friend has one just like it; I know all about it." "Please," begged the salesman, "let me show you how it works." "Ok," I said.

Well, the demonstration model didn't perform the way it should. The speed was too slow. The salesman shook all over. The more he tried to get it to work, the worse it became. I felt sorry for the poor man so I suggested that we try another machine. It worked fine. I learned a lesson from this experience. Don't oversell your product. Once a sponsor is sold, close the deal and let it go at that! Overselling is just as bad as underselling! You destroy your sponsor's confidence in you when you give the impression that you don't know how to sell!

Don't Cave In To Your Price-Cutting Competitor

One of the astronauts was asked what his greatest fear was when he was floating in outer space. He said, "The fact that I'm in a space capsule that was assembled by the lowest bidder." A good radio advertising salesman keeps cost firmly in the background. Make up your mind that you are not going to expose yourself to the process of having a sponsor rearrange your rate card. Even if the subject of price does come up, hang it in suspended animation by saying something like this: "Mr. Sponsor, how can you determine the value of anything unless you know all about the product. Let's talk about the cost after you've heard more about our radio station and what it can do for you." This bit of advice will work only if you can equate the quality of your station with your station's rates.

Dare To Be Different

I was one of 20 men summoned to a leading broadcasting school to present ideas for creating and implementing a sales training course to be added to the curriculum. I had a very simple presentation. I noticed that the other applicants had elaborate charts, graphs, etc. When I stepped into the presence of the four learned men who were to decide who got the job, I was apprehensive to say the least. Throwing caution to the wind I said, "Gentlemen, erase the degrees from your names and come with me while I visit merchants on Main Street. That's the battleground! That's where shirt-sleeve and face-to-face selling is done. I have battle scars to prove it. "Look here," and I proceeded to show them scores of testimonial letters from satisfied sponsors in my market. After reciting a few experiences, explaining how some of these merchants were persuaded to advertise on my station, I got the assignment.

You've got to take chances but they must be risks that are built on firm foundations. Just saying that you are the most qualified man to do the job is not enough! You must prove it with documentary evidence and mix it up with showmanship and integrity. Some sales presentations are founded on a bluff and run on the same principal. You be different. Build your presentation on a foundation of solid rock.

Simplicity Pays Off

The razzle-dazzle salesman is often a one-shot salesman. If he's all front and no back, he soon runs out of customers because his hot-shot reputation precedes him wherever he goes. Avoid this trap! Your presentation should be simple and honest. It need not be elaborate and filled with impossible claims. Examples of hot-shot claims: "My radio station can increase your business by 50 percent." "Let me show you how we can sell that junk you've been trying to get rid of the past 50 years," and so on. Established facts about successful campaigns run for other sponsors on your station go a long way toward encouraging a sponsor to buy a schedule from you. Let your presentation be animated yet simple and to the point.

Benjamin Franklin once asked some men if they could make an egg stand on end. "That's easy," volunteered one of the men. After a few minutes, the man gave up in disgust. "Can't be done," he said. Another man attempted to make the egg stand on end but he also gave up after some very good attempts. Each man in turn agreed that it was impossible. Ben Franklin then said, "Are you all certain this feat is impossible?" "We agree," said the men almost in unison. "Let me show you that it is possible," said the great Mr. Franklin. He then tapped the end of the egg on the table until it flattened out sufficiently to provide a platform and it indeed stood in its end. To a man, the audience said, "Oh, that's easy, anybody can do that!"

Take a lesson from Ben Franklin; be one step ahead of your competitors by having new, fresh ideas in your sales kit. If your ideas are new and presented with a little showmanship to substantiate them, you've got a winner. But exaggerated claims with no evidence of proof of performance will plummet your stock to zero. You can always make a presentation simple yet replete with showmanship.

How To Satisfy The Sponsor Who Has Everything

A general merchandise store has been in business for 80 years. According to all available information the store had never advertised. His customers had supported him through feast, famine, drought, floods, and depressions. These facts were confirmed by the owner when I called on him. "Never did advertise and don't have to; my customers are loyal and they've patronized our shop for the past 80 years. Always made money," was the way he summed it up. I collected the facts and went back to the radio station to analyze them.

It seemed to me that he **owed** something to his loyal customers. Careful research revealed that his patronage consisted mainly of people who enjoyed country and western music. Accordingly, I prepared a 30-minute C & W program with no commercials. It as a program of uninterrupted music with appropriate opening and closing credits. The credits merely said, "Jones' General Store presents 30-minutes of uninterrupted music in appreciation for your continuous support during the past 80 years." The music followed. The closing credit approximated the opening lines. The owner of the store agreed that our premise was correct. That he **owed** something to his loyal customers. Remember this, should you have some sponsors who think they don't have to advertise simply because business has always been good, simply because they think they have everything!

Eager-Beaver Selling

My salesman was elated because he finally sold an account he had been trying to sell for several months. The traffic order read: "Victory at last!" The order, however, was a complete disaster because it called for six announcements to promote a tire clearance sale. A radio station simply cannot afford bad publicity because of a campaign failure. Accordingly, I asked the salesman to suggest to the tire dealer that he take a meaningful schedule; at least saturation for several says. The salesman balked, so I took the initiative and called on the account.

"But your man called on me many times and convinced me that I was missing a bet by not advertising on your station," said the tire dealer. "Correct," I answered," and with your limited schedule, you might as well not advertise at all." "Why is that?" he asked. "Good question," I responded. "Although we never guarantee specific results, our experience has been that a saturation schedule of at least 15 announcements a day for five or six days has much more of a chance to accomplish your goal than a meager total of six sales messages."

"You've got a good point there," was the tire dealer's honest reply; please increase my order. And, also tell your salesman not to make extravagent claims." The sale was a success and the dealer became a regular advertiser after we discussed his yearly budget. Learn a lesson. Tempting as it may be to close a sale with an account that you've been trying to land over a period of time, don't take any old schedule. Unless you have reasonable assurance that you will be helping your sponsor, it is best to refuse a small handout. Don't be an eager-beaver salesman.

Don't Bury Your Sponsors

If you work hard, it is possible to get a lot of sponsors. The more sponsors you have, the thinner you must spread yourself. Unless you keep a tight list of service calls, the tendency will be to "let some of these sponsors wait because you can't call on them all very often." When you get an account to advertise on your station he feels like a tourist because you've given him the royal treatment. But if he is negelected too long after your initial sale, his resentment will build against you. Keep in touch with all of your accounts. If you cannot do this yourself, be sure that somebody on the station staff does. A bread and butter note is one good way to keep in touch. Send these brief notes or make a simple phone call. The main point is not to let your sponsors die of neglect because they'll be resuscitated by your competition.

Clip The Gossip

Rumors, whether they are true or false, do much damage. Stifle a rumor whenever you can. First of all, don't repeat that rumor. Second, don't bother to refute the rumor you hear; it only adds to the fuel. Take the information casually with a "so what" attitude and then change the subject. If you are the storm center of a rumor, try to find the source and then immediately confront that person. Ask for the facts outright, no holds barred. Plug the source of the rumor and you've smothered it. People who start or spread rumors generally want attention. A juicy bit of gossip holds people's attention. A rumor is about one percent truth and 99 percent icing to make it real tasty. Don't start or spread rumors and you'll sleep lots better every night.

How To Analyze Your Prospect's Objections

Most progress results from previous failures. Thomas Edison tested hundreds of filaments before he found the one that would serve in his Mazda Lamp. We could go on and on listing familiar stories about converting failures into successes. But at this moment we want to address ourselves to salesmen who bemoan lost sales. A sale is lost because an objection (or objections) were raised and were insoluble. Keep a meticulous list of these objections. Tape record them yourself and then answer them yourself. You must be able to recognize the normal stalls and excuses that are given at the beginning of your presentation. These are natural resistance to change. We are all victims of inertia. The objections that you want to tape record are the ones stated after you've made the presentation:

Prospective sponsor: I really don't believe that radio advertising will get me the desired results, after all.
You: That may be true, but when you decide on the medium that you want to use, please be certain that it has all the advantages that our radio station provides such as reaching the

major share of your trade area; low cost per capita; ability to make immediate changes in your copy if necessary, etc.

You see, when you practice how to contend with objections, you'll be able to cope with them whenever they arise. Please don't have all the answers for every objection. Be honest. If you cannot answer an objection, say so! Assure the sponsor that you'll get the answer for him. I doubt seriously whether any salesman has all the answers to every objection. Your constant effort, therefore, is to analyze objections and learn the difference between a normal excuse or stall and an objection that is valid. When you are able to distinguish between these, you'll have a much better chance to demolish them.

Wear A Different Hat

It is a must that you see the situation from the other man's vantage point. As a dedicated sales representative for a radio station, about all you can see is that a merchant or company must have rocks in their heads if they don't advertise on your station.

The best way to see their point of view is to actually play their part in a practice session with another salesman. You take the part of the sponsor and let the salesman try to persuade you to buy. Don't offer far-fetched or ridiculous reasons or objections. Just raise valid reasons why you, as the merchant or sponsor, will not or cannot take a schedule.

True, it is difficult to make an absolute switch to the role of the sponsor. But if you begin with just a little understanding of his position, your understanding will begin to grow. The more you can understand about the sponsor's feelings, the better you will be able to deal with him. Doctors are adept at this. A doctor knows that a patient will experience pain when he is pricked with a needle so he says to the patient "This won't hurt a bit," as he jabs the syringe into the patient's arm. Then when the patient complains that "it did hurt me doctor." The medico says, "What I meant to say was that it wouldn't hurt me a bit."

From Best To Pest

"Too bad, he made such a good first impression and now he's a downright pest." That is generally the fate of an overanxious salesman. There's a difference between adding to your original presentation with good, usable material and becoming a pest. Follow-up calls or letters must have meaning; not just be repeats of the same old pitch. It takes real, keen understanding to know when you are building a strong case or losing a sale because you are becoming a pest. Sometimes there are honest-to-goodness reasons why a decision to buy isn't made. Could be because of a merger, change of policy, etc. There is a certain amount of time required for a sale to hatch and if you try to hasten the process, you'll wind up in the file called "pests" and that's a toughie to get out of.

Two-Man Selling

If your sales manager elects to make some calls with you, be glad about it. Learn from him. After all, he is the sales manager and he must know a thing or two. Be sure, however, that you know the part that you are to play in this 2-man effort. He may want to watch you in action or he may want you to see him make the sale. In either case, play the part that you are supposed to. Sponsors are wary when two men take part in the oral part of the presentation. It looks as if you are ganging up on him. If you are to be the observer, be exactly that! Resist making comments or suggestions until you have left the sponsor.

Dare To Deviate From Routine Procedure

Have at least one feature that sets you off from the run-of-the-mill salesman. It could be either dress, speech, or an object of some kind. How about getting to be known as, "I'm the new idea salesman." This is a good way to have people remember you. But be sure that you can live up to the title that you bestow upon yourself. Another good way to set yourself off from the crowd is to pronounce the name of the man to whom you intend to make a presentation; then spell his name and pronounce it again. This technique helps you to remember names and how to pronounce them. A good friend of mine never fails to leave a piece of candy or a token of some kind with his sponsor. Sure, it's an added expense but it is a good impression builder. Another good salesman I know never fails to wear a small boutonniere. Give this idea lots of thought. Dare to deviate from the routine and people will remember you and seek you out.

Analyze, Analyze, Analyze

The job of analyzing should never end. Learn all about your sponsors. What appeals to them. What motivates them.

Then make your presentation appeal to his preference. Is he interested in making more profit? Does he need a tax write-off? How about the pleasure motive? Does he like to imitate his competitor? It's up to you to analyze your sales prospects and why he likes to buy. Then direct your presentation along those lines. A good salesman's homework never ends!

HOW THE ENTIRE TEAM FUNCTIONS

Teamwork! That's what makes a radio station function. The sales representative must know what the program director is planning. The announcers must know how important their work is in relationship to sales and programming. The traffic manager is the nerve center. She (or he) has to have her (or his) finger on the pulse of the entire organization. A well oiled team! Cooperation! Knowledgable! Expertise! The Right hand must know what the left hand is doing.

To make our point stronger, let's compare the operation of a radio station with the goings-on in a Government top priority secret security project. The building of the atomic bomb, for instance. Each part of the bomb was sub-assembled and then the bomb assembled in a different plant. It is safe to say that one, perhaps no more than two people knew the entire process from A to Z.

It's different in a radio station. Not knowing what the other department is up to can result in plenty of disastrous head-on collisions. Accordingly, I searched the country for the most complete set of ground rules. There were plenty of them. Out of the many submitted, I selected the Policy Book of Operations given to all KSEL-AM-FM staff members. It is complete. Fortunate is the person who is on the KSEL team in Lubbock, Texas. This station is a credit to the entire industry. Study the following pages carefully; little more can be added.

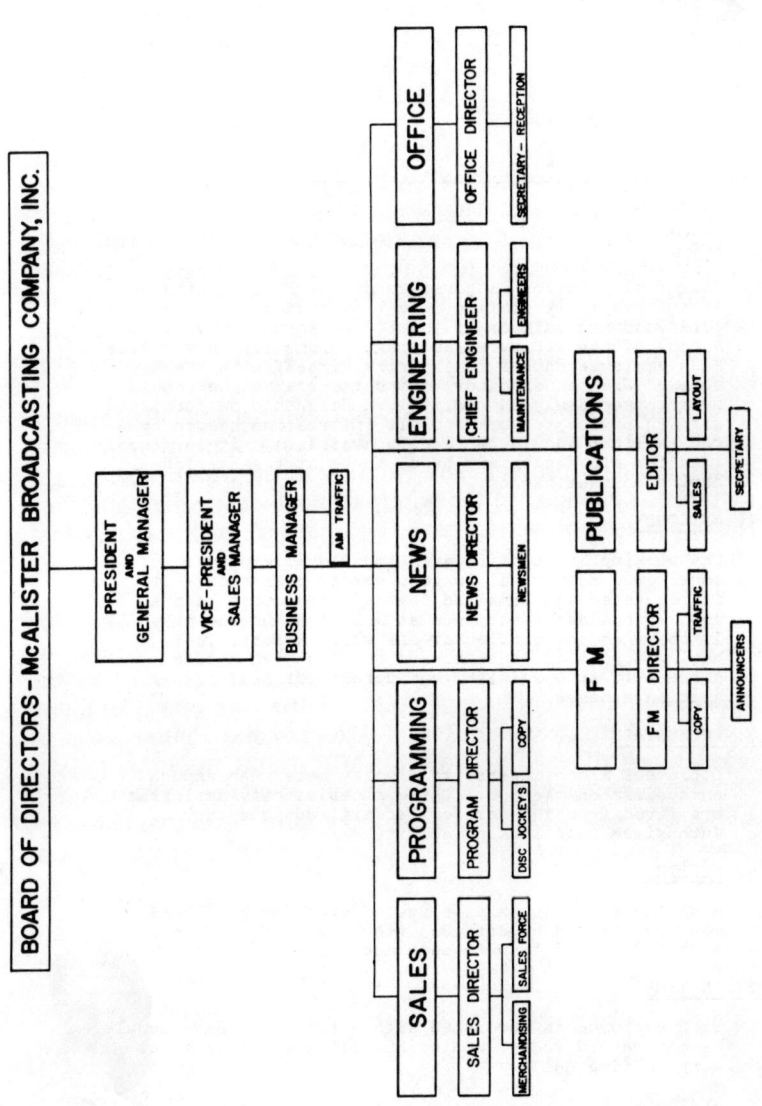

MCALISTER BROADCASTING OPERATIONS BOOK

GENERAL

1. FCC

This radio station is governed by the FCC, Washington. At no time is it station intention that any of the rules and regulations of the FCC be knowingly violated. A copy of the FCC rules and regulations are in the file. Each employee should familiarize himself with these rules. When an examiner visits the station he should be greeted warmly and politely. He should be furnished with an office to work and all information needed by the examiner should be readily available. It is a good idea for all department heads to be at the station during an examination.

2. ATTITUDE

The working attitude of each individual employee is considered most vital in good steady operation. It is requested and demanded that all employees keep a good enthusiastic attitude at all times on the job. If there is any problem at all which affects your having a good attitude toward the job then please discuss it at once with your department head or station manager.

3. ENTHUSIASM

Employees are requested to display more than enough enthusiasm on the job. Three times as many employees are fired from the job for bad attitude and lack of enthusiasm than lack of ability.

4. MEETING

A schedule of meetings is posted every week. These meetings should be attended regularly as if it were a shift. Be on time to each meeting.

5. ON TIME

Each employee is furnished with a time working schedule. We may be old fuddy duddies but it is vital to be at work on time daily.

6. NEATNESS

It is the responsibility of each employee that the radio station remain neat. You may be broke but at least you can be neat. Some messy employees will be made examples of for their lack of neatness.

7. DRESS

During the week all male employees should wear a shirt and tie. Female employees a dress and heels. Exception...engineers and maintenance men)...On weekends sport shirts and flats are permissible.

8. FRIENDS-KIN (CONT)

No employee should have friends or kin spend a great amount of time visiting at the station. The radio station is a business and a place for work not play.

9. GENERAL HORSEPLAY

It is most important that employees enjoy their work at the radio station...Horseplay can easily get out of hand. Large social gatherings are unwanted in the hall or someone's office. If any employee has nothing more to do than shoot the bull then there is something desperately wrong.

10. HALL CONVERSATIONS

Employees who congregate to discuss business in the hall are considered rank amateurs by station manager. Business transactions should be made in an office behind closed doors.

11. FRONT OFFICE TALK

Major discussion of station business is strongly discouraged in the front office. Again these discussions and problems should be solved behind closed doors. Any major problems should most definitely not be discussed in the front office while guest are present.

12. EXPENDITURES

No employee is permitted to spend any station money without first obtaining a purchase order from the bookkeeper.

13. READY TO WORK ANYTIME

In the radio business employees should realize they may be ask to come to work anytime day or night..7 days a week. Special promotions, emergency broadcasts, etc., are all just a part of the radio business. It is expected that employees accept these calls for work with the right frame of mind....... ENTHUSIASM.

14. PROFANITY

Profanity around the radio station is strongly discouraged. Announcers who make profanity a habit are apt to slip at one time or another when the mike is open. Non air employees never know when the mike is open.

15. VACATIONS

The KSEL staff vacations operate on the following schedule:
   Employment of 6 mos. or over..one week
   Employment of 1 yr. or more...two weeks

16. IDEA BOX

An idea box is located in the front office of the radio station. Employees are encouraged to place ideas for the improved operation of the Radio Station. The ideas should cover all departments and subjects. A $5.00 bonus will be paid weekly to the employee having the best idea of the week.

17. SICK LEAVE--TIME OFF

When an employee becomes ill he or she should report in to the station as early as possible. If an employee is ill over several days he should call the station and report his condition each day he is out. When an employee needs time off (except emergencies) he should request the time off several days in advance. No employee is to take time off without clearance.

18. COMPLAINTS

All complaint calls to the radio station should be given to the Manager or Assistant Manager. In the case they are out of the office the persons name and phone number should be taken.

19. WRITTEN MESSAGES

The old idea of writing it down holds true for good business operation. Employees are urged to use written memos and messages to fellow staff members. It is most important that copy notes from the salesman to the copy department be written out on the copy information sheets.

20. EMPLOYEE HOME NUMBERS

The home telephone number of employees are not to be given to callers. Exceptions would be accounts calling for a salesman or emergency telephone calls.

21. OFF DUTY PERSONNEL

Employees that are off duty should not make it a habit of hanging around the radio station. Those who are on duty do not have the time to visit with off duty personnel.

22. CONTROL ROOM..NEWS ROOM..OFF LIMITS

There are to be no visitors in the control room or news room. Station employees are not to spend anytime visiting in the control room or newsroom. When there is business to be conducted the employee should get in an out in a matter of minutes. The DJ's and newsmen are not to have friends or kin visiting in the control or newsroom. The only exception to this rule would be an organized group of visitors or a guided tour.

23. RAISES

There is no definite schedule for raises. Raises are on an individual basis and given as merited.

24. LOGGING PUBLIC SERVICE BROADCASTS

When the station conducts a Public Service or Local News broadcast such as tornado coverage, major fire, civic club special event, etc....this should be logged on the station program log. Responsibility is with the announcer on duty to be double checked by the program director.

25. HOURLY COMMERCIAL LIMIT

There are to be a maximum number of commercial announcements broadcast hourly on the station. The program log denotes the placement of commercial announcements. No one is allowed to insert extra commercial announcements during the hour.

26. TIME CARDS

All employee time cards should be turned in the day before pay day.

27. EMPLOYEE WORK LOCATION

Each employee is given a definite work location. It is the responsibility of each employee to see that his working area is straight and neat at all times.

28. FRONT OFFICE CARE

The condition of the front office is the direct responsibility of the girls. Neatness should always be the theme. The girls are not to leave their desk at night until the front has been cleaned and their desk cleared.

29. BUSINESS DISCUSSIONS

The girls are not to engage in business discussions or problems when there are guests in the front office.

30. VISITORS

Each person who enters the doors of KSEL are to be treated with upmost kindness. Coffee should be offered and the guest book should be signed. When a person comes to see a member of the staff their name and company should be asked and so told to the staff member. For example, Mr. None of Dunlaps to see you. Girls should be fast to learn the businesses of frequent visitors to save embarassment. When a person comes through the front door they should be immediately greeted. If a girl is on the telephone she should still make definite acknowledgement of a person's entry.

31. PERSONAL TELEPHONE CALLS

The office girls should refrain from making any personal telephone calls of any length at the front. Personal calls are discouraged period. If a personal call needs to be made the girl should move into one of the private offices.

32. AT THE DESK

The radio station does not approve of the girls up and moving around. They should stay at their desk and in the front unless extreme business moves them elsewhere.

33. ALWAYS AT THE FRONT

There should be always one girl at the front from eight to five-thirty. On lunch hours etc the schedule should be set to not leave the front empty.

34. KINDNESS

Kindness is the continued theme in answering the phone and greeting visitors. No matter who is calling and what is said the girls are to remain calm and kind. If any complaints are received on any employee mistreating a listener or guest they will be dismissed immediately.

35. SMOKING IN THE FRONT OFFICE

The radio station does not allow the girls to smoke in the front office.

36. TELEPHONE ANSWERING

When the telephone at the radio is answered the girls should have pep, and enthusiasm. No dead fishes please, good morning KSEL or Good afternoon KSEL..should be used. At times other greetings may be used.
ACT LIKE YOU ARE DELIGHTED THEY ARE CALLING KSEL.

37. BUSINESS ATMOSPHERE

The girls should see to it that a top notch business atmosphere is displayed at all times in the front office. Horseplay should be eliminated.

38. TELEPHONE CALLS AND MESSAGES

Telephone calls for staff members should be handled in the following manner:
1. Buzz the office.
2. If the office does not answer use the intercom.
3. If the person does not answer the call inform the caller he is out of the office and take the number.
4. If there is a call for an employee and they are in the building and do not want to take the call, tell the caller they are out of their office..Do not say they are in conference or in a meeting.
5. There is no excuse for a salesman or any employee not getting a message or call. This is one of the main responsibilities of the girls.
6. Do not leave messages or notes for any employee on the front desk. Calls for salesmen yes, but any messages or information, no.

39. SPECIAL JOBS

Before the girls begin a special project for any employee with the exception of the President, Vice President nd Business Manager, they should clear with the Business Manager.

40. COFFEE BREAKS

Morning and afternoon coffee breaks should be short and not a staff bull session. DJ's and other staff members should not enter in.

41. NOTEBOOK

    Each girl should have a personal notebook for instructions and notes...SALES INFORMATION AND CANCELLATION ON THE PHONE   REFER TO SALES MANAGER OR SALESMAN HANDLING THE ACCOUNT.

42. OUTGOING MAIL

    The girl responsible for the outgoing mail should check postage at all times if more than 2 sheets are enclosed. Air Mail stamps should be used on most mail going out of this area. (To Eastman Offices, etc.)

43. DON'T SAY, "I DON'T KNOW"

    When a person calls and asks a question the girl is not to say, "I don't know". Find a person on the staff who should know and refer the call to them.

44. WHEN YOU LEAVE

    It is the responsibility of the last girl leaving to inform news to answer the phone.

45. ON TIME

    The girls should be on time daily. Arrive five minutes early and be at the desk ready to go to work at the hour.

46. SUPPLIES

    Always use the standard telephone message slips for all calls. We don't like telephone messages on all kinds, shapes of paper. Watch office supplies you use regularly and inform Business Manager of anything we are getting low on, so that order may be placed before we run out.

47. LONG DISTANCE

    On all long distance calls get the person calling and where the call is from...The operator may not want to give out this information, but get it anyway.

48. SICKNESS

    In case of sickness or other emergencies call and inform Business Manager so we will know why you can't come to work or will be late.

49. MISCELLANEOUS ITEMS TO REMEMBER

    One very important thing to remember is when talking on the telephone to one party, if another line rings, immediately say "One Moment Please" and answer the other line, then say "Good Morning KSEL, One moment please", go back to your original call, etc.

    When necessary to go into control room or news room please be sure the light is not flashing indicating they are 'on-the-air'.

    Another important item that can create problems is leaving the date and time and signature of person who takes a message off the message. Please be sure and see that the message is completely filled out.

50. NOSY PEOPLE

Messages and notes on a persons desk or in their rack are not to be read by other staff members. Staff members are also not to pick up material from the desk in front and read the information.

51. DEPARTMENT HEADS

When Department Heads must be gone from the radio station during working hours their location and time expected back should be available.

52. OVERTIME

Staff members are not to work any overtime unless approved first by their Department Head.

53. ENGINEERING TROUBLE SHEETS

Any problems involving station equipment or facilities are to be reported by the written trouble sheet and placed on the trouble book in the Engineering Room.

54. INFORMATION TO ACCOUNTS

When an account calls for information about his schedule or spots, regular staff members are not to give out any information....His name should be taken and his salesman notified as soon as possible. Only exception would be bookkeeping information, copy by Program Director, etc.

55. TAKING HOME RECORDS, EQUIPMENT

No station employee is to take home records, equipment, or any station materials without first the consent from the department head.

56. ASSIGNING OF STATION EQUIPMENT

At times station equipment will be assigned out to employees. The equipment becomes the full responsibility of the employee and in the event it is lost or damaged the employee is expected to pay.

57. SALES PROPOSAL

A station copy of each sales proposal is to be made and retained by the station for the proposal file.

58. TRAFFIC-COMMERCIALS

The KSEL Program Logs are under the control of the traffic director. All commercials to be placed on the log are to be filled out on the KSEL sales contract. Salesman and others making out contracts need to be sure to see that all information is supplied. No verbal orders will be taken. All orders must be written out.

G-59. TELEPHONE MEMOS

>Information concerning station contests, promotions, auditorium shows, etc. should be typed out on a general information memo for the telephone operators. This can save much time for the girls.

G-60. RESIGNATIONS

>When an employee wishes to resign he should let this request be made in the form of a letter to the manager.

G-61. PROBLEMS TO DEPARTMENT HEADS

>When an employee has a problem he should first consult his department head for the solution.

G-62. HEARING MISTAKES

>When an employee hears a mistake on the air, wrong copy, incorrect news story, etc. he should report it at once.

G-63. TAKING ASSIGNMENTS

>Various staff members will be assigned special projects, promotions, remotes etc. It is most important that each employee accept his assignment responsibility with complete thoughtfulness.

G-64. POSITIVE ATTITUDE

>All goals are the same among all employees. To make KSEL the most efficient, best sounding, most profitable radio station in the nation. A positive attitude for this goal is most desirable.

G-65. MAINTENANCE PROBLEMS

>When there is a need for immediate maintenance the employee should notify Mr. Butler at once.

G-66. COFFEE ROOM

>It is the responsibility of each employee to keep the coffee room clean. Cups, sugar, spoons should be in place.

PROGRAM PRODUCTION

59. PROGRAM DIRECTOR

>The KSEL Program Director is in charge of all schedules involving the DJ's. All changes should be handled through the Program Director.

60. THE DEEJAY

>KSEL today has the largest radio audience in West Texas. The responsibility and dignity is great upon the man occupying the KSEL control room chair. He is talking to more people at one time than any other person in West Texas. Any DJ who considers his time on the air as just another Board Shift should have his head examined. Perfection is the goal. There should be no poor air performance at KSEL.

61. MUSIC PATTERN - CLASSICS

The airing of classics, oldies, etc. have always been a problem. For this reason here is a new policy concerning the playing of classics.

1. A classic play list will be prepared each day by the KSEL music department. The days Classic Sheet will be posted in the control room.

2. 20 classics will be chosen each day for air play. When the DJ plays one of the classic selections it is to be marked. After a classic is marked it is not to be repeated until all 20 classic selections have been played once.

3. Only the side of cut listed on the classic sheet is to be played.

4. If there is no classic sheet in the control room notify the Program Director at once.

5. At the end of the day the classics are to be changed by the midnight announcer.

62. VERY IMPORTANT

When playing a pick hit, spotlight tune, new song, always identify it as such. The people like to know the new songs. Many times ask them to listen closely and see what they think. In the same manner classics, top 20 and rebounds should be identified.

63. PACE

A fast lively peppy pace should be the rule day and night at KSEL. HUSTLE is the by-word. The DJ is to be bright, lively, friendly and enthusiastic.

64. CONTROL ROOM VISITORS

There are to be no visitors in the control room. This includes family, friends, employees, etc. At times a guided tour will come through but they are to stay only a few minutes. If a member of the staff enters the control room on business, he or she is to make their stay as short as possible. If the announcer has visitors during his shift he is to inform the front desk the time he is off duty so his visitors can see him then.

65. NEWSMAN MIKE

The Newsman will request the air for various news stories. It is his authority when and what the story should be. The newsman should get the air without question.

66. CONTROL ROOM CONDITION

The control room is the work room of the station. The control room must be kept clean at all times. Each announcer after finishing a shift must take a few minutes to clean up the control room.

67. ANNOUNCER'S BOARD

There is a bulletin board in the control room for the use of the announcers. Each announcer should check this board daily for important information and memos from the program department.

68. DJ IN THE CONTROL ROOM

The DJ is to stay in the control room during his shift. While an announcer is on the air he does not have time to be up walking around visiting in the News Center, front office etc. The job is much more important than that.

69. ANNOUNCERS OFF DUTY

Announcers off duty should not hang around the radio station. If the announcer should or wants to remain at the station after or before his shift he should not hang around others who are working. A work place is created for every announcer.

70. ANNOUNCERS COMING ON DUTY

When an announcer comes on duty he should arrive at the station at least fifteen minutes before his shift begins. This will give him time to check memos, select records, etc.

71. SMOKING IN THE CONTROL ROOM

It is alright to smoke in the control room, however, the announcer should do his best in keeping the ashes in the trays and keeping the surroundings as neat as possible. This is important, ashes are harmful to control room equipment.

72. CROSS PLUGS

It is important that the DJ's cross plug each other as much as possible. Many times the DJ promos, plug cards, etc. will promo DJ's; However, DJ adlibs cannot be beat. Especially so on the upcoming DJ.

73. PRODUCTION RECORDING

The production shift of the DJ is just as important as the board shift. The work in production is just as vital. The DJ should accept this important responsibility. KSEL charges almost double the price on commercials. Our commercials must be twice as good. As in the DJ show, perfection is the goal. A definite schedule for production and office hours is set for each individual DJ. The DJ's are to meet this schedule as they do their air schedules.

74. TWO MAN CONVERSATION

Ksel strongly discourages two man conversations on the air (between two DJ's, Newsmen, etc.) exception.. TTO. When D.J.'s do chat on the air together it should be brief. Very important, be sure both DJ's are on Mike and working the mike direct. The DJ is not to make any adlib comment introing the newsman. No funny intros for the newsman at all. No adlib intros at all please.

75. LIVE TAGS

On some commercials live tags are vital. Each cartridge tape that needs a tag will show a star on the label. It is important that the live tag be given every time. Watch for the stars, then the live tags in the copy book.

76. INFORMATION TO ACCOUNTS

At no time is the DJ to give any logging information to accounts on the phone. He should tell the account calling that he doesn't have that information and that the salesman will call soon. This is regarding copy and spot logged.

77. CONTESTS

This is a most important phase of our operation and at times a very tricky one. Here are some policies concerning contests.

1. The DJ in charge of the contest will type a complete copy of rules and regulations. This should be carefully read by all DJ's. At no time should the DJ adlib about contest rules, etc. An extra copy of the contest rules should be made for the FCC contest file.

2. When talking to a listener in a contest on the air, be as brief as possible. If they win don't bother to get their name and address on the air, hit a record and then get their name and address.

3. Make sure the names of contest winners get to the proper staff members or in the proper notebook file, etc.

4. Promos and contest winners should be broadcast a sufficient number of times after the contest.

78. ANSWERING THE PHONE ON THE AIR

It is not good for the DJ to answer the phone directly on the air in contest questions etc. If the calls are screened first, the DJ can usually detect trouble makers.

79. REMOTES

Ksel has some definite opinions concerning on location commercial remotes. The remotes will be sold with a one minute, 90 second, or 2 minute commercial. The DJ should respect these times and the remote commercial should not exceed the time sold. All unnecessary adlib should be eliminated. The main sales message should be sold hard. When interviewing, store equipment should be checked out at least ten minutes before broadcast.

80. COMMUNITY SERVICE ANNOUNCEMENTS

At regular times during the schedule the community service announcements will be logged. On light commercial days the DJ can throw in various announcements during his show in addition to those logged. These announcements are worth thousands of dollars to us in public relations.

81. MEMOS AND LETTERS

There is a mail slot in the production room for each DJ. All personal mail and station memos are placed in the slot. It is very important that the DJ check each day for mail and station memos.

89. OFF WORK

When a DJ must be off from his DJ show or production shift, he must clear in advance with the Program Director. When a DJ is sick and cannot work, he should check each day with the Program Director to state his condition.

90. COPY WRITING

The DJ's are expected to write copy under the direction of the Program Director. It is best to have the ideas and writing of several persons and not just one. We expect the written copy to be the same in quality as is the DJ show and production shift.

91. PREPARATION FOR SHOWS

The DJ's are expected to spend a minimum of from Fifteen to Thirty minutes daily in preparation for their programs. This time should be spent in gathering interesting news items, one liners, production gimmicks, etc.

92. PROJECTS AND RESPONSIBILITIES

Each DJ will be assigned certain inside responsibilities. At various times DJ's will be asked to head and direct a station project or promotion. DJ's are expected to shoulder the responsibility in fine fashion.

93. STACKING COMMERCIALS

The radio station does not like the DJ's stacking commercials. Running one commercial after another. The DJ should put the time, temp, promos, adlib, jingles, etc. between all commercials.

94. IDEAS

The radio station is built on good ideas. Not ideas from one or some, but from many. Any time you're struck with a good idea, let it be known.

95. MORE PRODUCTION DO'S AND DON'TS

1. Each DJ is responsible for putting production records back into the proper shelf after using.

2. Check with copy before putting cartridges into control room rack or taking them out and erasing.

3. Date and initial all copy produced and return to copy room for filing.

4. Before tying up the production room, for the DJ's own benefit, check with copy to see if there is any priority recording to be done.

96. INSTRUMENTAL BEFORE THE NEWS

With the use of the tone on the hour the news and tone should hit right on the nour. Many times the DJ will end up a couple of minutes or a minute before the hour and the news. The DJ can at this point play an instrumental which will carry him up to news time. This is not to be done on the half hour headlines. On the half hour the DJ is to run the headlines right after the song near the thirty. It does not hurt for the half hour headlines to be a couple of minutes early or late.

97. RECORDS IN PROPER PLACE

All records are to be kept in their proper places at all times. There is a place for every record. There are shucks provided for all records. No record should be left out of the shuck or its proper place. As soon as a record is finished playing it should be returned to its proper place.

98. RECORD AFTER THE NEWS

After the hourly news as soon as the news close has been given the DJ is to hit with a fast up beat song from the chart.

99. INTRODUCTION OF RECORDS

The introduction of records in a McAlister operation is very important. Here are some rules that apply to the introduction of records.

1. When a record is from the survey it is alright to introduce the song as being from the survey and give its number. It is important that the announcer watch and make sure he does not introduce every survey record by giving its number. Many can be played without any introduction. It is very important that the DJ get as much variety in his introductions.

2. Never take over ten seconds to intro a song.

3. Never introduce two records the same way twice.

4. When introducing a song over music, make sure your intro is completed by the time the vocal begins.

5. When introducing a song over the first few bars, be very brief.

6. Never intro a song at the beginning and end both.

7. At times it is good to play a song without any intro at the beginning or end.

8. The secret to a good introduction of a record is a simple brief varied introduction.

100. GIVING OF THE TIME

The KSEL time should be given between every record without fail. Only give the time once between records, except on a real commercial day, when two or three commercials are given in a row. Then it may be good to give the time once or twice.

101. GIVING OF THE TEMPERATURE

The giving of the temperature is one of the most important things the announcer does at certain times. Note the conditions and how the temperature should be given in accordance with those conditions. The present temperature should be given between every record between the hours of 5:30 A.M. and 8:30 A.M. This includes all programs all seasons in this time period.

A Clear Normal Day...On a clear normal fairly warm day the temperature should be given every fifteen minutes.

On Extremely Hot Day...In the summer when the temp reaches the 100 mark the temp should be given two or three times every fifteen minutes as it is a big talking point when it is so high.

A Cold Day...On a cold day in the early morning and morning hours up until nine or ten the temp should be given between every record. After ten on a cold day the temp should be given every ten minutes.

When the Temp is Falling or Rising Rapidly....The temp should be given between every record if it is rising or falling sharply. For example if a warm or cool front moves into the area rapidly the temp falling or rising is a fairly big news story.

102. THE DAY'S HIGH

The day's high would be given at least two times every fifteen minutes in the morning hours. The same is true at night when dealing with the night's low.

103. MUSIC PATTERN

There is a definite music pattern for KSEL AM and FM for each of the broadcast hours. This pattern is to be followed without deviation as it is posted in the control rooms. Here are some important rules concerning the selection of music:

1. Always play the correctly marked sides of records.
2. Abide by the "Play Only" sticker on the albums.
3. Keep the music on the upbeat.
4. Never play 2 slow songs in a row.
5. Never play 2 girl vocals in a row.
6. Never play 2 instrumentals in a row.
7. Never play 2 group singers in a row.
8. Never play 2 wild rock n roll in a row.
9. Never play a bad record.

104. PLUG CARDS

There are a definite number of plug cards in the control room for use by the DJ's...These rules apply to the Plug Cards.

1. A plug card is to be used between every record without fail.
2. The plug cards are to be rotated in order.

105. EXCHANGING SHIFTS

No announcer's shifts are to be changed unless cleared by the Program Director. If something comes up where announcers need to exchange shifts the Program Director is to be notified in advance.

106. SICK LEAVE

If an announcer is sick and can not work his shift he should contact the Program Director in time for his shift to be accounted for.

107. CONVERSATION BETWEEN THE ANNOUNCER-NEWSMAN

There should be no small talk conversation between the announcer and newsman. The announcer is not to spend his time in the news center nor is the newsman to spend his time in the control room. THERE ARE

TO BE NO FOOLISH CONVERSATIONS BETWEEN THE ANNOUNCER AND NEWSMAN ON THE AIR. FOR EXAMPLE THE ANNOUNCER IS NOT TO ASK THE NEWSMAN WHAT HE THOUGHT OF A RECORD, ETC. There is an intercom between the announcer and newsman. This is for the announcer and newsman to work out cues and such for better production. It also saves the announcer having to go into the news center or the newsman having to go into the control room to relay a message.

108. PROGRAM LOG

The program log is to be followed at all times. Everything that appears on the log should be taken care of on the air. When a commercial or promotion spot is logged at a certain time, it is to be run as close to the time called for as possible. If there is no copy or tape for a logged spot the announcer is to get in touch with the copy desk at once. It is the responsibility of the announcer to see that everything which appears on the log during his shift is run.

109. ANNOUNCING

THREE ESSENTIALS IN ANNOUNCING.....The Ksel announcer must have these three essentials in his announcing. PUNCH, PACE, AND PEP..Let's look at each one briefly.

PUNCH...Each announcer must have good punch in his announcing and voice. He should speak with punch and force, but never shouting or talking loudly. The announcer should be extra careful to punch with the proper punch and pronunciation all commercials and promos etc.

PACE...The announcer should have a good fast pace announcing style. The announcer should be able to

speak rapidly, and at the same time speak clearly.
It is important the announcer speak with a good
steady fast pace, but it is just as important the
announcer speak clearly and is clearly understood.
Production to the degree of perfection leads to a
desirable station pace. Split second production
is required by the station of all announcers. The
announcer should at all times avoid with the upmost
care, any pauses. Split Second Production leads
to a professional sounding radio station.

UP BEAT SHOWS...All DJ's shows on KSEL should be
on the up or fast pace style.

UP BEAT MUSIC...KSEL music is also to be on the
up beat. At least two thirds of all KSEL music
is to be on the up beat. Music and the pace of
music is discussed in another section.

PEP...A successful announcer must be a lively,
bright sounding announcer. He must have a great
deal of enthusiasm in his voice.

ENTHUSIASM ON COMMERCIALS...The KSEL announcer
always shows much enthusiasm when giving a commercial. The announcer must sound as if he is really
sold on the commercial and can hardly wait to inform
his listeners of the important news contained in
the commercial.

ENTHUSIASM IN GENERAL...Enthusiasm in general is
the mark of a good KSEL announcer. Both on the
air and off the air the announcer should express
much enthusiasm and desire in giving the people
of Lubbock the best possible radio program.

ANNOUNCER'S APPEAL...It is best for the announcer
to get in his mind who he is appealing to. All
KSEL announcers will pattern their shows in much
the same style and method. No DJ is to ever
pattern his personality or announcing to appeal
to the teenagers or kids. The station has other
means in getting the teenage audience. The announcer
should get in his mind who he is appealing to and
talking to. EVERY ANNOUNCER IS TO APPEAL TO THE
ADULT AUDIENCE, AT ALL TIMES THIS IS TRUE. For
this reason the radio station takes a stand on the
following rules and standards for a DJ and his air
personality.

THE PERSONALITY...KSEL likes for its DJ's to reflect
a definite personality in their shows. Appealing
to the adults, KSEL requires the DJ to reflect a
sincere, intelligent, and at times a humorous
personality. The station requests a good
personality show out of every announcer. The DJ
should work hard to make his show one of the top
rated shows in the market. The best way for an
announcer to reflect the correct and desirable
air personality is for him to be natural. You do
not have to put on to be a successful air personality. Along these lines here are more important
rules and ideas concerning the air personality.

FUNNY STUFF ON THE AIR ...It is alright for the DJ
to inject at times funny or humorous stories or
situations into his show. This of course can be
greatly overdone, but if used properly it can be
a big asset to one's air personality. There is,

however, a big difference between being humorous and silly. If the announcer does not watch closely he will begin to border on the silly stage. This does the station NO good whatsoever. The DJ should watch for clever material to inject into his show, but he should watch closely and not become silly or overdo his funny stuff on the air. Remember in selecting your material we are appealing to an adult audience.

HEP AND JIVE TALK...No hep or jive talk is allowed on KSEL. The station never likes to hear the announcers use sayings like, ALL THAT JAZZ, REAL COOL, CRAZY etc. Once again we are appealing to an adult audience.

CHANGE OF VOICE...NO KSEL announcer should try to use a character voice on the air. Please no BUGS BUNNY, OR MICKEY MOUSE THINGS. No Grandba or any other similar voices on the air. The only exception to this would be in the case where the station's copy writer uses a different voice on a taped commercial.

TRITE SAYINGS...All announcers have the habit of using trite sayings. That is to use the same expression or saying over and over again. Sometimes we get on a saying and run it into the ground. For example, one past announcer used the sayings: for your information, and for your entertainment. They were badly run into the ground. Keep away from trite sayings and when you start to labor on a saying, break yourself of it as fast as you can.

BACKGROUND MUSIC...KSEL does not like a large amount of background music used by the DJ. Before each hourly news the DJ might want to use some background music. This, however, may be used at times on recorded spots. The station does take a very dim view of the DJ taking background music and fading it in between sentences in a spot or adlib. If the music is used at the correct time, the music should be faded, the announcer speak his piece, and then the music be faded back. Not any of this up and down stuff.

THE BEST AIR PERSONALITY......The best air personality for a KSEL announcer to develop is a good, friendly, enthusiastic, sincere approach. It is truly important the announcer be as natural as he can. The use of friendly, enthusiastic, sincere, approaches will appeal to the adult audience and will make the DJ an outstanding announcer and a real asset to the station.

110. TELEPHONE CALLS...There are to be NO PERSONAL TELEPHONE CALLS PUT THROUGH TO THE CONTROL ROOM FOR THE DJ WHILE HE IS ON THE AIR. If a telephone call comes in for the DJ while he is on the shift, the number and name will be taken for the DJ to call back. Business calls will be placed into the control room, but these should be kept to a minority. KSEL does not accept telephone request as such. There may be times when the contest calls for telephone reaction and this will be overseen by the DJ and the station telephone operator. At times the DJ may ask for a personal reaction from the audience. In these cases the DJ should always see that someone is available to answer the calls. On all calls that consist of news calls, contest, personal audience reaction, etc. the contest and news number should be used and not the business phone.

At night when there is no one on the front desk the newsman should answer most of the calls. By the nature of the job the newsman will be using the telephone more than the DJ. At night the newsman should protect the DJ by not letting the run of the mill calls into the control.

111. STATION JINGLES...A good supply of KSEL jingles are in the control room for use by the DJ's. It is alright for the DJ to play a jingle between every record but it is most important that only one jingle be played between records.

112. TALKING DURING RECORDS-JINGLES COMMERCIALS

It is against station policy for DJ's to talk or make little comments during records, jingles or commercials. When a DJ is introducing a song over the instrumental beginning of a record he should make sure his comments are finished before the vocal begins.

113. ADLIBING ABOUT COMMERCIALS OR SPONSORS

The DJ is not to adlib or make comments about any commercial or sponsor unless that account is purchasing the DJ's personality show. This is especially true of national and regional accounts. Thousands of dollars can be lost by one DJ trying to be funny with an adlib about a sponsor.

114. EQUIPMENT TROUBLES

When there is an equipment breakdown in the control room or newsroom the real amateur in our business will talk about the breakdown on the air, thus telegraphing it to the audience. The real pro is the one who can continue his show or news in a manner that the audience has no idea about the trouble or breakdown.

115. TALKING ABOUT OTHER DJ'S, STAFF, ETC.

Usually the audience is not nearly as interested in KSEL Personnel and station surroundings as much as the DJ thinks. He should refrain from making many comments about staff members, physical surroundings, etc.

P-116. TALK BACK ON REMOTES

Remote broadcasts are not to be two man DJ shows. The DJ on the board is not to get in an on the air conversation with the announcer on the remote.

P-117. RECORDING ROOM CLEAN

It is just as important to keep the recording room clean as it is the control, news, etc.. A place for everything is provided, and everything is expected to remain in its place.

P-118. RECORD NUMBERINGS (COLORS)

To help the employees identify the record files easily here are some numberings and coloring.

1. CLASSICS-All AM album and single classics are labeled with a black pen and marked with a C before the number.

2. <u>FM</u>-All FM albums and singles will be marked with a <u>red</u> pen. <u>FM</u> will precede the number.
3. <u>PRODUCTION</u>-All albums and singles used for production only are marked with a <u>blue</u> pen. A PRO will precede all numbers.

All records are to be kept in there proper places at all times.

There is a card file for the above music classifications.

P-119. MASTER JINGLE FILE

There is a master jingle file for all accounts, commercial, and station jingles. No tape is to be erased and this file is to be kept neat at all times. This file will also include special news intros and station promos.

P-120. TAPE LABELS

Each tape cartridge placed in the KSEL control room rack should have a uniform tape label. On the label must be this information.

    A. Account name
    B. Length of commercials
    C. Starting date
    D. Expiration date or TFN
    * Red Star on cartridge label means the spot has a live tag.

P-121. A copy log is to be kept daily by the copy department. On this log should be the following:

    A. Spot recorded
    B. Writer
    C. Name or names of announcers recording the commercials.

P-122. NAME OF SHOW AND DJ

The name of the program plus the name of the DJ should be used a minute of every 15 minutes by the DJ.

P-123. TAPE CARTRIDGES FOR SHOWS

Most Deejays will have several cartridges for his show, intros, gimmicks, etc. It is most important the deejay keep his cartridges current. Much money can be wasted in old not used DJ cartridges. These should be culled at least once a month.

<u>NEWS POLICIES</u>

116. NEWS DIRECTION

The KSEL news director is in charge of all activities involving the news department and news men. All schedule changes, etc. should be and must be approved by the News Director.

117. LOCAL AND AREA NEWS

KSEL news center is built on local and area news. It is our desire to furnish listeners with 50% of our news from Lubbock and South Plains cities. The emphasis is always on local and area events and news happenings. A local story will always have precedence over a state, national or international story if they are of equal importance. Never should we give a newscast without local or area or both stories. This includes headlines during the hour. Local slants to many state and national stories are also desired. Remember, the success of KSEL news depends on our local and area news coverage.

118. NATIONAL-STATE STORIES WITH LOCAL TIE-IN

Many of the national and state news stories can have a local tie in. When a national or state story breaks the question should be asked...Is there a local opinion, background information, or follow up beep I can get? In at least 30% of the state and possibly 20% of the national, local tie ins can be effective.

119. EDITING THE NEWS

It is extremely important that we use the same thinking as our friends at the newspaper in editing the news. A good journalist realizes his responsibility only to the people of Lubbock and the South Plains. Every story broadcast on KSEL news should be of interest to a majority of the people in the Lubbock South Plains area. For example, a story concerning a traffic fatality in Dallas or San Antonio or Houston which does not pertain to a local resident is not of interest to this local area. Any story that affects another section of the state or another state in the union and does not affect or interest the people in our area should be deleted from the news. Whenever a newsman edits the news he should ask this question of every newscast. Will this and does this story interest the majority of our listeners? If this question is asked many useless stories will be deleted.

120. BEEPS

KSEL news has built the reputation of getting more telephone news beeps than all other stations combined. We cannot get too many beeps. It is vitally important from the news coverage standpoint and the public relations standpoint that we fill our airlanes with these news beeps. On every event that takes place in Lubbock there will be a chairman or a spokesman. This person should be contacted for a news beep, on stories of violence in Lubbock and in the state of Texas actuality beeps can be of great use. For example, in armed robberies the person robbed makes a wonderful beep. Other beeps can be obtained through our direct dial in the State of Texas. Our news department can build a fantastic reputation on actuality broadcasts, another terminology for local and area beeps. Beep assignments will be made every morning by the news director, however it is always advantageous for the newsman on duty to secure several beeps himself. Permission should always be asked of the person being recorded to use the beep on the air.

121. MOBILE NEWS

KSEL news again has built the reputation for mobile news broadcast. We cannot have too many mobile news on location broadcasts. KSEL news should establish the reputation of being there on the air. However, at times when there are two newsmen on duty one can do a mobile broadcast by use of the telephone in the news room. This will accomplish the same purpose as would a mobile broadcast on location. A few simple rules to remember on mobile broadcasts are:

1. Intro the mobile broadcast with the headline of the story, in other words, two people have been injured in an automobile accident at 5th and K. Do not intro, this is Bill McAlister, KSEL mobile news, 5th & K where two people have been injured. Use the headline first.
2. Mobile broadcasts should be kept short.
3. Names of accident victims should not be used from the scene without checking first to see if relatives have been notified.
4. All mobile news broadcasts should use the closing tag line blank name from the scene in a Ford, 950 and out.

122. NEWS DIRECTOR ALERTED

The KSEL news director should be informed and alerted on every breaking story of major consequence including national, local, state, etc. He should be informed of late breaking stories at night of consequence for supervision and direction.

123. AVALANCHE JOURNAL

The newsman should not be afraid to use stories in the Avalanche Journal. Every local story that appears in the AJ in the morning edition on the front page should be included in KSEL morning newscast. The same is true of the afternoon edition of the paper. Listeners do not know who had the story first the AJ or KSEL. However, one exception would be feature stories, they naturally are not to be used.

124. SPORTS NEWS

Lubbock and the South Plains have been termed the hot bed of sports. We at KSEL news concur and feel our sports news is important as is other KSEL routine news. In checking the paper, the sports page edition should be checked as carefully as the front page in the morning and afternoon editions. Any local sports story of consequence on the sports page in the morning or afternoon should be included in KSEL news that morning or afternoon. Newsmen should again watch not to get features. In most cases the headline on the sports page in the morning or afternoon should be included in KSEL news that morning or afternoon. Other radio stations do not emphasize sports in their regular news - KSEL does.

125. FIRE AND ACCIDENT INSERTS

KSEL news has built the reputation when you hear the sirens - tune 950 for information. The moment we receive information that a fire truck or trucks are moving in the Lubbock area the fire inserts should be used. The moment we have a report of a 77 in our area the accident with injuries insert should be used. If we get word that an ambulance is making a medical run the medical run ambulance insert should be used. These inserts should be aired as soon as possible without breaking a record. Here are some rules to remember in getting information on automobile accidents and fire in the city.

1. When a mobile is available it should be dispatched to the scene of a fire or automobile accident.

2. If there is no mobile unit available newsmen should try and contact a house, business or person closest to the scene to get vital information. The information desired on an automobile accident is how many persons are injured, whether they are male, female or children and some report on the automobiles, not so much damage but any spectacular occurance such as hitting a house, window, knocking down telephone poles, overturning, etc. Much of this information may be obtained from a person near the scene. The newsman will rely on the city directory heavily to find businesses or residences near the actual scene. On fires the information of course would be on what is burning, how badly etc.

126. NEWSMAN PRIORITY

The newsman has priority over the DJ in the decision of when to air a news story. The newsman should not take advantage of this authority and at all times use his better judgement. But the DJ is instructed to throw the mike to the newsman at any minute upon his request without question.

127. NAME OF ACCIDENT TRAGEDY, ETC.

One big problem in radio news is knowing when to air the names of accident or death victims. We are not interested in speed to the point we air a name knowing closest relatives have not been notified. In most cases the funeral home can give you this information or hospital. If there is some question as to whether closest relatives have been notified it is better to check with the news director for clearance before airing the name.

128. PURSUIT OF STORY

One of the greatest of weaknesses of KSEL news is the lack of pursuit in a big story. When a local or area story of any consequence breaks it should be our desire to obtain just as much information on the story as possible. In the incidence of a fatality or death the newsman should gain just as much background information on the victim as possible. The name of the person where he worked, what he was doing at the time of the death and other vital information like this should be aired as soon as possible. In the case of businessmen in accidents or businessmen in fatalities it is vitally important to get on the air the place of business. Many men are associated with the company they work for. The same is true in females when they are employed. This does not
only cover stories of tragedy but other stories where background information is desirable. Pursuit of stories to get all if not a little more than the paper should be the desire of all KSEL newsmen.

129. FRESHNESS IN NEWS

One of the most vital areas of our news presentation is freshness. Radio news is built on what is happening now or what will happen in the future. The more current moment by moment news we have the better our sound. The newsman should try to lead with a fresh story every hour and half hour in his news broadcast. At no time should the same lead story be read without a rewrite on the hour and half hour. Very Important the more current we can make our news in writing the more dramatic our sound will be. For example, Yogi Berra named the most valuable baseball player of 1964. Instead of just coming on and saying Yogi Berra named most valuable baseball player the introduction should be United Press International announced two minutes ago Yogi Berra as the most valuable baseball player, etc., or Lubbock police reported 30 seconds ago an automobile accident with injuries, or less than 5 minutes ago attorney general Waggoner Carr announced in Austin or President R. C. Goodwin announced this hour Texas Tech will etc. Immediancy is the answer, making it sound as if it just happened and KSEL got it on the news first.

130. LISTENING TO MONITORS

One ear of the newsman must be tuned to our police, fire, DPS and mobile unit monitors at all times. The secret of missing a big story is not to be listening to monitors. When on the telephone or in conversation with another newsman the number one responsibility of the newsman is to hear what is said on all those monitors. This comes before anything.

131. WEATHER COVERAGE

The weather forecast given by this radio station should be written and delivered in laymen's terms. Do not use big words or roundabout words to describe the weather. Is it going to be fair, is it going to be windy, is it going to be clear, should be clearly stated. Being in an agriculture country it is vitally important in most seasons if we are going to have moisture or if we are not. In these seasons each newscast should carry a small weather tag no rain in the forecast or showers predicted, etc. We should either say no rain or there will be rain. The clearer and more down to earth you can write the weather in layman's language the more original and clever our weather will be. A complete weather forecast should be given on all hourly news, a brief weather forecast on the half headlines with the present temperature.

132. LEAD STORY

As is important the lead paragraph of a story, the lead story of a newscast is vitally important in getting the attention of the news listeners. The lead story should be fresh and attention getting. In most cases the lead story should be changed every hour and half hour. In the case it is not changed it should definitely be rewritten before being used again...especially the first portion of the story.

133. DRAMA IN STORIES

This radio station is not and has not been known for sensationalizing or overplaying news stories. In fact we have gone the other direction in not giving enough drama in our news delivery. It is our hope in the days and months ahead that we can have more drama on stories of tragedy and stories of excitement and those that would warrant such a thing. If we have to border on sensationalism then this is the desire in adding the drama to our news delivery especially true on local and area stories. Let's get dramatic in news.

134. DATELINES

A city dateline is to be used on each and every news story given. The dateline should be the city only without the use of "From, in, at." For example Lubbock, Dallas, Moscow, New York, Los Angeles not in New York, In Dallas, from Austin, etc,. On stories concerning weather, say For the West Texas area or For the state. A Lubbock dateline should be used and an opening sentence from the KSEL weather desk.

135. WRITING NEWS

A vital area at KSEL news is the writing and creating of local stories. Much more creativeness plus cleverness and drama is needed in the writing of our local and area stories. This can be the big separator between this operation and other radio news.

136. NIGHT NEWSMAN WRITING TOMORROW'S NEWS

It is the responsibility of the night newsman to prewrite many of the stories to be used on tomorrow's morning newscast. The news director will assign each evening the stories to be written that night by the newsman for use the next morning.

137. NEWS SOURCES

It is highly important that each news source in the city of Lubbock be definitely assigned to a newsman. The newsman is much like a salesman in that he is completely responsible for that news story. The public relations, news information and general relationship between this news source and the radio station will be the responsibility of the newsman assigned. Every newsman will have a few news sources and each newsman should be working hard to see that we are in grade "A" condition with each source.

138. DON'T BUG THE PD

Many times our news department has been known to call and wart the police department too much. It is important to remember the police desk sergeant and dispatcher will only have so much information. For example, on a 77 it is ridiculous to call the police dispatcher for any information concerning the accident moments after. Our information must come from the scene, then from the hospital or ambulance. In cases of major accidents where information concerning the accident is desired, a call should be made for the police officer investigating. Most likely he will not be in service but can return the call to the radio station. Let's not get in the habit of picking up the phone several times a day to call the police dispatcher for a minor question.

139. URGENTS

There are many stories that are important however they do not warrant a bulletin intro...These stories should be classified as urgents. Injuries and local

fires etc. should be urgents. There is an urgent
intro in the control room for use each time.

140. REWRITING NEWSPAPER STORIES

We will lift many stories from the AJ and other newspapers...We should be careful not to use the same
composition as the newspaper especially in the case
of the AJ. For example, the paper says "A thief who
had a hunger for candied apples stole"..etc...our
newsman comes back and uses the same wording to open
his story, this is an OB steal.

141. FEATURE STORIES

We can't make news, we can only report it", is an
old newsman's cliche. True, we can't make news
but we can make a news story. We should always
look for some unusual angle in a news story that
could be developed into a good feature story, which
in effect, gives you an exclusive story.

142. MOBILE NEWS

It is the responsibility of the KSEL news director
to see that the station is completely covered day
and night for mobile news. If the news director
cannot cover-the responsibility should be passed on.

143. PRONUNCIATION

There is rarely an excuse for mis-pronunciation of
a word. There is a Webster's unabridged dictionary
in the newsroom which we should always use whenever
we are in doubt about the pronunciation of any word.
Listen to other newscasters on TV and other radio
stations. Any time we hear one of them pronounce a
word differently than we do, look it up. You'll
be surprised how many times they are right and we have
been mispronouncing the word. Proper names are a
bit trickier, they can be pronounced any way the person
or place involved wants them pronounced. Each area
has its own peculiarities in the pronunciation of
the names of persons and places. If there is ever
any doubt about the proper pronunciation of one of
these names, always ask someone else. There is
always someone around who has lived in the area
longer than you, who will know.

144. REPUTATION

KSEL has built a reputation of being first with the
news;while this is an enviable situation, it puts
a lot of responsibility on the news staff to maintain that reputation. We must think news at all
times. We must try to never miss a story. If we
do, we should ask ourselves, why? then, make an
effort to see that the same mistake is never repeated.

145. ON AIR MONITOR

The newsman is not to be a listener of the DJ show.
Off the air monitors should be off in the KSEL
News Center. The only time a newsman needs to
monitor is for cues and this can be done with head
sets.

146. NEWSPAPER STORIES

Every local news story that appears on the front page of the morning paper should definitely be used on the 7 A.M. and 8 A.M. KSEL news. Every local or area story that appears on the front page of the Bulldog should be used on the 12 noon and the evening paper should have coverage on our 5 P.M. and 6 P.M. news. This policy also holds true with reference to the front sports page of the papers. The headline on each paper should appear accordingly on the newscast regardless of its classification.

147. PUBLIC SERVICE STORIES

Public Service events will be used on KSEL news. Here are two important rules concerning public service.

1. Never lead off a newscast with a general public service story.

2. Keep the Public Service stories short. Many times a one sentence headline will be fine. Very few public service stories require more than a two sentence story.

148. STAY IN NEWSROOM

The important position for the newsman is in the newsroom. Time outside the newsroom should be seconds and not minutes.

149. UP DATING STORIES

The importance of updating continuing stories is paramount. When the station airs a story over a period of hours the story should be updated to sound current.

150. NEWS SIGNS

There is a sign in the news center for almost every need. These signs are to be used in notifying the DJ what is needed. Signs should be used each time except for the hourly and half hour news.

151. NEWS TEASERS

A news teaser is to be given before each hourly news. The teaser should be aired from 10 minutes before up until 3 before the hour. The teaser should be short, one line, and do what it says, tease, create interest in the story and upcoming news...There is a format for the teaser in the News Center.

1. The same teaser should never be used twice.
2. The teasers can be on local, Texas or National and International stories.
3. The bug sound is to be given before each teaser.
4. Here are some good examples of news teasers.

    BUG
    NEWSMAN....A BIG FIRE IN BIG D, THE STORY IN
              FIFTEEN MINUTES ON KSEL NEWS.
    BUG
    NEWSMAN....THE PRESIDENT MAKES A NEW APPOINTMENT
              DETAILS IN FIVE MINUTES ON KSEL NEWS.

    BUG
    NEWSMAN....MISSILE GOES UP AT THE CAPE, THE STORY
              IN 13 MINUTES ON KSEL NEWS.

5. The important thing to remember concerning a teaser should be clever, short, interest provoking, and plug the next KSEL news.

152. WEATHER WRITING

The newsman will have the responsibility of writing the weather. Here are some general rules in weather writing.

1. Keep it brief..Use few words.
2. Tell us if or if not we expect rain, if we don't just say, No rain in the forecast.
3. When there is rain give the percentage of chance. For example, a 40% chance of rain today.

153. LEAD SENTENCE

The lead sentence of a news story is like the lead story of a paragraph. It is to get attention and be the bannerline of the story. Newsmen should be imaginative, clever and original in their writing of the lead sentence.

154. ACCIDENTS AND FIRES

When there is an accident with injuries or a fire the specially written out insert is to be aired by the newsman immediately. The exact location is not to be given, but rather the area of the city. Most important....when an accident or fire insert is used it should be followed up on the air on the next hour or half hour newscast. Even if the fire was a false alarm or the accident without injuries this should be reported on the next hour or half hour news. Don't leave the listeners hanging.

155. BULLETINS

Major local area state and national stories should be given at once on KSEL. Use the bulletin intro. Read the bulletin slowly and then, repeat it once.

156. SPORTS HEADLINES

Sports headlines are to be aired by KSEL news once each hour. There are to be one line headlines including local, state and national sports. 3 to 5 sports headlines should be used.

157. FUNERAL ANNOUNCEMENTS

Death of a known local or area citizen is a story. The newsman should contact the news director for leadership in how to handle these announcements. When giving the death of a male, accident or natural causes, his occupation and the company he worked for should be given.

158. NEWS MEETING

There is a meeting of all newsmen each week. All newsmen are to attend this meeting.

159. NEWS CENTER

The KSEL News Center will be referred to on the air as the KSEL News Center only. It is against the policy of the station to call it anything but the news center. Please do not call it the News room, News bureau, etc.

160. CLEAN NEWS CENTER

It is the duty of the News Center and the newsman to keep the news center clean at all times. It is very easy to keep the center in a mess. There is a place for every piece of news. All news copy should be kept in the proper place. The newsman should keep his drinks in the News Center while on duty. The person that has a bottle or cup is responsible for that bottle or cup being put up.

161. BULLETIN BOARD

There is a Bulletin Board in the News Center for the use of the Newsmen. Important memos and information will be placed on this Bulletin Board. All newsmen should check this Bulletin Board regularly for information.

162. VISITORS IN THE NEWS CENTER

No visitors are allowed in the KSEL News Center. If a staff member has business in the News Center he is to make his stay as brief as possible.

163. NEWSMEN OFF DUTY

Newsmen off duty should not hang around the station or the News Center. The newsman should arrive around fifteen minutes before his shift begins to prepare himself for the shift.

164. NEWSMEN COMING ON DUTY

The newsman coming on duty will not do the hourly news when he comes on duty. For example if Jim Jones is coming on duty at 4 P.M. and Don Smith is coming off duty at four, Don Smith will do the four o'clock news. The men going off duty will do the news before he goes off duty. When a man comes on duty his first air work will be the half hour headlines.

165. SMOKING IN THE NEWS CENTER

It is alright for the newsmen to smoke in the KSEL news center. The newsmen should be careful to keep the News Center clear of ashes and clean.

166. CONVERSATIONS BETWEEN THE NEWSMEN AND ANNOUNCERS

There is to be no small talk conversation between the newsman and announcer while on duty. The newsman is not to spend his time in the control room. There is an intercom system between the announcer and newsman, and this is to be used for business only. There are to be no conversations between the announcer and newsman on the air. No exceptions to this rule. For example the announcer is not to ask the newsman what he thought of a record etc.

167. THE INTERCOM

There is an intercom system between the announcer and the newsman. The intercom is to be used for business only. The intercom is used for communications between the announcer and the newsman. When a bulletin comes in or the newsman has a special broadcast he can relay the message to the control room by the intercom. The announcer can in turn inform the newsman of his cues and such.

168. FORMATS

There are certain formats to be used in the News Center. There is a format for the hourly news, half hourly headlines, news teasers, and all news broadcast. These formats are to be used and read as they are written. The wording should not be changed.

169. ANNOUNCING THE NEWS

Newsman's air style...The KSEL news is to be given by the Newsman in this air style.

1. The newsman is to give the news in a rapid pace with plenty of punch and speed.
2. The newsman should as the DJ have plenty of uplift and drive in his voice.
3. The newsman should always give the news in a good sounding pace and punch tone.
4. The newsman should remember good production is also very important on the news. He is to be fast on his cues when he comes in on teasers, hourly news, half hour news etc. He should also have good production when using a tape broadcast on the news. The newsman as the announcer is to stray from pauses in his operation.
5. The newsman should follow closely all instrutions and policies concerning giving the news as outlined in this book.

170. HOURLY NEWSCAST

The KSEL hourly news can be the true success or failure of the News Center. If the hourly news

is done according to station policy and if it is done with much preparation and enthusiasm by the newsman it can be one of the greatest assets of the station. Here are complete instructions concerning the hourly news.

1. A taped introduction will intro the news every hour.
2. The moment the tape is completed the newsman should open the news with the general format opening or a sponsored opening if the news is sponsored.
3. Datelines are to be used on every story given on the hourly news. The word Dateline is not to be used, only the town or city the story is from, example, DALLAS, LUBBOCK, WASHINGTON, etc.
4. A lot of fresh and late breaking news is to be used on each hour's newscast.
5. The hourly news stories are to be briefed in content. This applys to both local, Texas, and national stories.

6. The newscast should contain from 12 to 15 stories each time. The only exception to this would be if you had a big story on which the newsman had a special tape broadcast that took up much time. In this case the newsman could reduce the number of stories used, The hourly news is to run from three to four minutes.

7. Special additions to stories are to be used as they are called for in the section for that material in this book.

171. NEWS

There will be certain stories that should have and include KSEL Additions in the stories. These additions should be included in the local stories and the wire news as well. Here are additions to be made to every story pertaining to the conditions listed below. These are for the hourly news only. The half hour headlines are not to include these additions.

172. ADDITION TO A WEATHER STORY

Every weather story whether it is a state weather story, national or local should have this opening line added with this dateline. The dateline Lubbock should be used and every weather story should open as below.

LUBBOCK.......FROM THE KSEL WEATHER DESK

173. ADDITION TO SPORTS STORIES

Every sports story given on the hourly news should have this dateline and addition made.

LUBBOCK.....FROM THE KSEL SPORTS DESK

174. ADDITION TO THE STOCK MARKETS AND STORIES CONCERNING BUSINESS

This dateline and addition to the stock market story and stories concerning business should be made.

LUBBOCK.......FROM THE KSEL FINANCIAL PAGE

175. ADDITIONS TO REGULAR STORIES

At least once on each news on the hour this addition should be made in a local and wire story. TELLS KSEL.....This line can be worked into any number of stories any number of ways. FOR EXAMPLE........ DALLAS...A BIG FIRE IN BIG D...DALLAS FIREMEN ARE BATTLING A FIRE AT THE GOODMAN BUILDING IN DOWNTOWN DALLAS. FIREMEN AT THE SCENE TELL KSEL THE FIRE IS OUT OF CONTROL ETC. Here you can see how the addition works in well with the story. Addition to the regular stories as the above is done this addition should be handled in the same way.

176. KSEL REPORTERS

Here is an example of the KSEL reporters....DALLAS A BIG FIRE IN BIG D, DALLAS FIRE UNITS ARE AT THE SCENE OF A THREE ALARM FIRE IN DOWNTOWN DALLAS. KSEL REPORTERS ON THE SCENE SAY THE FIRE IS OUT OF CONTROL. ETC.

177. A BIG STORY ON THE NEWS WIRE

This story will be given the moment it is received. The story and later information will be repeated by the newsman between every record. The program director or manager is to be contacted at once for further instructions.

178. A TORNADO ALERT

When a tornado alert is on in the area these rules will apply.

1. A special assigned man will take the control board during the tornado alert.
2. All mobile units will be dispatched to various parts of the city for weather broadcasts. If a tornado enters the city or is in the country side area, the mobile unit nearest the tornado will follow the tornado along its path at a safe distance and broadcast its path as it makes its way along. Other units will join in the journey from different directions.
3. There will be two men on duty in the news center. One man will be at the newsman's desk broadcasting late reports from police radio, wire and telephone information. The other will monitor police radio, the weather wire and other means for other important information. He will also handle the mobile desk and work with the units, to get them set up.
4. All mobile units will monitor their radios for off the air cues.

EDITING THE NEWS

179. LOCAL NEWS

KSEL feels a surplus of good local news is the key to our success as a News Department. The newsman should include just as much and many local news stories on each hour's news, and on the half hour news. He should be constantly searching for news on the local scene. The newsman should very carefully check each edition of the newspaper for all local news stories. These stories should be rewritten from the newspaper stories and used on our news. The paper will provide for many stories to be used. All stories from the paper should be rewritten and in most cases shortened. The newsman will have a CALL LIST for each hour in the newstime. These calls are to be made with no exceptions for tips on news stories. Many stories can be gained through the CALL LIST that otherwise would not be obtained. The CALL LIST and information to be gained will be posted in the KSEL NEWS CENTER. The sharpness of the newsman can be a great asset in the gathering and airing of local news. There are many national news stories that can be tied into local stories. If the News Center is on the ball many local stories can be obtained in this manner. For example, if the Congress announces an increase in the draft quota...the Newsman can get a report from the local draft board to see how this will affect Lubbock and Lubbock County. We will want to use our government leaders from our area for many official comments concerning governmental actions. This is not only true in the national government scene, but in the State government.

When a newsman has a local news story he should rewrite the news story several times giving a good variety in the wording of the story. Freshness is vital on all of our local news reports. In the action of radio news the right now pulse of the City is the important factor. Of course, there are many stories which require follow ups, but on the other hand, the KSEL News Center should be constantly reporting what is happening in Lubbock right now or what is going to happen in Lubbock. The current news is a great asset to the freshness and vitality of our entire news sound. We are sure the KSEL News Center can build a great reputation for complete, first and accurate news, if this is done through our local news coverage it will be of great value to all.

180. WEST TEXAS NEWS

KSEL, with its 5000 watts not only has a news responsibility to Lubbock, but to the area surrounding Lubbock. For this reason West Texas news is of vital importance to KSEL. The newsman should be well acquainted with the area towns and cities surrounding Lubbock. West Texas map is posted in the control room for the newsman. In ranking news as to its importance, West Texas News is second after local news. The area within a fifty mile radius of Lubbock is especially important in this respect. The KSEL newsman on duty can get many good West Texas stories from the editions of the local newspaper. The United Press Wire will at times offer a source for West Texas coverage. At times news tips from area towns will provide for good leads in West Texas news. In some cases the newsman will want a telephone report from one of the area towns. In this case the newsman should first clear with the Program Director or the News Director before the call is made. If a big story breaks and neither is available, then the newsman should use his judgment before making the call. If a feed is desired the station in the area town should first be contacted for a broadcast. If the town has no station or the station has no information, then the call should be placed to the proper agency. Good West Texas news coverage will help to build the vast area audience which is so desired.

181. TEXAS NEWS

Next in importance in the KSEL news cycle is Texas news. Although it is not as important as local, the station likes for its newsmen to include many Texas stories on the news. The newsman should keep a close watch on the wire for the latest breaking Texas news, always keeping in mind not all Texas news is of the greatest importance. A good question to ask, not only on Texas news but all news, is the news interesting to the people in Lubbock and on the South Plains.

Some Texas stories are not of interest to those in this area. Such as a killing in San Antonio or a stabbing in East Texas. Once again the judgment of the Newsman plays an important role in this field. Variety and freshness are also very important in the editing and giving of the Texas news.

182. NATIONAL AND INTERNATIONAL

Although national and international news is very important there are some good and some bad news stories in this classification. The newsman should keep the latest and most important national and international news stories on the air.. He should at the same time do a good job segregating the national news in keeping the most important on and the lesser off. Once again if the newsman is sharp he can find many ways to tie a national story into a local story.

183. WEATHER STORY

When a weather story rates the news it should be given as the KSEL additions call for. In the case of a severe weather warning the Newsman should follow these rules.

1. The warning can first be put on as a bulletin.
2. The most important phase of the warning is, "Does it include the Lubbock South Plains Area?" This should be given at the first and end of the story every time it is used on the air. If the warning DOES include the area then the newsman should give the DJ a copy to be used on the 15 and 45 minute weather.

Also in the case of snow warnings or other weather stories which relate to our area the DJ should have a copy for his 15 and 45 weather. It is always best for the newsman to realize the importance of weather news. Anytime there is a local weather story, rain snow, dust storm, etc. the newsman can use this for copy on his hour and half hour news.

184. SPORTS STORIES

There are many sports stories that come across the news desk which merit our coverage. Sports stories should not be in a separate classification. The story should be given in the classification of local, west Texas, Texas, national and international. The KSEL classification is used on all sports stories.

N-185. HEADLINE ON PAPER

The Headline on each edition of the A.J. should receive top attention from newsman. The headline story should be used on all morning, noon, and evening drive time , hour and half hour newscast.

N-186. LOCAL STORIES ON NEWS

Never should the newsman give an hourly newscast without any local stories.

The time should be rare indeed when the half hour news does not contain a local story.

N-187. SPECIAL NEWS PROMOS

When a major news story or report deserves DJ promotional coverage the newsman should type a promo card and instruct the DJ on its use.

N-188. IMMEDIACY NEWS

The alert KSEL newsman sounds his sharpest when he puts immediacy in his news. When a story breaks he should use some of the following.

1. Just in
2. Received minutes ago
3. Just off the wire
4. Only minutes ago
5. 2 minutes ago

N-189. MAJOR NEWSCAST

During the operations of the News Center many memos, special formats, broadcasts will relate to what we refer to as our "major newscast". Here are the major newscasts on KSEL.

6:30 A.M.	12:00 Noon	4:30 P.M.
7:00 A.M.	12:30 P.M.	5:00 P.M.
7:30 A.M.	1:00 P.M.	5:30 P.M.
8:00 A.M.		6:00 P.M.
8:30 A.M.		

ENGINEERING

1. All equipment to be repaired by engineers only.

2. All equipment to be handled with reasonable care; radio equipment is comparatively fragile.

3. Cleanliness around equipment is necessary as most trouble in radio equipment is caused by heat and dust.

4. Do not overdrive consoles and other equipment. It is designed to operate in the range indicated on the meter.

5. Tools are for engineer only. It is imperative that they be available when trouble arises.

6. Radio equipment can be dangerous...do not tamper with it.

7. Speakers should not be blasted, they can be ruined, also they disturb others.

8. Meters should be read each thirty minutes...Don't duplicate others or your past mistakes in logging.

9. All engineers should know how to read all meters and adjust equipment to stay within license requirements. If you don't know...ask...You won't learn any younger.

SALES DEPARTMENT

1. AVAILABLE ANYTIME

    The job of a salesman is a continuing one. It is not an eight to five proposition. The salesman is expected to be in a position to make a call at 5 A.M. or 11P.M.

2. SALES REPORTS

    The radio station will have a definite system for sales reports. These reports should be kept current and completely filled out by the salesman on a daily basis.

3. CONTRACTS

    No commercial announcements are to be logged without a written contract. Salesmen should be careful to make sure all information requested on the contract is completed.

4. CANCELLATIONS

    The telephone operators are instructed not to take cancellations over the phone. When an account calls to cancel his number should be taken and the salesman is to make the return call or visit. All cancellations should be turned into traffic on the written form.

5. COPY INFORMATION

    All copy information for the production of commercials should be written on the special copy memos.

6. CALL INS

    The salesman are to call the station at least once in the morning, around noon, and once in the afternoon for messages.

7. WEEKEND SHIFT

    Every weekend there is to be a salesman on call for sales calls. The salesman is to leave his whereabouts with the telephone operators.

8. BAD PAY ACCOUNTS

    The salesman is to be careful we avoid bad pay accounts. On new accounts the salesman should check with Don Garth for a credit reference.

9. IDEAS

    McAlister Broadcasting is not selling time, spots, ads, etc. We are selling ideas. Creative thinking from all salesman is vital.

10. SPONSOR REMOTES - PROMOTION

    When a salesman sells a special broadcast, promotion, etc. the success of that broadcast promotion is a large responsibility of the salesman. He should be on location and in close touch with the Production Department to see that everything is perfect.

11. RATE CUTTING

   Under no circumstance does the salesman have the
   authority to give a lower or special rate or
   package not shown on the official rate card.

FM POLICY

1. FM PROGRAM DIRECTOR

   The KSEL FM Program Director is in charge of all
   FM shifts, schedule changes, music and program
   material. He is to also supervise the traffic
   logging of all programs and commercials.

2. FM MUSIC PATTERN

   The KSEL FM Music Pattern consists of the following:

   a. Vocal
   b. Instrumental

   The vocal, instrumental rotation on a one for one basis
   is to be in effect during all programs with the exception of the hymns and jazz music.

   On each of the FM albums appears the PLAY ONLY STICKER.
   ONLY THE CUTS LISTED ON THIS STICKER ARE TO BE PLAYED.

3. DEFINITE MUSIC PATTERN

   KSEL FM will maintain a definite play pattern refering
   to the amount of songs from the special FM good music
   survey. This is to be followed at all times.

4. TALK PATTERN

   Announcer talk on KSEL FM is to be at 10 minute intervals. The pattern of breaks should be as follows:

   10 after, 20 after, 30 after, 40 after, 50 after,
   the hour and on the hour.

5. NEWS HEADLINES

   News headlines will be broadcast on the hour. These
   headlines should consist of loca, state and national
   headlines. Four to six headlines should be used
   with a brief closing weather forecast. A taped intro
   will be used for the news each hour.

6. HALF HOUR WEATHER

   On the half hour KSEL FM broadcast weather. A taped
   intro will be used for each half hour weather.

7. DURING THE HOUR BREAKS

   On the talk breaks at 10 after, 20 after, 40 and 50
   after the hour the following is to be included in
   every break:

   1. Commercials
   2. Time
   3. Temperature
   4. FM Plug Card

5. Music Selections for the next ten minutes.
6. FM jingle
7. An FM plug card should be used on the hour and half hour.

8. TELEPHONE REQUESTS

    KSEL FM will be taking telephone requests on its hotline telephone. When a person calls for a request it is better for the announcer to get the artist he wants to hear more so than the song.

9. LIVE COMMERCIALS

    When the FM announcer is reading a live commercial he should use an instrumental background music.

SUNDAY MORNING

The KSEL Hymnbook is most important in the station's programming. Here are some important rules concerning the presentation of our Sunday Morning Hymnbook.

1. BILLY GRAHAM

    The Billy Graham Program comes in during the week. It is the responsibility of the Program Director to make sure the Billy Graham tape is in the proper location for each broadcast.

2. THE SUNDAY MORNING RELIGIOUS MUSIC

    This music is to be played from the religious music tapes in the control room. The songs are to be played in order.

3. Talk by the announcer is to be on a ten minute basis. On the hour, ten after, twenty after the hour, half hour, forty after and fifty after.

    Each ten minute break should include the following. Brief weather forecast, time, temperature, and commercials, public service or promos if any.

4. NEWS

    Sunday morning news is to be broadcast in the following manner:

    <u>Hour</u> - Six to Eight short headlines with a complete weather forecast

    <u>Half Hour</u> - Five to Seven short headlines plus complete weather forecast.

5. WEATHER - TIME

    The Sunday Morning Weather and time is the most important material. It should be given on every 10 minute break.

THE IDEAL RADIO SALESMAN

There is a difference in salesman and <u>radio</u> salesman!

A good radio salesman has to have more than just "sales ability", selling an intangible such as radio takes much more ability than selling something such as cars; or hardware, etc! What it amounts to is that in radio you are selling "you" to the client, then you are selling your product. For this reason a radio salesman <u>must be</u>:

1. ENTHUSIASTIC
2. SINCERE
3. COMPLETELY SOLD ON WHAT YOU ARE SELLING
4. ABLE TO GET ALONG WITH AND KNOW WHAT PROSPECTS NEEDS.
5. IMAGINATIVE

Number 5 is important because in the final analysis you are selling not just radio but an idea. It has been proven that the average sale in a market such as ours is made on the third call (unless of course you are selling strictly a quick promotional pitch). If you haven't sold yourself to the client by that third call you need to be honest with yourself and if need be give the account to another salesman.

The most vital part in making a sale is, of course, the closing. You must know when to stop talking and make the client say yes or no. Many good salesman have lost a contract by talking themselves out of the sale.

<u>NEVER</u>: Talk about "that other station" they have all got some listeners but we have the majority here.

<u>ALWAYS</u>: Sell consistent advertising because in the long run this is what the foundation of a radio station is built on!

THE IDEAL NEWSMAN

A KSEL newsman should think news at all times. Everything he sees or hears about should be thought of in the terms of "is this news? Is this something that KSEL listeners would be interested in hearing about". Good big news stories are usually hard to come by because the people involved would much rather the general public didn't know about it. When your sixth sense tells you that there is a news story buried somewhere that you can't uncover, discuss it with the News Director. He may know avenues of approach that you are not familiar with. Of course, you don't run into this type of news story often but when you do, you certainly don't want to boot it. Good big exclusives are really feathers in our caps.

Big news stories are not the only place we can score "brownie points" though. People are news. Each person who accomplishes, achieves or performs anything noteworthy should be a news story on KSEL. Each person involved in a news story has countless friends, neighbors and relatives who are vitally interested in the story. They will tell the person involved and anyone else who will listen, that they heard about it on KSEL. Human nature being what it is, they will just automatically have a kind feeling toward KSEL because of the story.

News in Lubbock is very competitive. To stay on top we must stay sharp, be alert and work, work like the dickens. News is a 24 hour a day job. Everyone in the KSEL News Department must be available around the clock if needed. Of course on routine news, which will be most of the time, you will have an assigned shift but you must be available to work at any hour of the day or night on any important news story on which you are needed.

News is a serious thing. You should never "horse around" with a news story. KSEL newsmen must build an image with the listener of sincerity, authenticity and maturity. When they hear you read a news story, they must believe it, must believe in your integrity. There is no such thing as a slow day in news. There will be days when news stories are a little harder to come by. On those days we'll just have to dig a little harder and deeper for stories. On such supposedly slow news days we should contact all our news sources diligently. Sometimes checking in this manner we come across a good feature story. As you know, feature stories are the spice of our business. The listener enjoys a little relaxation from all the hard news, as in fact, do we.

Stay neat and act as if you're proud to be a KSEL newsman because you must be.

Wear your KSEL newsman name badge when your covering a story.

THE IDEAL DEEJAY

To give the DJ's an idea of what we are really looking for here is the description of an ideal DJ.

The ideal KSEL DJ should be a many sided individual. He should be a proud person who has great value in his program. The DJ should want to produce his show in a manner not to just help the radio station, but himself as well. At the same time the DJ should realize all air men need daily improvement. The DJ's style and pace should be molded to fit the stations format instead of the station being molded to fit the DJ's needs.

The DJ should not be arraid of hard work. He is not a clock puncher. The KSEL DJ should realize personal appearances are just as important as air shifts. The personal appearance is just as important to the DJ as it is to the station.

The DJ should remember no air personality can have a good performance without preparation.

The DJ should be alert to station promotions and changes.

Most important he should be creative. The DJ should always be coming up with good ideas on improving his program, performance, and station promotions.

Index

A

Account exchanges, 159
Affidavit forms, 31
Agencies, 42
Around-the-clock
 placement, 213
Associations, 20, 197
Attrition, 72, 89
Appreciation, time, 156
Approach, 144
Audience preferences, 72
Auto dealer, 52
Auto repair, 67

B

Bad habits, 84
Bait advertising, 175
Bank, 66
Barter, 46
Beeper phone, 240
Big accounts, 65
Big shots, 165
Billing forms, 31
Brochure, 26
Broadcaster's associations, 20
Budgets, 51
Bully, 51

C

Chain stores, 55
Change, 92
Character, station, 75
Chewing gum, 83

Closing, 64, 85, 146, 226
Collections, 47
Comedy relief, 88
Communication, 83, 104, 163
Complacency, 145
Compliments, 164
Compensation, 21
Competition, 70, 149
Confidence, 266
Consideration, 104, 257
Contest, 105
Conventions, 197
Copy, 59, 214
Coverage map, 24
Creativity, 66, 91, 150
Critcisim, 155
Customer is always right, 164

D

Deals, 171
Deception, 91
Decision maker, 69
Defeatism, 186
Delinquent accounts, 196
Despair, 71
Diagonal placement, 212
Dissappointment, 155
"Disposals", 256
Distractions, 203
Doodling, 84

E

Emotional bully, 92
Enthusiasm, 100
Extrovert, 62

F

Failure, 70
False objection, 93
Fear, 63
Fidgeting, 84
Five Ws, 157
Flattery, 164
FM, 150
Follow up, 186, 196
Fraternization, 159, 165
Frequency discounts, 41
Friendship, 156
Frowning, 84

G

Goals, 162
Good habits, 84
Goodwill, 257
Gossip, 270
Guaranteed times, 265

H

Habits, 84
Hair, 83
Handshaker, 83
Health, 204
Hollow shells, 166
Horizontal placement, 212
House accounts, 160
Humor, 88, 106

I

Ideas, 91, 149
Indecision, 99
Inertia, 92
"Influentials", 74
Introvert, 62

J

"Jellybeans", 53
Joiners, 188

L

Letters, 190
Listening, 182
Listeners' preferences, 72
Local rates, 38
Lack of interest, 91
Losers, 161
Lotteries, 175

M

Mannerisms, 83
Manufacturing your product, 58
Market data, 26
Marketplace, 16
Market research, 155
Market study, 57
McAlister Broadcasting Operations, 274
Memory, 261
Merchandising, 151
"Midivert", 62
Morgue, 165
Motivation, 153

N

National Association of Broadcasters, 20, 197
National rates, 39
Needs, 99
Negativism, 94
Newscasts, 211
Newsletters, 199
Nicknames, 260
Numbers, 238

O

Objections, 54, 62, 85, 93, 180, 235, 270
Opinions, 183

Organization, 157
Orientation, 13

P

Package deals, 171
Patience, 166
People classifications, 62
Personal inventory, 263
Personal standards, 103
Per inquiry commercials, 139
Personalities, 227
P.I.s, 139
Planning, 91, 206
Poetic license, 86
Prejudice, 238
Preparation, 206
Presentation, 92, 142
Prime time, 213
Priorities, 158
Priority, 65
Problem solving, 168
Products vs services, 154
Program logs, 33
Programming, 18
Promotion, 106
Prospect classifications, 63
Prospect weaknesses, 86
Publicity, 116
Public relations, 116
"Pushover", 54

R

Radio Advertising Bureau, 20
"Raiders", 76
Rates, 26, 38, 86
Rate cards, 39
Rate cutters, 55, 70, 76
Rate cutting, 266
Rate increase, 174
Rebate, 44
Rebuttals, 230
Remote broadcasts, 240

Repair shop, 69
Reports, sales calls, 160
Reps, 41
Reputation, 165
R.O.S., 265
Rumors, 270
Run-of-schedule, 265

S

Salary draw, 21
Sales messages, 15, 40
Sales reps, 41
Salvaging accounts, 244
"Samples", product, 24
Sarcasm, 194
Self-analysis, 60
Self-condemnation, 155
Sense of humor, 85
"Sequestering", 52
Service, 67, 246, 258, 269
Services vs products, 154
Short rates, 44
Showmanship, 265
Singing jingles, 68
Single-station market, 264
Slogans, 66
Small accounts, 66
Smiling, 84
Smoking, 83
Sound, station, 16
Sparring partner, 85
"Spec" announcements, 59
Speed reading, 257
Spot announcements, 15, 40
Squelches, 102
Staff rapport, 15
Standards, 149
State associations, 198
Statement forms, 31
Station sound, 16
Straight commission, 21
Straight salary, 21

Strategy, 89
Swings, 105

T

Team function, 273
Team work, 78
Teenagers, 52
Telephone, 194
Temper, 97
Testimonials, 29, 116
Time, 56, 101, 205
Time buyers, 41
Timidity, 85
Timing, 102
"Time" salesman, 14
"Tools, 23, 56
Trade association
   budgets, 52

Trade-outs, 46
Trade publications, 20
Traffic forms, 31
Training, 18
Transmitter logs, 33
Two man selling, 272

U

Understanding, 152

V

Vertical placement, 212

W

Wants, 99
Winners, 161
Writing copy, 214

HF
5439
.R36
W52